HEAVEN AND THE AFTERLIFE

The Truth about Tomorrow and What It Means for Today

ERWIN W. LUTZER

MOODY PUBLISHERS

CHICAGO

Interior design: Erik M. Peterson
Cover design: Smartt Guys design
Cover photo of "Earth Day" copyright © 2015 by Igor Zhuravlov / iStock (59060012). All rights reserved.

Library of Congress Cataloging-in-Publication Data

Names: Lutzer, Erwin W., author. | Lutzer, Erwin W., author. How you can be sure you will spend eternity with God. | Lutzer, Erwin W., author. One minute after you die. | Lutzer, Erwin W., author. Your eternal reward.
Title: Heaven and the afterlife : the truth about tomorrow and what it means for today / Erwin W. Lutzer.
Description: Chicago : Moody Publishers, [2016] | Contains three of Lutzer's earlier titles: How you can be sure you will spend eternity with God, One minute after you die, and Your eternal reward. | Includes bibliographical references.
Identifiers: LCCN 2016012468 | ISBN 9780802414366
Subjects: LCSH: Salvation--Christianity. | Assurance (Theology) | Eternity. | Future life--Christianity. | Death--Religious aspects--Christianity. | Heaven--Christianity.
Classification: LCC BT785 .L88 2016 | DDC 236/.2--dc23 LC record available at http://lccn.loc.gov/2016012468

We hope you enjoy this book from Moody Publishers. Our goal is to provide high-quality, thought-provoking books and products that connect truth to your real needs and challenges. For more information on other books and products written and produced from a biblical perspective, go to www.moodypublishers.com or write to:

Moody Publishers
820 N. LaSalle Boulevard
Chicago, IL 60610

1 3 5 7 9 10 8 6 4 2

Printed in the United States of America

*This Trilogy is dedicated to the elders of Moody Church,
both past and present who have supported me, guided me and
prayed for me for 36 years. Your reward is waiting for you.*

*"And when the chief Shepherd appears,
you will receive the unfading crown of glory"*
(1 Peter 5:4).

CONTENTS

HOW YOU CAN BE SURE
YOU WILL SPEND ETERNITY WITH GOD

ONE MINUTE AFTER YOU DIE

YOUR ETERNAL REWARD

How You Can Be Sure You Will Spend

ETERNITY
WITH GOD

Interior design: Erik M. Peterson
Cover design: Smartt Guys design
Cover image of silhouette in sunrise copyright © Galyna Andrushko / Shutterstock / 198507053. All rights reserved.

ISBN-13: 978-0-8024-1310-9

CONTENTS

WELCOME TO ETERNITY

Five minutes after you die you will either have had your first glimpse of heaven with its euphoria and bliss or your first genuine experience of unrelenting horror and regret. Either way, your future will be irrevocably fixed and eternally unchangeable.

In those first moments, you will be more alive than you ever have been. Vivid memories of your friends and your life on planet earth will be mingled with a daunting anticipation of eternity. You will have had your first direct glimpse of Christ or your first encounter with evil as you have never known it. And it will be too late to change your address.

Two contrasting scenarios come to mind. One is the self-assured rich man who died and went to hades, where Christ said he, "being in torment, he lifted up his eyes" (Luke 16:23). All of his faculties were intact: he could see, feel, hear, and remember his life on earth. And even today as you read this book, he is still fully conscious, knowing there is no way out of his predicament.

The other picture is of the crucified thief to whom the dying Christ said, "Truly, I say to you, today you will be with me in Paradise" (Luke 23:43). All of his faculties were intact too; and today he still enjoys the presence of Christ in paradise.

Would you be surprised if I were to tell you that Christ taught that more people were en route to agony than destined for ecstasy? More will be in conscious anguish than in rapturous joy.

Is it possible for us to know in this life where we will spend eternity? Some think not, insisting that about all we can do is hope for the best and count on the mercy of God. After all, we are sinners, and God is holy. There are, the argument goes, too many unknowns, too many hidden premises, too many opinions. "Besides," said one man, "I can wait to be surprised!"

On the other hand, it would seem strange indeed if God were to keep us wondering, suspended somewhere between a flickering hope and a persistent doubt. If He is our heavenly Father as Christ taught, we would expect that such crucial information would be revealed to us. Thanks be, it has been.

Many good people will join the rich man in hades, not because they are rich but because they are good and are depending on their own goodness to save them. For all their sincerity, they will find themselves on the wrong side of heaven's door. Or perhaps they are counting on the mercy of

God, not knowing that it is given only to those who meet an important requirement.

No doubt some surprises await all of us five minutes after we die; but it is much better to be surprised about the indescribable glories of heaven than the indescribable agonies of hell.

Be wrong about Social Security; be wrong about baseball; be wrong about your career choice; but don't be wrong about where you will spend eternity.

This book will lead you on a journey. We will discover why we can know, even now, where we will be after we have said our last words and breathed our last breath.

With your Bible in one hand, and your doubts and questions in the other, let us begin our journey.

CHAPTER 1

THE TRAGEDY OF MISPLACED FAITH

Faith can destroy you!

As residents of Chicago, my wife and I clearly remember the Tylenol tampering episode that happened here years ago. You might remember that someone bent on random murder put cyanide in a few capsules. The poison did its work very well. One woman who bought her Tylenol from a drugstore near our church died within minutes after taking a single capsule. In all, seven unsuspecting people died.

Two unforgettable lessons emerged from this tragedy. *First, faith does not in itself have any special merit; it does not have the power to change the nature of a drug from harmful to helpful.* Seven people firmly believed they were taking medicine, not poison. But their faith did not save them. In fact, their faith killed them.

Faith is only as good as the object in which it is placed. Or, to put it differently, *what* we believe is more important than the fervency of our belief. That old cliché, "It doesn't matter what you believe as long as you are sincere," just isn't true, as the victims of the Tylenol episode proved. Better to believe the truth with trembling hands than to believe error with steady confidence. What you believe really matters.

A second lesson we must learn from the Tylenol episode is scary indeed: *Sometimes a false belief resembles a true one.* To the casual observer, the cyanide looked just like the Tylenol powder. The label had all the earmarks of being authentic, so there seemed to be no need to distrust the contents. The promise was that these pills would relieve pain, yet taking a single one brought death.

Christ taught that many people who have a strong and abiding faith will someday discover that their faith cannot save them. To their everlasting chagrin, they will live to see the door of heaven slammed in their faces. They will spend eternity on the wrong side of the celestial entrance.

Maybe we can best capture the feeling if we use a story from this side of heaven's gates. Imagine standing in a swamp while a rescue plane flies overhead. You wave your weary arms and moan, but you know that the pilot does not see you. You do not have the strength to walk to civilization, and because your sense of direction is confused, you would not know where to walk if you could. Since the other members of your party died when your plane went down in the swamp three days ago, you are completely alone.

You stare into the night, knowing that you must simply

lie down in the mud to die. You long for someone to be with you, but you must bear your despair alone. Waves of fear dissipate the courageous thoughts you had yesterday. You have a burning fever, and now you hysterically wait for the end.

Translate that feeling into cosmic proportions. You see the inside of heaven, catch a glimpse of some of your friends, but are told by Christ that you are permanently disqualified. There is no second chance, no opportunity to return the next day with the right documents in your hands. You can't reroute your travel plans. You turn away, never to see heaven again. You stare into the darkness ahead of you, conscious that you are entering the realm of moral chaos, loneliness, and darkness.

The words of Dante, long since forgotten, flash into your mind: "All hope abandon, ye who enter here!"

I wish it weren't so. And I know you do too. Yet Christ taught that many who expect the gate of heaven to swing wide open will be shocked to see it swing shut on them. Their exclusion from His presence is final, personal, and eternal. The words of rejection that they hear from Christ will ring in their ears forever.

Let us hear it from the lips of Christ Himself:

> Not everyone who says to me, "Lord, Lord," will enter the kingdom of heaven, but the one who does the will of my Father who is in heaven. On that day many will say to me, "Lord, Lord, did we not prophesy in your name, and cast out demons in your name, and do many mighty works in your name?" And then will I declare to them, "I never knew you; depart from me, you workers of lawlessness." (MATTHEW 7:21–23)

These people never dreamed that they would be banished by Christ. After all, they acknowledged Him to be Lord and served Him. They had a whole bag of spiritual experiences that ordinary people like you and me could envy. I get chills when I visualize their contorted faces.

These religious types did not lack faith; if anything, they had too much of it! They had the confidence that they would enter into heaven. To hear them tell it, you would think they had a reserved seat in the front row of the balcony in the celestial cathedral. And now *this*!

If you did a personal inventory, their profiles would prove that these were not halfhearted souls who mouthed a commitment to God on Sunday and then did their own thing during the week. They were the dependable people who kept the church doors open year after year. They did miracles in the name of Christ. They even cast out demons and performed a litany of wonderful works. They thought of Christ as their Savior, not their judge. These good people were fooled into accepting cyanide in a Tylenol capsule.

Of course, it's easy for us to think we know who the people are that Christ was talking about. The other day I heard a preacher on television talk as though God didn't do anything unless He consulted with him first (that's an exaggeration, but you get my point). He told glowing stories about his work among the poor. He described all of the miracles God seemed to be doing through him. Maybe it was all true; maybe it was all false; or more likely it was a bit of both. Safe to say, God is His judge.

Let's not misread Christ's point: He does not want us to think that only those who make extravagant religious claims will be deceived. His warning is more basic: *If the people who seem the most likely to make it will be shut out of heaven, then plenty of other ordinary people will have the same frightful experience.*

Many sincere people who are devoted to their faith, many who would never brag about their relationship with God, and many who just quietly believe and have good works to prove it—these, too, just might miss the heavenly kingdom.

I'm glad that Christ didn't leave us confused about why some people will find themselves on the wrong side of heaven's door. To keep us wondering would not have been kind, but would have left us with our doubts to brood over our uncertain future. What we need is light to find the right path.

I once read about a very tired man who checked himself into a motel late at night. He peered out of the darkened window as he closed the shades, then sank into a deep sleep. When he awoke and pulled back the shades, he saw majestic Mount Rainier through the motel window. The mountain had been there all the time; it was there even in the darkness. But he couldn't see it until the light of the sun showed him where he was.

That's the way truth is. We can't make it up. We can't create it by sleight of hand. All we can do is discover it in the presence of God's light as revealed in the Bible. Just as the light of the sun can enable us to see where we are geographically, so the light of another Son (Christ) can help us see where we are spiritually. *And I believe He wants us to know whether we will spend eternity with Him.*

The purpose of this book is to help us understand all that Christ has done to make it possible for us to know where we are going and that we do have a place reserved for us in heaven. I believe that we can be just as confident as the early disciples that our eternal future is secure. Just listen to what Christ promised them:

Let not your hearts be troubled. Believe in God; believe also in me. In my Father's house are many rooms. If it were not so, would I have told you that I go to prepare a place for you? And if I go and prepare a place for you, I will come again and will take you to myself, that where I am you may be also. (JOHN 14:1–3)

The New Testament invites anyone, regardless of his or her past, to have the assurance that he or she will be escorted by Christ into the glory of a personal, heavenly existence. It is interesting that Christ taught that only a few would take advantage of this offer. Before I explain why, let's hear Christ's description of the two roads that are going in opposite directions.

A Fork in the Road

Recently I was discussing the credentials of Christ with a woman who said, "I believe that there are many paths to God. People can come in their own way." I told her I wished that were true, but I was confronted with a choice—do I believe her well-intentioned opinion, or do I believe in what Christ Himself had to say? He was not as broad-minded as many of the gurus who occasionally make headlines.

Christ insisted that there was a narrow road that led to eternal life, but, in contrast, there was a broad road that led to spiritual death. Clearly, there are two separate gates, therefore, two roads and two very different destinations. Hear it in His own words:

Enter by the narrow gate. For the gate is wide and the way is easy that leads to destruction, and those who enter by it are many. For the gate is narrow and the way is hard that leads to life, and those who find it are few. (MATTHEW 7:13–14)

Visualize an expressway with several lanes of traffic. Each lane has its own religion, philosophy, and point of view. Popular culture today tells us that we can choose our own belief, church, or personal philosophy. We can even switch lanes if we like. Everyone makes it to the finish line; everyone has a good time; everybody wins. The fun is in the journey.

Of course, it is quite true that when you are on an expressway, it really doesn't matter which lane you choose. And, yes, you can switch lanes as often as you like. In the end, you will get to the same destination as the folks who are zooming by on your left or the slowpokes you are passing on your right. It's not what lane you are in, but the expressway you are on that determines your destination. Your lane is your choice. Your final address is not.

Now it gets tricky. According to Christ, this wide expressway, which is thought by many to be labeled "The Way to Heaven" is actually "The Way to Destruction." Even in the Old Testament we read, "There is a way which seems right to a man, but its end is the way to death" (Proverbs 14:12). The cyanide is labeled "Tylenol."

In contrast, Christ says that the way to life is narrow and "those who find it are few." Here there is only one lane of traffic. The travelers come in various shapes and sizes, but, as we shall see, they share a common core of beliefs. The lane is too narrow to accommodate a host of different opinions about religion in general and about Christ in particular. But I'm ahead of the story.

There are more people on the broad way than the narrow one. And if we are not careful, we will get the two roads confused. Just ask the people who expected to enter heaven but were told by Christ to leave. He consigned those otherwise good people to the same destination as those who "practice lawlessness."

No wonder that John Bunyan, in his classic allegory *The Pilgrim's Progress*, wrote, "I saw that there was a way to Hell, even from the gates of heaven." And so there is.

The Three Lanes

There are many wrong paths to God but only one right one. We don't have to be experts in identifying all of the false paths, for, if we are observant, we will notice that, despite differences, they all have a common characteristic. Try to find it as I describe three lanes of the superhighway that is going in the wrong direction.

The Ladder Climbers

While riding on a plane, I had a conversation with a man who said to me, "My greatest fear is to stand behind Mother Teresa on the day of judgment and overhear the Lord saying to her, 'Lady, you could have done a whole lot more!'" This man was an achiever who was trying to climb a ladder to God, but he wasn't sure whether he had even made it to the first rung!

Though it has variations, you have probably heard it a dozen times: God has given us a conscience, a moral nature that can distinguish (however imperfectly) between right and wrong. He gives us the ability to do good works that have the power to purify the soul. Our task is to use these gifts to the best of our ability.

Devotions, prayers, and disciplines help lift us rung by rung. And though we might not do all that we should, we can depend on God's grace to get us the rest of the way. As the cliché says, "God helps those who help themselves."

Chances are your friends believe this. Maybe you do, too. If you are a perfectionist, or if you have had to work for everything you have ever had, this route will be particularly appealing. According to a Barna Research report, almost all Americans believe they are good enough to get to heaven. That doesn't mean they think they are perfect, but that they think they are as good as, or better than, others. Even those who don't go to church see themselves as decent enough to have a good chance of "making it."

I often ask people this question: "If you were to die today and God were to say to you, 'Why should I let you into heaven?' what would you reply?" Nine out of ten say something like this: "I'm a pretty good person, and I'm trying hard to do better."

For now let's just file this answer in the back of our minds. We'll reflect on it later.

The Religious Types

Perhaps you are surprised that I've put religion in the "mistaken" category, that I'm listing it as just another lane on the broad expressway. "After all," you might say, "if religion does not get us to God, what will?"

But think about this for a moment. The people who were banished by Christ were certainly religious. I get the impression that they didn't just serve God occasionally but actually made it a way of life. When they were knocking on heaven's gate, the reason they expected to gain entrance is that they had done so many religious works in the name of Christ.

Religion can take many forms. For some, it involves sacraments, which are believed to be channels of grace for the faithful. The church, the argument goes, has the power to complete our incomplete deeds.

For others, religion is studying the ethics of Jesus and trying to live by those precepts. Knowledge linked with proper motivation helps us live a religious life, we are told.

We've all met those who believe they have met God through nature. The contemplation of the works of God leads to a knowledge of God, they say.

As you well know, there are dozens of different religions in the world, and each has its own creeds, ethics, and expectations. Religion, if understood broadly, is much more diverse than most people realize.

However, religion is really just another version of the "ladder theory." Religion defines the rungs more carefully and states the expectations more clearly. And, of course, God's help is often sought. But religion, as such, is not the way.

Reasons will be given later.

The Mystics

Of course the mystics are religious too, but I've given them their own category because they are unique people who usually seek God with more intensity than others. Throughout the years, some devout souls (bless them) have renounced the world and secluded themselves in monasteries to find God. Maybe there are not many people who do that today, but the idea that we can find God within us through meditation and concentration is gaining adherents.

I've often admired the Christian mystics, those hardy souls who can take their faith that seriously. These men and women took the words of Christ, "You shall love the Lord your God with all your heart and with all your soul and with all your mind" (Matthew 22:37) as their compelling vision. They fasted and they prayed; they meditated on the Scriptures or other devotional literature. They tried to deal with the sin that cropped up in their own hearts so that they could love God with pure motives.

Certainly some mystics found God, but not in the way or for the reasons that they thought. The temptation was to fall into some form of the ladder theory, to strive within the soul to make oneself worthy of God. Finding salvation through mysticism was such hard work that few mystics knew when they had finally made it. Indeed, most thought one could never know.

Today there are many who are into a different kind of mysticism, a form of spirituality that seeks an inner encounter with whatever God or gods there be. Techniques of meditation and self-help promise that God is just waiting to be discovered. Usually the goal is to lose one's identity and "become one" with the ultimate, or the divine.

These folks believe God is accessible to anyone who seeks Him. Often they also believe that He can be found in any one of the religions of the world. After all, if God is within us all, He is available to everyone, at anytime, anywhere. We just need to find the key, and the door to spirituality will swing wide open.

But, as we shall see, the door is jammed.

Beyond Good Deeds

Certainly these lanes on the expressway look as if they might be right. If salvation (that is, being reconciled to God) does not come by my striving to make myself a better person, what is left? What could appear to be more right than the view that we accept God's grace to do the best we can and expect Him to do the rest? And what could possibly be wrong with trying to find God within ourselves? Yet the travelers who follow these paths encounter bumps along the *way—barricades* might be a better word.

A friend of mine told me how guilty he felt when, as a youngster, he switched a sign on a street and watched as the motorists were misled. Signposts are important; if they are incorrectly labeled, the consequences can be disastrous.

Each of the three paths above shares a common error. *They overestimate our ability and underestimate God's holiness.* They operate from a skewed perspective of ourselves. We see shades of goodness and badness, and as long as we compare ourselves to others, we can be quite confident that we are worthy of God's love and forgiveness.

We've all had that satisfied feeling that comes from doing our "good deed for the day." When we go the extra mile by taking care of our neighbor's children, giving some money to charity, or making an honest deal, we feel smug about our goodness. And when we pick up the newspaper and read about those who kill and steal, we feel pride at how different (and better) we really are. We might even think about how much better the world would be if everyone was just like us.

Our problem is that we are looking at ourselves through the wrong end of the telescope. We are actually much farther from God than we can imagine. The better we understand God, the more convinced we will be that there is no recognizable common moral ground between us and Him. It turns out that we are like the boy who told his mother that he was eight feet tall, at least according to the yardstick *he* had made!

I can't speak for you, but my problem is that I'm not very good at climbing a ladder to God. No matter how hard I try, my basic nature remains unchanged. I can resolve to be better, and I might even improve, but I am fundamentally the same within. My problem is that after I climb the ladder a foot, I often fall back a yard. I mess up. If we could grasp how holy God is, I am sure we would quickly agree that we have misjudged how far up the ladder we have come. Fact is, we even hide our true selves from ourselves, for, beneath it all, we are nasty sinners. I agree with Augustine, who said, "He who believes that God is holy will despair trying to appease Him."

Later in this book I will explain why some people who take steps toward God might actually be taking steps away from Him. As we shall see, the harder we work to attain heaven, the less likely we are to make it. *Our good works give us a false sense of assurance because they mask our real need.*

Church rituals don't help much. The problem is that if I am accumulating grace through the sacraments, good works, and learning, I still don't know when I have enough. Even if I could take care of my past sins, tomorrow is another day.

Even the mystics had to admit that the more carefully they looked into their hearts, the more they realized that they could not love God unselfishly. The closer they got to God, the more clearly they saw their mixed motives. Yes, they loved God, but perhaps they did so out of fear of hell or out of a desire for self-fulfillment. Who can say that he loves God with pure, unselfish motives?

To really love God means we should hate sin. So these sincere souls tried to get themselves to hate what they knew they secretly loved! Try as they might, however, they could not uproot sin from within their hearts. Greed, lust, envy, self-will—those still lurked within the soul. Left unresolved was the question of how a holy God could meet them within their souls, which had not yet been purified. The more they contemplated their own hearts, the more sin they saw.

Whatever else may be said about the path of the mystics, it was simply not accessible to everyone. The common person who had to work long hours to earn a living had neither the time nor the opportunity to devote his life to mystical contemplation of God. And if those who did have such an opportunity confessed that they died without the assurance of salvation, the question was: Why bother?

When our oldest daughter was about ten years old, she talked us into buying a hamster. I felt sorry for that little animal, running on his wheel at all hours of the day. My response was to put a drop of oil on the wire axle so that I didn't have to hear the squeaking that came from his cage. If you are going to run on a treadmill, at least you should do so without disturbing others!

There is such a thing as a religious treadmill. When we are on that treadmill, there is no relief from the daily recognition that what we do is never enough, and there is no escape from the worry that, after we have expended all this energy, God just might put the bar a notch higher. We sympathize with the man who feared hearing the Lord tell Mother Teresa that she should have done more. Some people have chosen to get off the treadmill altogether. They have left religion behind and seem to be content just doing the best they can, hoping that everything will turn out right. Many of them feel better because of it.

The Way to Reassurance

C. S. Lewis said, "The safest road to Hell is the gradual one—the gentle slope, soft underfoot, without sudden turnings, without milestones, without signposts." Or, as we have learned, it is the attractive, well-traveled road with mislabeled signposts. You're convinced that this crowd of well-meaning people couldn't be wrong.

But if the lanes that look so right are really on the "broad way that leads to destruction," as Christ put it, how can we recognize the narrow way that leads to life? And how can we be sure that the path we chose is the right one? These questions will be answered more fully later on, but for now let's just think about what the narrow road would have to look like, given our predicament.

Since we will always fail at climbing the ladder to God, we need God Himself to come down the ladder and rescue us. We need God to initiate a plan that is so radical, so drastic, that it is independent of our own tainted efforts. We need a grand scheme that will overcome all of our shortcomings.

We need a way that doesn't appeal simply to those who have a bent toward religion; we need a help that isn't limited to those who were brought up in fine homes and have managed to stay out of trouble. The narrow way has to work for people regardless of their racial origin or their social and financial advantages or disadvantages.

Realistically, this path should be open even to those who have failed "big time." You might know an alcoholic, a rapist, or even a murderer who is too morally weak, or too run-down, and has done too much damage to climb even the most user-friendly ladder to God. Some people, figuratively speaking, have fallen off the ladder completely. In fact, we all have.

Pastoring in downtown Chicago for so many years, I have come to realize that many people (more than we would like to admit) have done terrible things that they cannot change. I have met people who have destroyed other people's lives through abuse, drugs, and crimes. Some have broken marriages, angry children, and ruined careers. Some have well-hidden skeletons that torment them in moments of quietness and solitude.

These folks don't know where to begin in coping with their guilt and failure. They have done too much damage to be saved by good works. Nobody knows how much grace they would have to accumulate to become holy enough for God to receive them. For them, the paths that we have briefly explored simply will not do.

Finally, if there is a path that really does lead to God, we should know it. To put it differently, we should have the *assurance* that our relationship with God rests on a solid foundation.

What I long for, and what I think every person longs for, is the knowledge that my relationship with God is secure—permanently secure—not just for today, but for tomorrow and for all of eternity. And such knowledge should be available to all who sincerely desire it, no matter how messed up, no matter how great their sin or crimes.

Neither you nor I want to be among those who are banished from heaven because we were on the wrong path. We should welcome, rather than fear, an examination of our convictions. Christ taught that our eternal destiny is dependent on what we believe and on what we do with those beliefs.

So we must approach these questions with an open mind and a willingness to learn and have our convictions challenged. Someday many will have to admit ruefully that misplaced faith is worse than no faith at all.

The question is not whether a path looks good or even feels right. The question is: Is it God's way, or is it what I *think* is God's way?

Stay tuned.

CHAPTER 2

WHY GRACE IS SO AMAZING

I was capable of anything. I had not the least fear of God before my eyes. . . . I not only sinned myself, but made it my study to tempt and seduce others."

Those words were written by John Newton, who was such a notorious sinner that he challenged his friends to think of some new sin he had not yet tried. He was a cruel slave trader who convinced himself that he was an atheist—and with God pushed out of his consciousness, anything was permissible.

But on March 10, 1748, while on board the vessel *Greyhound*, which was being ripped apart in a powerful storm,

Newton remembered God. After hours of pumping water from the ship, Newton, convinced that he was now to die, made a suggestion to the captain as to how the ship might be spared, and then he added, "If this will not do, the Lord have mercy on us!"

This was the first time he had consciously spoken of his need for the mercy of God. Now the question lodged in his mind: "What mercy can there be for me?"

He returned to his pump as the icy waves drenched him and his companion. Eventually, he and his mate stopped during a lull in the storm to tie themselves to the pump to be kept from being thrown into the sea. In his terror, verses from the Bible that his mother had taught him now raced through his mind. "Because I have called, and ye refused; I have stretched out my hand, and no man regarded; I also will laugh at your calamity; I will mock when your fear cometh" (Proverbs 1:24, 26 KJV). He had laughed at God; God was now laughing at him. The words kept coming back.

Every time the ship plunged and a watery mountain engulfed it, he was convinced that in a moment the vessel would be smashed to bits. Even yet, he wasn't convinced that the Christian religion was true. He had ridiculed the miracles of the New Testament for so long it was now difficult for him to believe.

The next day, when the storm subsided, the sailors went back to their responsibilities without giving thanks to God that their lives had been spared. Newton, however, found a New Testament that was on board and began to read it. He read chapter after chapter until he was convinced that Christ's death on the cross was for him. "It met my need exactly," he wrote later. "I needed someone to stand between me and a holy God who must punish my sins and blasphemies. I needed an Almighty Savior who would step in and take my sins away. . . . I saw that Christ took my punishment so that I might be pardoned."[1]

Twenty-seven days later, weak and starving, the crew reached land and were saved. Newton saw this rescue as from the loving hand of God. Years later, he wrote what has become the most beloved hymn of all time:

> *Amazing Grace! how sweet the sound,*
> *That saved a wretch like me!*
> *I once was lost, but now am found,*
> *Was blind, but now I see.*

John Newton never again doubted God's grace—God's undeserved favor toward us. But many people who have never had an experience like his don't understand why grace is truly amazing. Or maybe they think that a sinner like Newton needed special grace, but they do not. They see grace as nice, helpful—even necessary—but not really *amazing*.

Here is something you can count on: *The better you believe yourself to be, the less grace you think you need.* The more self-confident you are, the more convinced you'll be that you could get by even if God were stingy with grace. Sure, you struggle with sin, but that's just a part of the human predicament. All you need is some help from God and a bit of personal determination. You can make yourself good enough for God to accept you. You just need to get desperate enough to clean up your act. If grace can help you—fine.

John Callaway, a well-known interviewer on the television program *Chicago Tonight*, was asked about his religious faith. He said, "I'm struggling and I'm not winning that struggle. I'm living in the classic state of sin in that I think I'm separated from God. And my only saving grace is that I know it and I think I'll do something about it if I live long enough." He added that he "just needed to get serious about it!"[2]

Someday, when I get serious, I'll do something about it!

Even if Callaway had added, "With God's help I will do something when I get serious about it," he would not have understood grace. For him, apparently, grace is appreciated but not amazing. If he put his mind to it and did his part and if God graciously did His, together they could "pull it off."

God sees us quite differently. The New Testament paints a damning portrait of what our life is like without God's grace. Sure, hard work and discipline might change us, but they will not help one whit in bringing us closer to God. Our condition is far worse than we have ever dreamed. *Not until we know how bad off we are will we appreciate how good God is.* Grace then turns out to be amazing indeed.

Life without Grace

So, how bad off would we be without grace? In the New Testament, Paul likened his readers to corpses in a cemetery. "And you were dead in the trespasses and sins in which you once walked, following the course of this world, following the prince of the power of the air, the spirit that is now at work in the sons of disobedience" (Ephesians 2:1–2).

This does not mean that people who have never received God's special grace are always mean-spirited or do bad things. I have met people who are generous and kind who would not want to be called Christians; they may not believe in grace (as described here) at all. But even so, because they are sinners like the rest of us, the Bible teaches that they are "dead in trespasses and sins." There is a barrier between them and God that only grace can overcome.

So let's jump into our passage and try to understand this unflattering description. It is not a pretty picture, but I think you will agree that it rings true.

We Are the Walking Dead

We have all walked through cemeteries, with their rows of tombstones lining small paths. It is not just that the bodies lying beneath the surface are weak or sick; they are entirely helpless. *If they are to come alive, they will need more than help—they will need a miracle.*

Imagine the surprise if at a funeral the preacher or priest were to turn to the corpse and say, "If you just got serious about it, you could sit up, get out of that coffin, and walk!" Chances are, someone would call for help and people in uniforms would lead the minister away.

Spiritually speaking, we are dead toward God; and unless He gives us the miracle of life, we will stay dead. Of course, the people Paul is talking about in Ephesians are not dead physically, but spiritually. People who are "dead in trespasses and sins" might go to the symphony, watch a movie, or walk their dogs. Some might even be reading this book, proof that we can do many things while being alive in this world but dead toward God.

When our daughter Lisa was about four years old she said, "Mommy, my teddy bear knows that he isn't real!" We laughed, of course. When you stop to think about it, only a real teddy bear could know that he wasn't real.

Don't miss my point: Teddy bears can't know that they are real (or unreal), and they don't have the power to make themselves real. The same goes for people interred in cemeteries. A dead body can't make itself alive. Only God can return the spark of life to it. To continue the analogy: to expect people to rectify their relationship with God on their own is expecting the impossible. We cannot raise ourselves to life, even if we were to get serious about it.

Left to ourselves, we are disconnected from God just as surely as the plug of an electric lamp that has been pulled from the wall. And we cannot restore the current. Without Christ, we are "The Walking Dead."

Paul now explains in more detail what this means.

We Are Deceived by Satan

Years ago a comic popularized the catchphrase, "The Devil made me do it!" Well, the Devil might have had something to do with it, but he didn't make us do it. We at least cooperated. But yes, we are deceived by Satan and his demons. Paul said that we are "following the prince of the power of the air, the spirit that is now at work in the sons of disobedience" (Ephesians 2:2). We are influenced by the one who is "the prince of this world" and who is continuously at work "among the sons of disobedience."

Christ taught that Satan has the ability to put thoughts into our minds that we think are our own! But he cannot do that unless we have already chosen to follow our own wisdom and our own desires. Whether the influence is direct or remote, great or small, an evil spirit with many helpers roams the earth trying to keep people from understanding the truth. That only adds to our deadness, the spiritual vacuum that fills the heart.

We make the problem worse through denial, by thinking we are something that we are not. Whether or not you agree with all that Luther wrote, you would have to agree that he had an interesting way of describing how deceived we really are without God's intervention. He wrote that the natural man was "bound, miserable, captive, sick, and dead, but who by the operation of his lord, Satan, adds to his other miseries, blindness: so that he believes he is free, happy, at liberty, powerful, whole and alive."

Bad enough to be blind and dead, but imagine being blind and dead and thinking of yourself as seeing and alive!

We Are Depraved

Paul also said, "We all once lived in the passions of our flesh, carrying out the desires of the body and the mind, and were by nature children of wrath, like the rest of mankind" (Ephesians 2:3). We sin as naturally as a bird sprouts feathers. We are not sinners because we sin; we sin because we are sinners.

Sin is nothing more than putting myself first, serving myself as best I can. Sin is not first and foremost committing adultery, stealing, or even becoming involved in crime. The first commandment is that we love the Lord our God with all our mind, soul, and strength (see Matthew 22:37; Deuteronomy 6:5). It follows that when we love ourselves more than God, we are committing what might be the greatest sin.

Sin is choosing to do what I want without doing it in submission to God's will and plan. That is why I can be sinning even when I think I'm doing just fine on my own. In fact, I might be *especially* sinning at the moment I think I am doing just fine.

And though I think I am doing fine on my own, honesty compels me to realize that life without God has little real meaning.

"If this is living, why do I feel so empty?" That is what many people ask themselves even though they might have all the friends money can buy. Even religious folks can experience spiritual "lostness." Anyone who looks for meaning in the wrong places will, if he is honest, confess that life seems trivial and without a grand purpose.

Perhaps you think that I have overstated the problem. But remember, I'm only helping us to understand what Paul wrote in the New Testament. By now it should be clear that we are in no condition to take care of our relationship with God. We need a heavy dose of grace. We need a big miracle, a breath of spiritual life from God. We need God to come to our rescue. Nothing less than a resurrection will do.

Grace has to be amazing or we are lost.

CHARACTERISTICS OF AMAZING GRACE

If the grace of God is to come to our rescue, it has to be powerful enough and merciful enough to meet us where we are and bring us into the presence of God. Paul continued, "But God, being rich in mercy, because of the great love with which he loved us, even when we were dead in our trespasses, made us alive together with Christ—by grace you have been saved—and raised us up with him and seated us with him in the heavenly places in Christ Jesus" (Ephesians 2:4–6).

God has entered the cemetery!

Grace Is Given Apart from Works

God surveyed the human race and concluded that He could not expect us to cooperate in reconciling ourselves to Him. Our fallenness permeated our entire being: Our minds are tainted with sin, our souls are stained, and our wills are paralyzed. Good people or not, we are in deep trouble.

The apostle Paul would say to John Callaway, "Not only are you unable to do something about it, but your very act of

38

trying to do something about it will complicate the problem! *Don't do anything about it until you have understood what God has done!"*

At last, I hope we are ready to define the word *grace*. Grace means God's undeserved favor. It is a gift that sets aside all human merit. It does not simply give us a hand; it gives us a resurrection. Grace is all one-sided.

Grace means that God takes the first step toward us. Yes, we do take a step because, unlike our daughter's teddy bear, we do have mind, emotions, and will. But our small step is simply a response to what God has already done. Grace means that God speaks a word, gives us spiritual life, and fits us to stand before Him. He descends the ladder we were trying to climb, scoops us up, and takes us all the way into His presence.

If God's rescue program had included our efforts, grace would be diminished and salvation would not be wholly the work of God. "But if it is by grace, it is no longer on the basis of works; otherwise grace would no longer be grace" (Romans 11:6). Some things can exist together, but human works and the grace that brings salvation cannot.

To clear the field for His own activity, God eliminated every work of man—past, present, and future. His action had to be pure, uncontaminated by our own best efforts. He had to act alone. Our self-effort was put on a shelf labeled "Unsuitable for Use."

If God had found something truly good within us that He could have used, He would have been obligated to recognize it and reimburse us for it. If God had owed us salvation, the whole system of grace would have collapsed. But His analysis concluded that every good work we do is tainted. Even on our best days, our motives are mixed. It's not just our actions, it's also who we are: sinners with an infinite gap between ourselves and God.

Grace means that we deserve nothing and can do nothing. *God comes along and does what we cannot do.*

Grace Is Unaffected by the Degree of Our Sin

What about those who have really messed up in life? I am talking about those who are in a tangled mess, without much hope of recovering from their misdeeds. Just think of the person you believe has blown it more than any other. Can grace save him?

Let us suppose that you have two corpses. Is one more dead than another? Does one need a bigger miracle to be restored to life? Fact is, the good person who lives next to you and the criminal you read about in the newspaper are essentially in the same predicament—both *need the life that only God can give.*

John Wayne Gacy was one of the most notorious serial killers in American history. He was convicted of killing thirty-three boys and hiding them in the crawl space under his house in suburban Chicago. Even now, decades after his execution, stories surface about some family who lost their son to his predatory evil. When his crimes came to light years ago, the media wanted to make him out to be some kind of monster who was scarcely a member of the human race. What struck me, however, was how normal he looked. In fact, he looked a lot like someone I know.

Gacy did not have horns. He did not look as if devils were coming out of his body. What got lost in the news stories was that he was an ordinary man with whom all of us, as members of the human family, share a great deal. He was simply a human being who decided to follow perverted sexual desires wherever they might lead.

Gacy's story is a reminder of some words of wisdom I read somewhere: "Sin always takes you further than you intended to go, keeps you longer than you intended to stay, and costs you more than you intended to pay." When he began his sinful odyssey, he had no idea it would end where it did.

Aleksandr Solzhenitsyn, who had a better grasp of the human heart than most of us, realized that the evils of the gulag do not belong to one race, country, or ideology. He wrote, "If only there were evil people somewhere insidiously committing evil deeds, and it were necessary only to separate them from the rest of us and destroy them. But the line dividing good and evil cuts through the heart of every human being."[3] Apart from grace, we are all on the same road. Some people just slide into the ditch and stay for a while. Others slide in, drag others in with them, and set up house.

Think of it this way. The Willis Tower (formerly Sears Tower) in Chicago is much taller than the nearby Union Station. From our vantage point there is a great contrast between the height of these buildings. But let's suppose we changed the question and asked which one of them was closer to the constellation Orion, which is a few thousand light-years away from the earth. Sure, the top of the Willis Tower is closer to this stellar constellation than the top of the train station, but does it really matter? *In the presence of thousands of trillions of miles, there is no appreciable difference in height between the two.*

Don't misinterpret what I'm saying. Of course it is better to be a decent citizen than to be John Wayne Gacy. Of course it is better to be honest than to be embezzling funds at work. From our point of view these distinctions are very significant, and they are also important to God. *But spiritu-*

ally speaking, even the best of us is still an infinite distance from God. If we forget this, it is because we have overestimated our goodness and underestimated God's holiness.

The good news is that God can save big sinners just as wonderfully as He can save lesser ones. God has declared that all of us are sinners and every mouth must be closed in His presence: "For there is no distinction: for all have sinned and fall short of the glory of God" (Romans 3:22–23). Some fall short more dramatically than others, but since the standard is God's glory, we all miss it. That's why we read that, from God's point of view, "there is no distinction."

Elsewhere Paul wrote, "For God has consigned all to disobedience, that he may have mercy on all" (Romans 11:32). We are equal in our unbelief, equal in our sin, and therefore equal in our need for grace.

There is no evidence that John Wayne Gacy accepted God's grace as given in Christ, but if he had, he too would have died a forgiven man. Here is a message of hope: *The issue is never the greatness of the sin, but the willingness of the sinner to be saved.* And even this willingness, this desire to accept what Christ has done for us, is given to us by God's grace: "No one can come to me unless the Father who sent me draws him. And I will raise him up on the last day" (John 6:44). Those are Christ's words, not mine!

Grace Is a Free Gift

If you have followed the logic so far, you know that grace has to be a free gift. Since it is independent of works and wholly of God, it must be given without strings attached. We now follow Paul's argument one step further. "For by grace you have been saved through faith. And this is not your own doing; it is the gift of God, not a result of works, so that no one may boast" (Ephesians 2:8–9).

When I was a child, my parents would have us listen to radio programs. There was one man who had a particular fascination for me because of his gruff voice and no-nonsense approach to teaching the Bible. But I also recall him saying something that did not make sense. At the end of the broadcast he said, "If you will send me five dollars, I will send you this new book, absolutely free!"

Even at the age of ten, I knew this was a contradiction. If he had really meant that the book was free, he would not only have sent it to anyone who requested it, he would have even paid the postage required to make the request. *That's what God does!*

Paul put it this way: "For the wages of sin is death, but the free gift of God is eternal life in Christ Jesus our Lord" (Romans 6:23). Yes, it has to be a gift—unearned and undeserved—and it is too expensive to repay.

Somewhere I read a story about a missionary who became a good friend of an Indian pearl diver. They had discussed salvation for many hours, but the Hindu could not believe that it could be a free gift. He believed that salvation could come by walking the nine hundred miles to Delhi on his knees. But the missionary said that salvation was so costly that Jesus had to buy it for us.

Before he left on his pilgrimage, the Indian gave the missionary the largest and most perfect pearl he had ever seen. The pearl diver explained that his own son had lost his life in getting this pearl from the bottom of the sea. The missionary thanked him, but then insisted that he pay for it. The Hindu was offended, saying that there was no price that could be paid for a pearl that had cost him his son.

Then and there the truth dawned: That is why Christians

insist that no one can pay for salvation. It cost God the death of His only Son. To think we can pay for that is an insult indeed. *Grace is free to us but very costly to God.*

God is so rich, we surmise, that He would not have had to buy anything. But there is one thing that God has purchased, and that is His people. We were not redeemed with perishable things, such as silver or gold, "but with the precious blood of Christ, like that of a lamb without blemish or spot" (1 Peter 1:19). To think that we could repay Him is an affront. It is a special insult when we attempt to repay Him with works He says He finds contemptible!

We will be indebted to God forever, but He has no expectation that we shall repay Him. If we think we can repay Him, we not only misunderstand the value of the gift, we also tarnish the word *grace.* God's favor toward us is undeserved, entirely a gift from Him to us. God doesn't expect to be paid back. He knows we can't. And we won't.

Grace Is Difficult to Accept

You'd think that everyone would be flocking to accept God's grace. Not so. There are reasons that the way to life is narrow and that "those who find it are few" (Matthew 7:14).

Intuitively, we think that we have to have some part in our salvation, to do some work, some deed that will make us worthy of the gift. Some do this by working up a sorrow for sin. Such sorrow is proper and to be expected, but it is not the basis for God's loving favor toward us. Sorrow does not make us more worthy of God's grace. It might lead us to cast ourselves upon His grace, but it will never make us more "presentable."

Someone said to me, "When I become older, I will come to God because then I will be less prone to failure." Whenever you meet a person who talks like that, you know that he has not yet understood grace. He is still thinking that he cannot come to God just as he is.

Many years ago I counseled a husband and wife who had come to church because their marriage was falling apart. I got the impression that the wife had dragged her husband to the meeting. I could tell that he wanted to be there about as much as a counterfeit coin wants to be seen on an offering plate.

They had belonged to a wife-swapping club, and the wife had recently come to understand the grace of God. She received the miracle of life that Christ offers, and it changed her. Now she wanted to get her husband to repent and experience the same miracle.

When I spoke to him, he said, "I would be lying to you if I told you that I won't continue in the club—I'm hooked." Of course he admitted that what he was doing was both sinful and destructive, but he felt that the temptation was too great. He could not change. He felt locked into his lifestyle.

I asked if he would be willing to admit his sinfulness and helplessness, to confess that he could not change himself. I urged him also to acknowledge that only Christ could forgive his sin and give him the miracle of eternal life. I explained that he didn't just need God's help; he even needed more than God's forgiveness. He needed God's power from start to finish.

For the first time in his life, he humbled himself to receive the grace of God, to accept Christ as having died in his stead as his sin-bearer. For days I wondered about him, hoping that the gospel would prove powerful in his life. To my relief, he made an appointment with me a few weeks later to say that he had left the club and was applying to a Bible school to train for Christian ministry.

He learned two things. First, *grace is free to helpless sinners who know how bad off they really are.* And second, *once the gift of grace is received, no one can ever really be the same again.* We come to God as we are, but He does not leave us as He found us. You can come as a homosexual; you can come as an alcoholic; you can come as an adulterer; but you come to the only One who can give you the gift of grace.

There are two kinds of people who shy away from God's grace. We ourselves have probably felt torn between both ends of the spectrum.

First, those who are awash with guilt find grace difficult to accept. They think, *If you really knew . . . If you knew what was in my past . . . If you knew my secret life . . . you would know that I'm too great a sinner to accept God's grace.* They are convinced that God is so mad at them there is no hope. They compare themselves to others and revise their estimation of themselves downward.

Second, the religious types, the Goody Two-shoes who think they have never done a very bad thing, find it difficult to accept God's grace. I remember a person saying that the worst thing he ever did in his whole life was to hit a golf ball through a window. Whew!

The folks who pay their bills, volunteer to work in the hospital, and raise good families find it difficult to accept God's grace because they don't think they need it. They know a dozen people who are worse than they. They look deeply into their hearts and realize that they could never do what John Wayne Gacy did. They see themselves as better than a whole host of other people. As one man told me, "I have just as good a shot at heaven as anyone else!"

These folks are offended when they are told that, in themselves, they are as far from God as John Wayne Gacy.

They bristle at the suggestion that the distance between themselves and God is infinite. They compare themselves to someone who is worse than they and revise their estimation of themselves upward.

That explains why Christ said that the prostitutes will enter the kingdom of heaven ahead of the religious types. Those who are in despair are more likely to see their need of God's grace than those who are self-assured. *Those who know they need a miracle are more likely to receive grace than those who think they just need God's help.*

Grace Can Be Received

Sometimes preachers who should know better speak of receiving God's grace as if we were expected to make a bargain with Him. I have a friend (bless him!) who in his witness for Christ used to tell people to "pledge their allegiance to Jesus Christ." An evangelist gave an invitation and told the people coming forward that they were making a "promise to follow Christ." I shake my head in dismay!

The potential convert is thinking, *If I have to pledge my allegiance to Jesus Christ or promise to follow Him, what will happen if I make such a decision and then break my promise the next day?* Certainly, accepting God's grace will result in a change of lifestyle. But we cannot expect the dead to walk until they are raised and the blind to see until they are healed. Sinners who have never been reconciled to God do not have the power to change their lifestyles, even if they were to get "really serious" about it.

To the person who says, "I want to do something about my broken relationship with God," grace says, "If you really understood the issues you wouldn't talk that way. God *did* something about your broken relationship with Him, and the only thing you can do is to humble yourself and accept it!"

Let me be clear. When you come to Christ, you do not come to *give*, you come to *receive*. You do not come to *try your best*, you come to *trust*. You do not come just to be *helped*, but to be *rescued*. You do not come to be *made better* (although that does happen), you come to be *made alive!*

Augustus Toplady had it right:

> *Nothing in my hands I bring,*
> *Simply to Thy cross I cling;*
> *Naked, come to Thee for dress,*
> *Helpless, look to Thee for grace:*
> *Foul, I to the fountain fly,*
> *Wash me, Savior, or I die.*

You do not come to Christ to make a promise; you come to depend on His promise. It is the faithfulness of God and not your own that gives the gift of grace.

Two Men, Two Beliefs, Two Destinies

Christ told a story about two men who both believed in grace. Yet interestingly, only one experienced the miracle of God's acceptance. The other, good man though he was, was rejected.

When the religious Pharisee went into the temple, he prayed thus: "God, I thank you that I am not like other men, extortioners, unjust, adulterers, or even like this tax collector. I fast twice a week; I give tithes of all that I get" (Luke 18:11–12).

If we think he was bragging, let's remember that he believed in grace. He *thanked God* that he was not like other men; he knew that his good works were done because of God's goodness, and he admitted it. I can hear him saying,

"But for the grace of God, there go I." If he was better than others, God deserved the credit.

In contrast, the tax-gatherer who was standing next to him was so overwhelmed by his sin that he would not even lift his face to heaven but smote his breast and said, "God, be merciful to me, a sinner!" (verse 13).

Christ added, "I tell you, this man went down to his house justified, rather than the other. For everyone who exalts himself will be humbled, but the one who humbles himself will be exalted" (verse 14).

Yes, both men believed in God's grace. The self-righteous Pharisee thought that God's grace was only needed to do good deeds. God's grace, he thought, helps us do better.

The tax collector saw God's grace differently. He knew that if he were to be saved, it would take a miracle that only God could do. He didn't need just a little help; he needed the gift of forgiveness, the gift of reconciliation. Only God could do what needed to be done.

The Pharisee said, "God, if You help me, I'll do better and save myself!"

The tax collector said, "God, You save me, or I'll damn myself!"

Was it difficult for this sinner—this tax collector—to receive grace? Depends. On the one hand, no, for he was relieved to discover that there was grace for the needy. But on the other hand, the grace of God was very difficult to accept. The crushing experience of having to admit total helplessness apart from God's grace is not easy for anyone. *And that is why the way to life is narrow and few there be who find it.*

Suppose you were standing at the door of the temple, and, as the Pharisee brushed by, you told him that he was spiritually lost. He would have been insulted. He would have admitted that he was a sinner but, with a shrug, would have reminded you that he was doing something about it and could do more if he got more serious! Grace was helpful and even necessary, but not amazing.

And that, at the end of the day, is the difference between those who are saved and those who are lost. Those who think they can contribute to their salvation think that God's grace is wonderful, but only the humble, who see themselves as God does, believe it is amazing indeed. *The difference is between those who know that God has to do it all and those who think that they can help Him out.*

The fourth stanza of the well-known and loved hymn "Amazing Grace" captures the wondrous nature of grace. Neither our life on earth nor our stay in heaven will exhaust our wonder.

> *When we've been there ten thousand years,*
> *Bright shining as the sun,*
> *We've no less days to sing God's praise*
> *Than when we first begun.*

Yes, grace is all one-sided. We bring nothing to the table, except our sins. God brings everything we need to lift us into His presence.

Amazing indeed!

CHAPTER 3

THE GIFT WE CAN'T
DO WITHOUT

I'm sure you've met someone who enjoys making a nuisance of himself!

A friend of mine attended the prestigious annual Christian booksellers convention. He went about asking the participants a pesky question and recorded their answers. These were the folks who wrote books about Christian living and the latest trends in theology, and every one of them should have known the answer to my friend's query, but most didn't.

Specifically, what he asked was, "Do you believe that we have to be perfect to enter into heaven?" A few knew the answer, but most stumbled through their reply, saying, with a shrug, something like, "No, we don't have to be perfect. Thanks to God's mercy, He doesn't require this of us or we wouldn't make it!"

God, they believed, is lenient, and we have reason to assume that He will allow us as sinners into His presence. In fact, He is so gracious that, thanks to Christ, the standards have been lowered. "Christians," they said, "are not perfect, just forgiven!" With a bit of His help, a dose of His forgiveness, and a tad of His grace, we can make it. How would you have answered that question? Perhaps you have never thought of it before, so I'll answer it for you. *Christianity, both Catholic and Protestant, has always taught that we have to be as perfect as God to stand in His presence.* Nothing less will do. So let me be as clear as possible. If you are not as perfect as God, don't even think you will ever be admitted into the heavenly realms! Give up your dreams.

The answer every delegate should have given was "Of course I have to be as perfect as God if I expect to stand before Him and be welcomed and received into His presence!" Come to think of it, this is not only the teaching of the Bible, but it also makes good sense. How could an infinitely pure and holy God who passionately hates sin have fellowship with people who are still regarded as sinners?

God's grace does not mean that the standard has been lowered. It doesn't mean that God can overlook our sin. Yes, God's grace means that we can be forgiven, but it means a lot more than that. But I'm ahead of the story.

Now, if we have to be as perfect as God to enter into heaven (and we do), then we have an obvious problem. In the last chapter I described as best I could how bad off we really are when left to ourselves. We are sinners by nature and sinners by choice. Some of us have done some wretched things. I have never yet met anyone who believes that he or she is as perfect as God.

So the question is this: How can we become as perfect as the Almighty Himself? That's a tall order, and it is also the subject of this chapter.

One Man's Struggle to Achieve Perfection

I have some Roman Catholic friends who think that Martin Luther was a turncoat, a deranged man who was angry at the church of his time for petty, personal reasons. Well, I'm not going to defend everything Luther did or wrote. Luther said and did some foolish things. Sometimes he was coarse, often angry.

But whether you are Catholic or Protestant, you have to appreciate his personal struggle. I myself am not a Lutheran, but Luther's experience has something to say to us all. Let us push back the curtain and understand the war within his soul.

Luther was troubled by what is known in German as *Anfechtungen*, a recurring despair of the soul. He was plagued by a keen sense of his own sin. Try as he might, he could not find peace.

He was taught a truth, apparently lost to our generation, that we have to be as perfect as God to enter heaven. But the path to becoming perfect, or holy, was tortuous and fraught with obstacles. Those who were serious about their faith would avail themselves of the means of grace offered by the church, and Luther did this to the best of his ability.

The church held out to people the possibility of embarking on the journey toward holiness. Those few who attained this perfection were canonized as saints, apparently qualified to enter heaven immediately at death. Those who did not attain this high degree of sainthood went to purgatory for as long as was needed until they were purged of their sins. Eventually, they, too, would qualify for the perfections of heaven, although no one knew when.

Luther longed for the assurance that he would meet whatever standard God required. He fasted so long that his friends feared for his health. He often wore rough clothing and slept in his cold cell without blankets to "put to death" the desires of the flesh. But no matter what he did, it never seemed to be enough.

Second, he took advantage of the sacraments of the church. Confession was of some comfort to him. To remind himself of his failures, he would begin by reciting the seven deadly sins and the Ten Commandments. Sometimes he confessed his sins for up to six hours and then later would go to his confessor, Staupitz, because he remembered a sin he had overlooked. One day Staupitz was so exasperated he said, "If you expect Christ to forgive you, come in with something to forgive—parricide, blasphemy, adultery—instead of these peccadilloes!"

Some have suggested that Luther was mentally unbalanced because he was so concerned about trifles. But he was perhaps the only sane man in the monastery. He knew that it mattered not whether the sin was big or little, but whether it had been forgiven. Even the smallest sin was enough to keep one from heaven forever. He knew that one blemish would bar us from the unimaginable majesty of God.

In his quest for perfection, Luther reached an impasse. He had been taught that if sin were to be forgiven, it had to be confessed. His problem was (1) that he could not be sure that he could remember all of his sins; (2) that he might have done some things he didn't realize were sins, so they would remain unconfessed; and (3) that even if he remembered and confessed all of his sins, tomorrow was another day, and the process had to begin all over again.

To make matters worse, he realized that his whole nature was corrupt. He was not a sinner because he sinned. Rather—and this was much more ominous—he sinned because he was at root a sinner. There were not only deeds that had to be confessed but thoughts too. The longer he lived, the more there would be of them. More penance, more confessions, more prayers.

Somewhere I read this bit of advice: "When you are in a hole, the first rule is to stop digging!" Well, Luther was in a hole, and he kept digging—trying to get out of the swamp of sin that lay in his heart. But he could not make himself free, even though he called on God for help. In desperation, he went beyond what the church had prescribed. Yet he was not sure that he had satisfied God on so much as a single point. To Luther, being promised eternal life was like a blind man being promised a million dollars if only he opened his eyes to see. The promise was wonderful, but the conditions were impossible.

In 1511, Luther was assigned to teach philosophy at the fledgling university in Wittenberg, which had been founded by the Elector Frederick. Luther enjoyed his work, but his conscience could not be silenced. One day when Staupitz visited him, he suggested that Luther should begin to teach the Bible in hopes of finding some solace for his soul.

And so it was that in 1513 Luther began lecturing on the Psalms and came to the first verse of Psalm 22: "My God, my God, why have you forsaken me?" He knew that these were the words Christ quoted on the cross. Christ, too, had *Anfechtungen,* for His soul was in despair. Luther realized that this was because Christ had taken our sin upon Himself.

In his study of the book of Romans, he soon came to these words: "For I am not ashamed of the gospel, for it is the power of God for salvation to everyone who believes, to the Jew first and also to the Greek. For in it the righteousness of God is revealed from faith for faith, as it is written, 'The righteous shall live by faith'" (Romans 1:16–17). Luther struggled with the expression "the righteousness of God," which he correctly understood as an attribute that stands over us and judges us and finds us to be unworthy. It is the righteousness of God that exposes our puny righteousness and makes us look so deficient.

"Sometimes Christ seems to me nothing more than an angry judge who comes to me with a sword in His hand," Luther remarked. The revelation of the righteousness of God, he believed, was bad news, not good news. Since we are punished for falling short of God's righteousness, it was not exactly comforting to know more about how holy God is! It makes us only the more convinced that we are sinners. We can increase our performance, but God's standard is far beyond us. The thought of trying harder sent Luther further into depression.

He described his struggle. "My situation was that, although an impeccable monk, I stood before God as a sinner troubled in conscience, and I had no confidence that my merit would assuage Him. Therefore I did not love a just and angry God, but rather hated and murmured against Him." Strong words, but the man was desperate.

Fortunately, he continued to study the next chapters in Romans, and the light dawned. He discovered that there is also a righteousness *from* God, which is given as a gift to sinners. For us, this is an alien righteousness because it is not a part of our nature, nor is it something that is fused into us. It remains external to us. *It is a righteousness that God credits to sinners who believe in Christ.*

Listen to Paul: "But now the righteousness of God has been manifested apart from the law, although the Law and the Prophets bear witness to it—even the righteousness of God through faith in Jesus Christ for all who believe. For there is no distinction: for all have sinned and fall short of the glory of God" (Romans 3:21–23). There is a *gift* of righteousness from God that comes apart from works.

We are thankful, for Luther and for us, that God can give us what we can never achieve. "For we hold," Paul wrote, "that one is justified by faith apart from works of the law" (3:28). There is a sharp distinction between the righteousness of God and the righteousness of man. God's righteousness is not simply man's righteousness lifted to a higher level; no, it is of an entirely different sort. Just as a billion bananas added together will never make an orange, so all the human righteousness performed since Adam, added together, could never change God's attitude toward a single sinner. There is an infinite chasm between God's righteousness and ours.

Christ's righteousness is the exact kind of righteousness God requires—obviously so, for it is His very own! With it, a man can stand before God.

The question then becomes, "What must we do to receive this righteousness, this right standing with God?" The answer is that this righteousness is a gift that has to be received by faith. It is given to those who turn away from their own efforts and trust Christ to receive from Him something they do not have. This righteousness, once received, carries a man safely all the way to heaven. Little wonder Luther said that embracing this discovery caused him to be "reborn and enter into the gates of paradise." Christ did for him what his works could never do! This is known as "justification by faith," which can be defined as *God's decision to declare us to be as righteous as He Himself is*. The penalty for our sin has been paid by Christ, who met requirements that were infinitely beyond us.

In California, I am told, a man pleaded guilty to a traffic violation. The judge read out the sentence, then left the bench and paid the fine he had assessed. That is what God did. We owed Him what we could not pay; Christ, the second person of the Trinity, paid our debt for us. God's requirements were legally met. Those who believe have their debt canceled.

This, then, is *justification by grace alone, through faith alone, because of Christ alone*. Justification by faith changes the way God sees us, not the way we see ourselves. It refers to the work of God outside of us, namely, the gift of righteousness we receive.

Paul goes out of his way to show that even the Old Testament patriarch Abraham was justified by faith, for he *believed God* and it was "counted to him as righteousness" (Romans 4:3). That means simply that the righteousness of God was legally credited to his account. No one past or present can be saved without it.

In another passage, Paul explained, "For our sake he made him to be sin who knew no sin, so that in him we might become the righteousness of God" (2 Corinthians 5:21). So there are two incredible transactions that happened when Jesus died on the cross. *Christ was regarded as a sinner when He bore our sin; we are regarded as saints when we receive His righteousness.*

Just as Christ did not personally commit any sin, and yet we read, "He was made sin for us," so, though we personally are not righteous, we nevertheless are accounted as such. We have "become the righteousness of God." We are declared to be as perfect as God. In His presence God does not see us standing alone. He sees only His Son standing alone, and we are "in Him." And when sin has been laid on the Substitute, it can never be laid back on the sinner.

The cross was not simply an expression of mercy. It was also a display of justice. To put it clearly, Christ became legally guilty of breaking every one of the Ten Commandments. He became legally guilty of genocide, sexual perversions, and hatred. Those sins were never a part of His nature or a part of His practice. They were alien sins borne by Him for us. Our debts were transferred to His account.

The result is exactly what we need. With God's righteousness ours, the legal logjam was broken. The dilemma of how a holy God could have fellowship with fallen humanity was solved. This explains why the New Testament can say that we are Christ's brothers: we are "heirs of God and fellow heirs with Christ" (Romans 8:17).

Sometimes justification has been defined as "just as if I'd never sinned." But that is only half the story. It is not just that our slate is clean, wonderful though that is. It is also that God looks at us as if we have lived lives of perfect obedience. He sees us as being loving, submissive, pure. *He sees us as having done everything Christ has done.*

If you have been reading this book for a while, this might be the place to put it down, get on your knees, and thank God for His incredible generosity. Or, if you have never received this gift of righteousness, receive it right now, by faith. This is grace indeed.

And the good news gets even better when we begin to contemplate the characteristics of this gift of perfect righteousness.

CHARACTERISTICS OF THIS RIGHTEOUSNESS

No wonder Paul kept returning to the theme of the righteousness of God! To the church in Philippi, he wrote that his goal was to be "found in him, not having a righteousness of my own that comes from the law, but that which comes through faith in Christ, the righteousness from God that depends on faith" (Philippians 3:9). No doctrine is more central to our faith; none is as liberating; none is more necessary.

This Righteousness Is a Gift

Obviously the righteousness of God would have to be a gift, for we neither have it nor deserve it. To quote Paul once more, we are "justified by his grace as a gift, through the redemption that is in Christ Jesus" (Romans 3:24).

Luther described this righteousness as "passive righteousness," for we receive it without doing anything. When we see the law, we see our sinfulness. All that we can think of are the sins we have committed and the things we should have done. Satan will take advantage of those weaknesses, and our consciences will be troubled, terrified, and confused.

Luther continues, saying that just as the earth does not produce rain but must simply receive it as a gift from above, so we can do nothing but receive this gift of righteousness. The soil cannot brag, for it neither deserved nor caused the refreshment. The parched ground is passive. It simply receives blessings by the mercy of God.

Once the earth has been watered, it can bear fruit, just as we will bear fruit for God after we have been granted the righteousness by faith. As for the terrors of the law—those penalties for sin we know we deserve—we need no longer fear, for Christ covers us. He is our refuge and strength.

While counseling a man who believed he had committed too many evils to be accepted by God, I asked him to visualize his life as a road on which he had carved some deep ruts, some leading right into the ditch. There were sins (or crimes) done against others that could never be rectified. All roads have their messes, but his was particularly ugly.

Then I asked him to visualize a blanket of two feet of snow covering the trail he had left behind. No matter how much the mud and gravel of the trail have been disturbed, no matter how deep the ruts or untidy the ditch, the snow covers it all. His past could be similarly covered, just as much as the path followed by the person next to him who all his life has tried his best to stay on the road. "'Come now, let us reason together,' says the LORD: 'though your sins are like scarlet, they shall be as white as snow; though they are red like crimson, they shall become like wool'" (Isaiah 1:18).

Again I have to stress that I'm not saying that it doesn't matter what we do in life because God just comes along and covers our mess. Obviously, it is better to live a decent life than to live a destructive one. The lives we live have repercussions that continue after we have been justified. But as I emphasized in the last chapter, my point is that when it comes to the righteousness of God, the "good" person and the criminal must both receive it as a gift—a gift that covers the sins of the past, no matter how great or small.

God does not have to do anything "extra" to save hard-boiled, great, cruel sinners. Nor does He have an easier time saving decent, respectable sinners. The gift of righteousness—the snow, if you please—is able to cover a trail that is unusually ugly as well as one that has been carefully traveled. In either case, God has to do everything that needs to be done.

The grace of justification stands entirely alone. One

writer, describing the relative differences between people, put it this way, "Grace . . . is not less than it would be had they sinned less. It is not more than it would be had they sinned more. It is wholly unrelated to every question of human merit." So it is. The righteousness of God is a gift given to all who truly believe.

Don't forget that God does not owe us this gift of righteousness. Fact is, If He gave it to us because He was obligated to, it wouldn't really be a gift. If we even partially deserved it, we could say that God was under some kind of obligation to give it to us. Grace means that what we received is completely undeserved.

That is why all the credit for our salvation goes to God alone. There is no room for boasting, no opportunity to say that we deserved it or helped Him with it. All we did was receive it by faith, which itself is not a work but a special gift of God.

I want the most wicked person reading this (I'll let you be the judge!) to know that Christ came to justify wicked people. We do not have to merit the merit of Christ!

This Righteousness Is Unchangeable

Obviously, everyone who receives this gift receives the same kind of righteousness. Whether it was the apostle Paul, who wrote much of the New Testament; or Billy Graham, who has preached to millions; or Bernard of Clairvaux, who inspired generations—these folks all received the same righteousness we do. Even ordinary people like us have the same acceptance before God, the same spiritual privileges.

Because I am a minister, I am usually asked to pray at church functions, whether they be picnics, banquets, or weddings. Somewhere, people have picked up the notion that pastors are closer to God and have a better chance of having their prayers answered. But anyone can pray just as effectively; anyone has the same friendship with God, providing that he or she has been made perfect through receiving this special gift.

This doctrine of equality is called "the priesthood of the believer." Every believer has the privileges of sonship. Every believer has the same attention, the same opportunity to serve God.

Nothing can ever be added to God's righteousness to make it better; nothing can be taken from it to lessen its value. A million years from now, it will still be as pristine as it was the day Jesus gave His life that we might have it. It is as unchangeable as God.

You don't have to know how to pronounce the name Nicolaus Zinzendorf to be blessed by these lines that he wrote:

> *Jesus, Thy blood and righteousness*
> *My beauty art, my glorious dress; Midst flaming worlds,*
> *in these arrayed, With joy shall I lift up my head.*

This Righteousness Is Permanent

We learned that when Martin Luther was confessing his sins in a monastery, he always feared that he might have forgotten some or simply didn't recognize others. What frustrated him was the realization that even if he could somehow settle his accounts with God today, tomorrow the process would have to begin again. He always felt off-balance in his relationship with God. To confess his sins was like trying to mop up the floor with the faucet running. What Luther needed was a divine act that would settle his relationship with God once and for all. He needed the assurance that despite the sins that he would commit tomorrow, his future with God was taken care of.

Similarly, there are people today who confess their sins but still have no assurance that they have satisfied God's requirements. And with good reason. They, like Luther, must discover that confession is not the same as accepting the righteousness of God for all of our sins. We are not saved by confessing, but by believing.

Confession is to be practiced by those who are *already* God's children through justification by faith. Confession keeps us in fellowship with God. But before we do that, we need to have our legal relationship with God taken care of. God needs to do a lasting act that will make us His children forever.

Confession is not the starting point for sinners, but follows once salvation has been received. Confession keeps me in agreement with God, but I have to belong to Him before it has meaning. The good news of justification is that the righteousness of God covers us from now through eternity. Two thousand years ago, sins that we would one day commit were laid upon Christ. To trust Him is to receive the completed gift of righteousness that will settle our legal obligations with God forever.

Justification is not a long, tortuous process with an uncertain ending. Justification is trusting Christ to meet the continual demands of God in our behalf. Twenty-four hours a day God demands perfection; twenty-four hours a day Christ is my righteousness before God. He will be there for me tomorrow and the day after. As we shall see in a future chapter, He is committed to bring us all the way home.

Notice how clearly the author of Hebrews teaches the completeness of Christ's sacrifice and the finality of our justification before God. "By that will we have been sanctified through the offering of the body of Jesus Christ once for all. For by a single offering he has perfected for all time those who are being sanctified" (Hebrews 10:10, 14). There was but *one* offering of Christ, and those who trust in it are "perfected for all time." We are not justified bit by bit as we perform religious duties. We are justified in *one* complete act.

Obviously, if justification took care of only our past sins, our future relationship with God would be in constant jeopardy. Tomorrow would be another day, with its temptations and sins, and I could commit a big sin and die. If all of my confessions and good deeds were not up to date, I would lose what I had yesterday. I'm glad that's not what the Bible teaches.

I have known a number of Christians who committed suicide. One woman showed me her husband's suicide note, which said that he could not "bear the thought of further suffering." Though he was a committed Christian, had led Bible studies, and brought others to faith in Christ, he decided to end his pain.

A girl felt so unloved that she reasoned that she was doing her family a favor when she took sleeping pills. Some people think that all who commit suicide go to hell, because they have committed a sin for which they cannot ask forgiveness. But the good news is that those who have had the righteousness of God credited to them will be saved, even if they should end in such failure. Suicide is a serious sin (murder), but thanks be, Christ died even for such sinners.

Once Luther grasped the fact that Christ's death paid every whit of the righteousness he owed God, he dropped the teaching of purgatory, which, interestingly, is not found in the Bible. The idea that we have to add our agony to the work of Christ, or that we still have to be further purified, diminishes Christ's work for us. Christ paid our debt *in full.*

When we die, there is no intermediate stop.

Augustine, well aware of his own sin, cried out, "O, God, demand what you will, but supply what you demand!" And when God supplies what He demands, we can be sure that those demands have been fully met. The hymn writer Elvina Hall had it right:

> *Jesus paid it all,*
> *All to Him I owe;*
> *Sin had left a crimson stain,*
> *He washed it white as snow.*

Just think: The works of Christ belong to us just as much as if we personally performed them! We owe God no righteousness, for we are accepted on Christ's merit.

This Righteousness Guarantees God's Unconditional Love

In most American homes children get the impression that their parents' love for them is conditional, that is, dependent on the child's performance. I don't know how many times I've heard someone tell me, "If I got a B my dad would chide me for not getting an A. If I got an A, he wondered why it wasn't an A+." Inevitably, the child grew up believing he would be loved only if he would perform.

Consider: Because we are accepted in Christ, it would be heresy to say that God would love us more if only we were better. God loves us through Christ and, therefore, He loves us just as much as He loves Christ.

If you think I have overstated the case, ponder these words in Christ's prayer to His Father: "The glory that you have given me I have given to them, that they may be one even as we are one, I in them and you in me, that they may become perfectly one, so that the world may know that you sent me and loved them even as you loved me" (John 17:22–23).

God loves Christ. Therefore He also loves us, for we are seen as being "in Christ," clothed with His perfections. Christ does not have some sort of righteousness we lack, for He shares His with us.

William Cowper, whose story will be told later in this book, wrote:

> *How Thou canst think so well of me*
> *And be the God thou art*
> *Is darkness to my intellect*
> *But sunshine to my heart.*

Of course, once we are God's children we can either please God or displease Him by the way we live. We must distinguish between our legal acceptance in Christ (our *position)* and our *practice* in daily living. Now that we know that we are loved, we will seek to love God. "We love because he first loved us" (1 John 4:19).

This Righteousness Unites Us with Christ

We've all seen movies where the good guy is fighting the bad guys and as he tries to stand up, the bad guys kick him down—again and again.

That is a picture of the conflict within our souls. Being "saved" (that's a word often used in the Bible to describe those who are justified) does not mean that we are exempt from trials, temptations, and sins. Often when we want to stand, we find ourselves tripped up or beaten down.

But we *can* stand. We are united with Christ by faith, so we can stand in His strength. We are not overcome by pressures or even our own failures. We rejoice that today Christ is to us everything we need: "Because of him you are in Christ Jesus, who became to us wisdom from God, righteousness and sanctification and redemption" (1 Corinthians 1:30).

The expression "in Christ Jesus" occurs more than one hundred times in the writings of Paul. Sometimes Bible teachers have called our union with Christ positional truth; that is, it refers only to our legal standing with God. Correct though this is, being "in Christ" is *reality;* it does not get any more real than this! This new relationship not only affects the way we see ourselves but becomes the basis for our encouragement and strength.

A woman, spiritually defeated because of a failed marriage and having little hope for a happy future, wrote to me that she had "given up on trying to ever please God." I replied that she need not feel helpless despite her setbacks, for, if she trusted Christ, He had already pleased God for her! Of course, she should try to please God in her daily living, but her efforts could never be the basis for her acceptance with God. The only sure basis for her relationship with God would always be Christ, not herself.

When the voice of conscience tells us that we are unworthy, when we are overcome by the consequences of our actions, believing that we can never forgive ourselves, we can confidently affirm, "Today God accepts me just as He accepts Christ. Today Christ is my representative, and He is standing in on my behalf."

Being "in Christ" gives us the assurance that we are heard in prayer. Calvin wrote, "It is a plain matter, that we cannot come boldly before the tribunal of God, unless we are certainly persuaded that He is our Father; and this cannot be without our being regarded as righteous in His sight."

A Tale of Two Books

In a discussion, a friend said to me, "There are so many different religions in the world, how can I possibly know which one is right?" I replied by saying that I would simplify matters for him. I would show that there are only two religions in the world.

I took a sheet of paper, drew a line down the middle, and above one column wrote, "All religions that teach we help save ourselves." Above the other column I wrote, "All religions that teach that God has done everything required to save us."

In a moment it became obvious that all the religions of the world belonged on the left side of the page. Christianity alone belonged on the right side.

The chasm between these two views is infinite and unbridgeable. The distance is as great as between heaven and hell, God and Satan, hope and hopelessness.

Some time ago I presided at the memorial service of a young man named Roger, who had died of AIDS. Though he had accepted Christ as his sin-bearer, and thus had the righteousness of God credited to his account, he still struggled with homosexuality until he was infected with HIV. Thereafter, he broke with his past behavior and lived a life of devotion to Christ. In the hospital, he was a witness to Christ's grace, especially to those who struggled with the same lifestyle and the same disease.

In his final days, it would have been easy for Roger to focus on his past behavior, the messy ruts he had made along the path of life. But he didn't. He focused on his acceptance in Christ, that gift of perfect righteousness which gave him the assurance that he would be welcomed into heaven. I am convinced that at death he entered heaven as perfect as God.

Imagine a book entitled *The Life and Times of Jesus Christ.*

It contains all the perfections of Christ: the works He did, His holy obedience, His purity, His right motives. A beautiful book indeed.

Then imagine another book, *The Life and Times of Roger*. It contains all of his sins, immorality, broken promises, and betrayal of friends. It would contain sinful thoughts, mixed motives, and acts of disobedience.

Finally, imagine Christ taking both books and stripping them of their covers. Then He takes the contents of His own book and slips it between the covers of Roger's book. We pick up the book to examine it. The title reads, *The Life and Times of Roger*. We open the book and turn the pages and find no sins listed. All that we see is a long list of perfections, obedience, moral purity, and perfect love. The book is so beautiful that even God adores it.

This exchange is known as justification. It is crediting the loveliness of Christ to those who are woefully imperfect. *Of course we have to be perfect to enter into heaven, and, thanks to Christ, we are!*

> *The errors of law and of God*
> *With me can have nothing to do*
> *My Savior's obedience and blood*
> *Hide all of my sins from view*
> *My name on the palm of His hands*
> *Eternity cannot erase*
> *Forever there it remains*
> *In marks of indelible grace!*

And the story is not yet over.

CHAPTER 4

THE MIRACLE
WE NEED

Religion can be boring.

    You don't have to do any research to prove the point. Just compare the crowd at church with the crowds that attend baseball or football games. Apparently there is no excitement at church that compares with that of the NBA, especially when the Chicago Bulls are in the play-offs!

Why this monotony, this lack of excitement?

It is not easy being faithful to rituals, even if we do understand their meaning. Nor is there much excitement in trying to live up to a moral standard we know we can't meet. One person told me, "I find myself expending my energy for church, but I just don't get anything in return."

This is not a new problem. By nature, we humans define our religion by what we expect ourselves and others to do. And "doing" becomes wearisome. Boring—at times, boring indeed.

In New Testament times, there was a group of religious leaders who weighed out their religious commitments to the last gram. They had more red tape than you could measure; some regulations defined other regulations. Their religious system seemed designed for failure. No matter how much you did, there was something you either forgot to do or more you should have done. Not only was the excitement gone, so also was the hope of the common man, who couldn't even remember the regulations, much less keep them.

These religious leaders were the Pharisees, good folks in many ways but specialists in misusing the Old Testament law, interpreting it as a set of complicated rules rather than as a means to experience God's grace. No wonder Jesus said of them, "They tie up heavy burdens, hard to bear, and lay them on people's shoulders, but they themselves are not willing to move them with their finger" (Matthew 23:4). They loved to strap religion on people's backs and see them squirm.

But one of these men, bless him, was so desperate to find reality in his religion that he came to Christ to ask some important questions that just might help him get the load of religion off his back. We have to commend him, because he knew how critical Christ was of his self-righteous crowd. But then, finding the narrow way that leads to life is not always easy.

This man was Nicodemus, a Pharisee who sat on the highest legislative body in Judaism. He shared a seat on the bench, representing the final court of appeal for the enforcement of Jewish law. He was a part of that brotherhood, one of those who thought themselves a cut above everyone else. He was a religious man among religious men.

Interestingly, though he had *rules,* he did not have *reality;* though admired as *good,* he did not have *God.* No matter how pious he was on the outside, he was rotting within. In fact, though he didn't know it yet, his religion was more of a hindrance than a help.

He came to Christ by night, possibly because he did not want to be seen conversing with the Man he was supposed to hate. Christ, you remember, embarrassed the pious Pharisees by bypassing their hocus-pocus and getting down to the issues of the heart.

The Judean night was no darker than Nicodemus's soul, spiritually speaking. Later, he would leave the darkness and come into the clear light of day—but that's getting ahead of the story.

Let us summarize the conversation as recorded in John 3:1–7, beginning with a question from Nicodemus.

> Now there was a man of the Pharisees named Nicodemus, a ruler of the Jews. This man came to Jesus by night and said to him, "Rabbi, we know that you are a teacher come from God, for no one can do these signs that you do unless God is with him." Jesus answered him, "Truly, truly, I say to you, unless one is born again he cannot see the kingdom of God." Nicodemus said to him, "How can a man be born when he is old? Can he enter a second time into his mother's womb and be born?" Jesus answered, "Truly, truly, I say to you, unless one is born of water and the Spirit, he cannot enter the kingdom of God. That which is born of the flesh is flesh, and that which is born of the Spirit is spirit. Do not marvel that I said to you, 'You must be born again.'"

What It Means to Be "Born Again"

What did Christ mean by that? We use the expression today to mean "remade." In the newspaper there was an article about a dilapidated tombstone that was restored, and the headline says it is "Born Again." A politician who switches from the Republicans to the Democrats is said to be "born again" (or is it the other way around?). Or perhaps an actor has reinvented himself, and the press now says he is "born again."

We had better find out what Christ meant by the term, because He said no one can see heaven without it. It really means "to be born from above." Christ was speaking of the work of the Holy Spirit within us; he was helping us grasp a miracle that only God can do.

Another word for the new birth is the fifty-dollar term *regeneration*. But even that word is not as difficult as it sounds. It just means "the act or process of being generated again." The Bible uses both words to refer to the same work of God by which He implants spiritual life within our souls. It is the creation within us of a God-like nature. This act changes us fundamentally. We are "new creations" in Christ.

Why do we have to be born again? God had warned Adam and Eve, "Of the tree of the knowledge of good and evil you shall not eat, for in the day that you eat of it you shall surely die" (Genesis 2:17). And die they did. Awash with shame and regret, they tried to run away from God. They were banished from the garden, their intellects became darkened, and the communication lines between them and God were jammed. We inherited their sin, and though we did not lose the ability to reason, we did lose the ability to reason our way to God. Worse yet, we were left with no way to repair the damage.

Adam and Eve began to die physically on the day they

sinned, and they would have died eternally—that is, forever separated from God—if God had not intervened. Just as a short circuit causes a light bulb to go out, so sin tripped the switch. Morally and spiritually, the human race (that's us, folks) was plunged into darkness.

To be "born again," or "regenerated," means that the circuit breakers are repaired and we are put back into contact with God. God renews our spirit and gives us a new nature; eventually, in the resurrection, we will receive a new body. We're talking about a serious transformation!

To put it differently, just as our physical birth made us members of our earthly family, so being born spiritually is necessary to make us members of our heavenly family. And just as a newborn baby has only a future and no past, so God comes to forgive our past and give us a new future. No wonder Christ said, "Unless one is born again . . . he cannot enter the kingdom of God" (John 3:3)! Nicodemus didn't get it. He heard the words *being born,* and his mind homed in on obstetrics. That's why he asked, "How can a man be born when he is old? Can he enter a second time into his mother's womb and be born?" (verse 4)

Christ replied, "Truly, truly, I say to you, unless one is born of water and the Spirit, he cannot enter the kingdom of God" (verse 5). This birth has nothing to do with your mother, but it has everything to do with your Father—your Father in heaven, that is.

We must be "born of water and the Spirit." You probably know that many people see the word *water* and think that Christ is referring to baptism. But the word *baptism* is nowhere in this passage. I would like to suggest respectfully that baptism would not have crossed Nicodemus's mind—and remember, Christ expected Nicodemus to already know the things they were speaking about that evening (see verse 10).

If baptism were really necessary to enter the kingdom of heaven, then virtually no one in Old Testament times would have qualified. Baptism began with John the Baptist during Christ's ministry, but it was not practiced by the Jews. Yes, the priests were to wash themselves with water, but that was not their entrance into the kingdom of heaven. God never makes His salvation dependent on a ritual.

Nicodemus would have known that in the Old Testament, *water* and *Spirit* are often joined to refer to spiritual refreshment that comes from God. A passage from Ezekiel would probably have come to mind: "I will sprinkle clean water on you, and you shall be clean from all your uncleannesses, and from all your idols I will cleanse you. And I will give you a new heart, and a new spirit I will put within you. And I will remove the heart of stone from your flesh and give you a heart of flesh" (Ezekiel 36:25–26).

Whenever *water* is used symbolically in the Old Testament, it always refers to renewal or cleansing, especially when it is joined with the word *Spirit*. There is a pouring out of the Spirit referred to in many passages (see, for example, Isaiah 32:15; 44:3–5). When the Holy Spirit does His work, there is the miracle of transformation but also the miracle of cleansing. The cleansing of the Holy Spirit does what water can never do.

There is a second reason to think Christ was using water as a symbol of the Holy Spirit's work. He did not say that we must be "born of water and born of Spirit," as if there were two separate births. He said, rather, that we must be born "of water and the Spirit." Water and Spirit are joined together, but there is only *one* birth, the one that is "from above." That is why the phrase is sometimes translated "born of water *even* the Spirit."

This new birth is done by God without human assistance.

Keep this in mind: Justification and the new birth happen at the same time. They are two different blessings that come to us when we experience saving faith. Although they cannot be separated, they must be distinguished. Justification happens *outside* of us; it is God's declaration in heaven that we are as righteous as Christ. The new birth happens *inside* of us. We are given spiritual life and are connected to God.

CHARACTERISTICS OF THE NEW BIRTH

Christ contrasted our physical birth with our spiritual birth, as He explained to Nicodemus: "That which is born of the flesh is flesh, and that which is born of the Spirit is spirit" (John 3:6). Flesh begets flesh, and Spirit begets Spirit.

You'll be surprised, I think, at what a great miracle the new birth really is. Clearly, this is something we cannot do, but, thanks be, God can.

The Work of Our Heavenly Father

We were born the first time as a result of the sperm of our father uniting with the ovum of our mother to produce a zygote. I inherited the characteristics of my parents but also their nature (a sinful nature, I might add).

Just so, two elements come together to cause us to be born into God's family. The Word of God (the gospel) unites with the Spirit of God to perform the miracle of God, the new birth. Listen to the words of Peter: "You have been born again, not of perishable seed but of imperishable, through the living and abiding word of God" (1 Peter 1:23).

Our physical birth was of corruptible seed; our spiritual

birth is of incorruptible seed. Our parents were incapable of cleansing the line of corruption we inherited. But the second birth, since it is of incorruptible seed, did what the first birth couldn't do.

On October 3, 1941, I was born into my family, thanks to my father and mother. Fourteen years later, after I had become so aware of my sinfulness that I could scarcely sleep, God graciously gave me the gift of faith, and I was reborn into my spiritual family. The Word of God combined with the Spirit of God to beget new life in me.

Two humans can beget a child in their own likeness, morally and physically (we've all marveled at how strikingly similar to his father or mother a child can look). Just so, God begets us in His own likeness. Don't get me wrong. God always remains God, and we always remain human. But when we are born again, we do receive His nature. *We don't become perfect in our everyday living, but we* are *made different.*

Neither you nor I can give the new birth to anyone. We are begotten by God alone, without human assistance. There are many things we can do, but bringing about the new birth is not one of them. When God regenerates, He is acting through the Word and the Spirit. The new birth is a direct act of omnipotence.

That should clinch it for us. Paul wrote, "Therefore, if anyone is in Christ, he is a new creation. The old has passed away; behold, the new has come" (2 Corinthians 5:17). Scientists have done many wonderful things, but one thing they have never done is to create so much as a single molecule. Creation is God's work, and we can only stand in awe of His power. He created the universe ex nihilo, that is, out of nothing. Even if we had been living on the day when the heavens and the earth were created, He would not have needed us to make His job easier. There was no need for our help because it was just "a bit much" for the Almighty. No, He acted alone— and with good reason.

When we are "born again," God creates within us a new nature that was not there before His intervention. Light was also created by divine fiat. Just so, the spiritual light that produces the new birth is the sovereign work of God. "For God, who said, 'Let light shine out of darkness,' has shone in our hearts to give the light of the knowledge of the glory of God in the face of Jesus Christ" (2 Corinthians 4:6–7). The shaft of light that causes us to be reborn has to come from God alone. He acted alone, creating it ex nihilo.

In the second chapter, I used the apostle Paul's analogy of resurrection to illustrate salvation. When Christ came to the tomb of Lazarus, He didn't expect help from the disciples, nor from Lazarus. He didn't say, "Now Lazarus, you should at least lift your elbow if you want Me to raise you from the dead!"

Once the miracle happened and Lazarus staggered out of the cave in which he had been buried, the disciples were able to remove the grave clothes. They were able to get something for Lazarus to eat. They could help him get reoriented into earthly existence. But when Lazarus lay in the grave, they could but watch as Christ did what only God can do.

Of course, when God saves us, there is one difference. We do agree to let Him do His work; we do exercise trust in what Christ has done. Whereas inanimate nature has neither mind, emotion, nor will, we have all three. And yet, our response is really the result of God's working in our hearts. God makes us conscious of our need for Christ; God gives us the ability to believe. Salvation is His work from start to finish.

The creation of the world and the creation of light are,

of course, great miracles. The new birth is different in that it doesn't affect the whole universe; the new nature within is not as great as the starry heavens; the light of the mind is not as blinding as the light of the sun. And our resurrection unto life is not as spectacular as Lazarus staggering out of the tomb.

And yet the new birth may be an even greater miracle! In the creation of the universe we see only the awesome *power* of God; in the miracle of regeneration we see the *mercy* and *grace* of God. The stars are the work of His fingers, symbolically speaking, but salvation is the work of His arm. God created matter and then put it in its place; but when He saved us, He had to overcome our blindness and the stubbornness of our wills. He brought us into agreement with what He was doing.

Back in 1954, soloist George Beverly Shea of the Billy Graham team sang this song to a packed crowd in London's Harringay Arena:

> *It took a miracle to put the stars in place;*
> *It took a miracle to hang the world in space.*
> *But when He saved my soul,*
> *Cleansed and made me whole,*
> *It took a miracle of love and grace!*[1]

An Englishwoman, who had obviously misunderstood the words, came to Shea later and indignantly remarked, "What do you mean by saying 'it took *America* to put the stars in place'?!"

America has done some wonderful things, has even trained astronomers who have diligently studied the stars, but, as yet, none of them has been able to create even one new star. We have put men on the moon, but only God could have created the moon. We must sharply distinguish between what we can do and what God can do. Only God can cause us to be reborn from above.

Other religions try to make men better, but only Christianity makes men alive. The new birth reconnects the switch that was turned off when Adam and Eve sinned in the garden of Eden. The miracle is all one-sided. Charles Wesley understood God's sovereign work in salvation when he wrote this hymn we love to sing:

> *Long my imprisoned spirit lay,*
> *Fast bound in sin and nature's night;*
> *Thine eye diffused a quickening ray–*
> *I woke, the dungeon flamed with light;*
> *My chains fell off, my heart was free,*
> *I rose, went forth, and followed Thee.*

We are the prisoners; God is the liberator. He shines light into the dungeon, cuts the chains, and tells us we are free. If He did not act, we would be lost forever.

The Will of Our Heavenly Father

Now I'm going to say something that might make you feel uncomfortable, but stay with me. Did you choose to be born physically? No, that was a choice made by your parents. (I've met some people who have complained about the fact that they arrived on earth without having a say in the matter!)

Who made the choice that you should be reborn spiritually? If I told you that our Father in heaven made the choice, you might complain that that isn't fair. And what is more, it seems "obvious" that you made the decision. And, I must agree, it was your decision, for no one was ever born again against his will. Anyone who desires to be born again can be.

Yet listen to the words of Christ to Nicodemus: "The wind blows where it wishes, and you hear its sound, but you do not know where it comes from or where it goes. So it is with everyone who is born of the Spirit" (John 3:8). Christ makes a connection between the breeze that He and Nicodemus heard above the roof of the house and the work of the Holy Spirit.

Note: In Greek, the word for *wind* is the same as the word that is translated *Spirit* in this passage (only the context tells us how it should be translated). Wind is beyond our control and is often unpredictable, blowing in one part of the country but not in another. It is also mysterious. Meteorologists can now make rather accurate predictions short-term, but they cannot predict the speed of the wind a year from today, nor can they tell how many tornadoes will develop next spring. Similarly, the work of the Spirit is beyond human explanation, and the Spirit does as He wills.

Although I memorized John 1:12–13 many years ago, I did not take the time until quite recently to think through the meaning of the verses. The text reads, "But to all who did receive Him, who believed in his name, he gave the right to become children of God, who were born, not of blood nor of the will of the flesh nor of the will of man, but of God." Did you notice how John credits the work of this new birth wholly to God? He says that we were "born not of blood"; that is, we are not born again by human lineage. No one is ever born again simply because his parents were Christians. God has many children, but no grandchildren.

Being born again is not a decision our parents can make for us, nor are we born again by being reared in a fine church

or a pious family. We don't "catch" the new birth from someone else in the same way we might "catch" a virus. God must
act or we are lost.

John continues: Nor are we born again by "the will of
the flesh," which means that we were not the ones who came
seeking for God. Finally, the new birth was not by "the will
of man, but of God." John here has eliminated any possibility
of tracing our new birth to ourselves, our family background,
or even our own decisions.

James confirms this. "Of his own will he brought us forth
by the word of truth, that we should be a kind of firstfruits of
his creatures" (James 1:18). We are born again because God
exercised His will and chose to show mercy to us. What I
once thought was the result of my will turns out to be the
result of God's will!

I can hear a chorus of objections. "What do you mean,
'God made the decision'? I am born again because I chose to
be! And what about those who were not chosen!"

This is not the place to answer all those questions, except
to say that here's what happens: God brings many circumstances into our lives, perhaps a Christian family or Christian friends, and we become aware of the good news about
Christ's coming to die for sinners. As our curiosity grows,
so does the recognition that we are sinners who need to be
saved. We are given the conviction that if there is any hope at
all for us, it must be found in Christ. We finally see that we
must choose to put our faith in Christ as our sin-bearer. At
that moment, God completes the new birth within us.

But don't miss the point. The reason we choose Christ
is that God worked in our hearts to bring us to that point
of trust. The decision that I would be born physically was
made entirely without me; the decision that I would be re-

born into God's kingdom was made with my consent to be sure, although my exercise of faith was God-given. Salvation is entirely God's work.

In New Testament times, there lived a woman named Lydia. When she heard Paul preach, "the Lord opened her heart" (Acts 16:14). She didn't open her own heart. Paul didn't open her heart. God did what only He can do. He showed her the truth and gave her the ability to believe on Christ.

Have no fear. The invitation to believe on Christ is extended to everyone. No one who wishes to be born again is ever denied the privilege. Some respond; some do not. Those who have the desire to receive the gift of God's grace do so because that desire has been implanted there by God. But by nature, we do not seek God. God seeks us.

The Way of Our Heavenly Father

Obviously, we cannot cause someone to be born again. And yet, in the history of the church, people have often thought they could. That is one reason there are so many people who claim to be Christians but cannot give evidence that God has done a miracle in their hearts. They assume they are saved because they have a certificate to prove it.

Let's take infant baptism. Many people regard it simply as a form of dedication, a sign of God's covenant within the church and their own family. But others believe that baptism washes away sin and makes the infant "a child of God." In fact, I remember reading one liturgy that says, "It is through the waters of baptism that we are reborn."

This teaching assumes that the new birth is under our control, that the decision to be born again can be made for us by our parents or even by the ministers of God. We can thus be born again without any knowledge of our sins and our need to trust Christ as our substitute.

Others believe they are born again through adult baptism or by belonging to the right church. They are taught that faith in Christ plus some other man-made ritual will bring about the miracle they need. Not until man acts, they say, does God act.

Is it any wonder that there are so many people who have been baptized but have no desire to walk in obedience to God's Word? They might be told that they are Christians but wonder why life is so boring, so powerless. Or they might continue to work hard to be saved, believing that if baptism is necessary, other rituals might be necessary too. Like Nicodemus, they might be very religious, but also very lost.

And what shall we say of "decisional regeneration" practiced so widely in evangelical churches today? A potential convert is told he must know that he is a sinner, pray a prescribed prayer to "accept Christ into his heart," and answer a few questions. Then he is told that he is now a Christian. No wonder there are many people who say they are trusting Christ as their Savior but only *think* they are.

This kind of teaching is often accompanied by invitations to come forward at evangelistic meetings. The impression is given, even if not stated, that coming to Christ means walking down an aisle or signing a card. Although most who use this kind of appeal know that coming to Christ and coming forward in a meeting are not the same thing, they do give the impression that the first step for sinners is to walk to the front, perhaps to the platform or the altar.

An invitation might be properly used if those who come forward do so to have their questions answered, receive prayer, or be given counsel. But by confusing coming to Christ with coming to an altar, many people have been misguided. Some think they are saved because they came forward and did all that they were told. Others think they cannot be saved because they are too shy to walk in front of a crowd.

Getting the chicken out of the egg can be dangerous. Although the need to believe is urgent, we cannot put pressure on people to be converted until they are ready. We must present the gospel and let God do what we cannot. Luther, with perhaps a bit of exaggeration, said that we must descend into hell before we can ascend into heaven. That was his way of saying that we should not get people saved until we get them lost.

Let us never forget that sinners cannot regenerate themselves. Let us also remember that a sinner can pray the right prayer, sign the right card, answer the right questions, and go to the right altar without having believed. To be saved, a person must transfer his trust to Christ alone and accept Him as his sin-bearer. Only such faith is evidence that God has regenerated him.

The great preacher Charles Haddon Spurgeon not only refused to give altar calls but even discouraged people from coming to be counseled in an inquiry room. He feared that they might be lured into a fictitious confidence that their conversion actually took place. He urged them, "Go to your God at once, even where you now are. Cast yourself on Christ, ere you stir an inch!"

Better that people be urged to seek God on their own, believe the promises, and ask God to confirm that they have transferred their trust to Christ. Better to let doubt (which is the subject of a future chapter) do its work.

By now you might be wondering what good it is to witness to the gospel of Christ if salvation is in God's hands and not ours. What part, if any, do we play in helping men and women believe?

The prophet Ezekiel was standing in a valley of dry bones, which symbolized the spiritual deadness of the nation Israel. The physicians of Israel would have been able to classify the bones, but they couldn't give them life. The mighty men of Israel would have been able to move the bones, but in doing so they would only succeed in transferring deadness from one part of the valley to another.

There *was*, however, something the prophet could do. He could preach to the bones and trust God to do what only God could do, namely, give them the miracle of life. So he preached, "O dry bones, hear the word of the Lord" (Ezekiel 37:4). Within a short time, he heard a rattling, and the bones came together, bone joined to bone. Then flesh grew around the bones. When the bodies were fully formed, he prayed, and breath came to the corpses, and they stood on their feet as a great army

Just so, we have the responsibility of sharing the good news of the gospel. We are to pray, discuss, and communicate. But we know better than to think that we ourselves can give life. We trust God to do what only He can do. And we also know that if He doesn't do it, it won't get done.

The new birth is instantaneous. It happens at a specific moment of time. Though there are many events that lead up to it, once it happens it is sudden and complete. We have passed "from death to life" (John 5:24). It is supernatural, instantaneous, invisible, and eternal. We are "delivered . . . from the domain of darkness and transferred . . . to the kingdom of his beloved Son" (Colossians 1:13).

The new birth is never repeated. Medieval theology taught that conversion was a process, a never-ending, often tortuous experience. The route to perfection was long and fraught with many possibilities for failure.

Not so. A healthy child is born complete, everything in place. The baby will have ten toes, ten fingers, and even little fingernails. Its ears will be perfect, a tribute to God's creative ability. In the same way, when we are born spiritually, everything is in place: we are God's children, partakers of the divine nature. "And in Him," says Paul, "you have been made complete" (Colossians 2:10 NASB). Now our responsibility is to grow. That's what newborn babies do.

The dry bones are resurrected in a moment of time, but their service to God continues after that. An old but true saying goes like this: "I have been saved, I am being saved, and someday I shall be fully saved." Though we are raised from death to life in a moment of time and are therefore "saved" when we believe on Christ, we are also "being saved" in the sense that God continues the work He has begun in our hearts. And, of course, in the future, when we arrive in heaven, we "will be saved" completely from even the presence of sin.

Only Christ could raise Lazarus, but once he was out of the grave, he was able to serve God. Just so, once we have been born again we must grow in our faith, not in order to be fit for heaven but because we want to serve Christ acceptably on earth.

We cannot take our blind eyes and make them see; we cannot give life to our spiritually dead natures; and we cannot cause our deaf ears to hear. Even so, we are commanded to believe, to repent that we might be saved. When we do, we know it is a miracle of God. And, as Ezekiel learned, if we share the message of life with others, the rest is in God's hands.

THE LOOK THAT SAVES

If you are somewhat rattled at God's sovereignty in the miracle of the new birth, you can take comfort in this: you can discover whether or not you are among those who will receive the benefits of His gracious work. What you must do is trust Christ alone, which confirms God's work in your heart.

Christ reminded Nicodemus of the Old Testament story of how Moses put a bronze serpent on a pole and invited those who had contracted a deadly disease to look at it. If they did so, this act of faith would bring about healing. These are Christ's words:

> And as Moses lifted up the serpent in the wilderness, so must the Son of Man be lifted up, that whoever believes in him should not perish but have eternal life. For God so loved the world, that he gave his only Son, that whoever believes in him should not perish but have eternal life. (JOHN 3:14–16)

Just imagine what happened that day in the wilderness. Many people complained, saying that this invitation didn't make sense. How could looking at a serpent (or any object) that wasn't even touching the sick folks be a remedy for the disease within them?

A good question, but the fact is that God chose to do a miracle; He chose to act on behalf of those who had the faith to obey the command of Moses. Just so, we look to Christ for the remedy of the disease called sin. We do not understand how someone who died and was raised two thousand years ago can do a permanent miracle in our hearts, but God says that if we look, we will live.

This look is a humble recognition of our sinfulness, a decision to receive Christ's work for ourselves. It is a look that embraces the wonder of God's love for us and invites Him to declare us righteous and make us one of His children forever. This faith is a ticket to the narrow way that leads to life.

For some, this act results in an immediate experience of peace and freedom from guilt. For others, it is a quiet moment with little emotion or deep feeling. For all, it is the beginning of a whole new relationship with God. The broken communication lines have been restored. At last we know God.

This was not the last contact Nicodemus had with Christ. After Jesus died on the cross, His body needed burial, so Joseph of Arimathea came to take His body away: "Nicodemus also, who earlier had come to Jesus by night, came bringing a mixture of myrrh and aloes, about seventy-five pounds in weight. So they took the body of Jesus and bound it in linen cloths with the spices, as is the burial custom of the Jews" (John 19:39–40). This was a bold step for a man who was a Jewish leader. Christ was supposed to be his enemy, but Nicodemus cared for Him as a friend.

We can be quite sure that only someone who had experienced the new birth would have had the courage to be counted along with Christ's disciples, risking ostracism and even death. Nicodemus had moved from opinions to convictions, from death to life. He came to Jesus by night, but later he identified with Christ in broad daylight.

Can religion be boring? Yes, as long as God appears distant and removed from our experience. As long as Nicodemus lived at the level of ritual, he found his religion empty; when he came to faith in Christ, his life became full. Of course, we can still fall into boring routines even after we have been born again. But now we do have a reason to be excited. Life has new meaning. Even religious people must be born again.

And now I ask you: Are you, my friend, born again? Even while you have been reading this chapter, God just might have "opened your heart." If so, let Him finish what He has begun. Go to God right now. Accept Christ as the One who died for you. Believe and be saved.

Nicodemus needed this miracle. So do we.

CHAPTER 5

HELD IN GOD'S HANDS

So *that's* what you believe!"

The man spit out his words like a chess player who was about to move his queen and declare, "Checkmate!"

"If *that's* what you believe," he continued, "then I can receive God's grace once for all and then live like the Devil and still go to heaven!" It was a deal that sounded too good to be true. The idea of having a reservation in heaven that could not be canceled no matter how he lived was appealing indeed.

So is it true that salvation once received cannot be lost?

Let's ask Ted Turner, the wealthy media magnate.

"I was saved seven or eight times, but when I lost my

faith, I felt better about it," Turner said when speaking to a group of humanists. He was raised, he said, in an extremely religious environment, including six years in a Christian prep school with Bible training and daily chapel services and regular meetings with evangelists.

He continued, "With no other influences in my life at the time and the way it was pounded into us so much, I think I was saved many times." He said he even considered missionary work, but when his younger sister got sick, "I prayed and nothing happened, of course." When she died, Turner said, he couldn't understand why this loving God he had heard about would allow someone who was innocent to suffer.

Turner still was not finished:

> I thought about it and said to myself, I'm not sure I want any part of this; if God is love and all powerful, why does He allow all these things to happen? This interpretation that it's just God's will . . . well, I can't get enthusiastic about that. I began to lose my faith and the more I lost it the better I felt![1]

So there you have it. Here is a man who was saved "seven or eight times," but no one can accuse him of being a believer today. He represents many others who apparently were at one time "born again" but lost their faith along the way.

The question of whether a born-again believer can lose his or her faith and be lost in hell forever has been controversial in the history of the church. I cannot pretend to settle hundreds of years of disagreement in a single chapter, but I can give you a few of the reasons why some of us think the Bible makes the matter very clear. And I might also have an explanation for the Ted Turners of this world.

Of course I know that some people think we are saved

only as long as we keep ourselves "in the faith." Often this is based on the depressing idea that if we die with sins that have not been confessed, God undoes all the work that He did for us. Our justification is canceled; the new birth is undone.

I sat next to a man on the plane who was taught this as a child. He was afraid he had committed some sin that he had not confessed. If he died during the night, he would be damned. When he reached his teens, he realized that he could never "stay saved," so he decided to save the faith until some future date, possibly just before he died. "I'm on furlough from living the Christian life," he told me.

Harry Ironside, for many years the pastor of Moody Church in Chicago, said he met a man who claimed he had been saved ninety-nine times. (Actually, if he believed he lost his salvation every time he sinned, I think the total would be much higher!)

A woman who was brought up with this kind of confusing theology said that in her church the town drunk got saved every Sunday morning and was drunk every Sunday evening. One day the pastor said to him, "Next Sunday we ought to shoot you right after you get saved!"

He was joking, of course, but you get the point. If you believe a person gets "unsaved" every time he falls into sin, you would be doing the man a favor to shoot him the moment he's saved. Better that than to die tomorrow unsaved.

Others say that we lose our salvation only when we commit a willful sin and are no longer in a "state of grace." This might happen through moral failure or turning away from the Bible into serious doctrinal error. If you are convinced of this, then all those who commit suicide are lost in hell. At any rate, the argument goes, we can't be sure today that we will be saved tomorrow.

I've even known some people to say that we should never comfort others with the thought that we can be sure of heaven because they will become complacent and "live like the Devil." They fear that people will get a ticket to heaven and then be careless, doing just as they please. And we have all met individuals who appear to be doing just that.

But is that a good reason to abandon a doctrine that is taught in the Scriptures? And what is more, I want to show that our security can be motivation for living a committed · Christian life.

Saved Today, Saved Forever

You have already guessed that I'm going to insist that God not only takes the initiative in saving us but is committed to those whom He saves, committed to the very end. He will bring all of His children home to heaven.

The Bible is a consistent book and cannot contradict itself. I believe that it overwhelmingly confirms that a true believer will never be lost. The work of God in the human heart is both miraculous and irreversible. Salvation, as we have learned, is God's mighty work. Our decision to accept Christ is rooted in His sovereign plans and intentions.

When the Holy Spirit comes to take up residence in our hearts we are "sealed for the day of redemption" (Ephesians 4:30). We are like a letter mailed on earth that is guaranteed to arrive in heaven. God is both the sender and the recipient. We can say that He seals us here; and despite the turbulence en route, no one can open the seal until we have arrived safely. And God will be there to do it.

Let's plunge in and take a careful look at a passage of Scripture that paints a rather complete picture of the panorama of God's purposes. You might be surprised at the detailed attention God gives to those who become members of His family.

Just stay with me, and we'll take a fast ride over some interesting theological ideas to show that God will never disown His children. They will never be lost in a child custody battle; they were purchased by His Son, and He is committed to keeping them even when they misbehave.

Five Unbreakable Links

You've seen a building under construction: boards, bricks, and steel girders are stacked close to the freshly dug excavation site. Day after day the work crews piece the material together. Gradually, a new building emerges from the seemingly unconnected materials.

How does such a transformation take place? By following a blueprint. Before construction ever began, an architect, or perhaps several of them, spent countless hours drawing plans that included everything from the apex of the roof to the electrical outlets.

If humans are smart enough to know that a building cannot be constructed without a master plan—if we have to choose every brick and window to fit the blueprint—we can just as easily see that God would not have created us without a specific plan in mind. We were chosen and designed for a purpose.

God was already preparing for our arrival on planet Earth long before we arrived on the scene. In the Scriptures, the curtain is pushed back, and we are allowed to peek into the plans and aspirations of almighty God. There we discover we are not an afterthought.

In Romans 8:29–30, the apostle Paul uses five verbs to describe God's great works on our behalf. Read the passage. If some of the terms are unfamiliar to you, don't be discouraged. We'll define them in a moment.

> For those whom he foreknew he also predestined to
> be conformed to the image of his Son, in order that he
> might be the firstborn among many brothers. And those
> whom he predestined he also called, and those whom he
> called he also justified, and those whom he justified he
> also glorified. (ROMANS 8:29–30)

You have just read a passage containing five verbs that form links in an unbreakable chain. God begins, says Paul, with those "whom he foreknew" and ends with those "whom he . . . also glorified." There are no loopholes; there is no possibility that one of God's children can fall through the cracks. All of them belong to Him in the beginning, and they are still His in eternity.

"Whom He Foreknew"

This means much more than the fact that God knew about us ahead of time. It means that He "foreloved" us. Long before we arrived on planet earth, He had already chosen us to be His; we were already cherished.

The Old Testament uses the phrase *to know* with the same meaning. The King James Version of Amos 3:2 says, "You only have I known of all the families of the earth." Interestingly, the *New American Standard Bible* translates the phrase as "You only have I chosen among all the families of the earth." And that, of course, is the idea. Perhaps the best way to translate it is to say that those who are foreknown are those upon whom God has "set His affection."

If you are a born-again Christian, you can stop right here and thank God that you mean so much to Him!

"He Also Predestined"

The word *predestined* means "to mark out ahead of time." Sometimes it was used by town surveyors, who arrived long before the people to mark out where the streets and buildings would be. In the same way, God mapped out ahead of time that we would be "conformed to the image of His Son." His plan will be accomplished, for God delights to honor His Son by giving Him "brothers." Of course, we will never be like Christ in His essence, but we "shall be like him, because we shall see him as he is" (1 John 3:2).

"He Also Called"

Third is the verb *called*. When we are "called," we experience the conviction of the Holy Spirit and respond to the gospel of Christ. This particular call is effectual; that is, it accomplishes its intended result. The Holy Spirit enlightens our minds, opens our hearts, makes us aware of our need, and gives us the ability to put our faith in Christ.

When we transfer our trust to Christ, we think that the decision is entirely ours and that our destiny is in our own hands. But, as we've been learning, we must trace our decision back to the inscrutable and certain plan of our heavenly Father.

"He Also Justified"

Since we discussed justification in a previous chapter, I need only point out here that this means more than the fact that our sins are forgiven. Justification means that I have been declared as righteous as Christ Himself and will be considered as such for all of eternity.

"He Also Glorified"

Finally, we come to the word *glorified*. Look into the mirror, and we will all agree that not a one of us looks very glorified in the here and now. Glorification, that is, receiving our new bodies and sinless natures, seems so far off that we wonder what it all will mean. Today we are not glorified, and everyone around us knows it. And yet this is the goal toward which we are moving.

The first two links in this chain begin in eternity past, the third is on earth, and the last two end in heaven. Notice that God is the subject of each of these verbs; that means He does all the acting. We are the objects; we do all the receiving. We are "acted upon" by the providential hand of God. And what He begins He finishes.

What is more, every one of these verbs is in the past tense! Even the word *glorified* is considered as something that God has already done. God writes the future as if it were history. Looked at from His point of view, we are already in heaven. Someone has said that this is a "daring anticipation." What a stupendous guarantee!

Those who were "foreknown" in eternity past are the same ones who end up glorified. Neither Satan nor they themselves can cause God to withdraw His love and faithfulness. He will bring them to where He says they already are!

Christ Our Attorney

If you are out of breath trying to grasp how much attention God is pleased to give us, there is more. Paul himself seems to be at a loss as to how to continue. Immediately after listing the five "links," he writes, "What then shall we say to these things? If God is for us, who can be against us?" (Romans 8:31). Though he wonders what to say, he does not stop there. Under the guidance of the Holy Spirit, He continues to assure us of God's faithfulness toward His people.

He visualizes a courtroom scene. "Who shall bring any charge against God's elect? It is God who justifies. Who is to condemn? Christ Jesus is the one who died—more than that, who was raised—who is at the right hand of God, who indeed is interceding for us" (verses 33–34).

This is not a municipal court; nor is this the Supreme Court of the United States. It is the Supreme Court of the Universe. God is hearing cases, and if we use our imaginations, we can listen to the proceedings.

Picture yourself as the defendant. You are at one end of a long table. The Devil, who is in cahoots with your conscience, is at the other end. Seated between the two of you is your attorney, Christ, who has chosen to take up your cause. On an elevated throne across from the table is the Judge of all the earth, God Almighty.

The Devil gives his opening arguments. He gives reasons (plenty of them) you should be barred from heaven. What makes it embarrassing is that he does not just mention some rather common sins you have committed but exposes nasty secrets that you thought were safely hidden. Like it or not, your dirty laundry is strung out across the courtroom. Added to your shame is the fact that what is being said is true. You cannot put your own spin on the details because you are in the presence of God, who has knowledge of all things both actual and possible. You are already embarrassed, but there is more to come.

Satan shouts the damning conclusion, "This person cannot be a member of God's family. He must be cast away from the presence of God forever." In his closing arguments he says that if the Judge does not agree with his conclusion, more accusations are in the offing. There is a briefcase with lists of sins that have not yet been mentioned. Indeed, a U-Haul trailer full of sins is parked outside the door.

What are your options? You cannot deny the accusations. God knows better, and so do you. It does no good to compare yourself to others, arguing that you are not as great a sinner as those who lived next door. You are being tried—you alone—a solitary human being in the Courtroom of the Universe.

What you once considered a speck of sin that was easily rationalized now looks like a mountain. The excuses you were planning to use evaporate like dew in hot sun.

Your best option, or more accurately, your *only* option, is to turn to your attorney. You let Christ handle the accusations for you. You tell Him, "This is all Yours."

Christ agrees with the accusations but points out that His death settled your account. He announces, loud enough for the cringing Devil to hear, that this particular sinner has been declared just as righteous as God. And the Judge has already agreed to accept the terms of the acquittal.

Who would dare impeach the Judge? Who would dare call you a sinner if God has chosen to call you a saint? That is why Paul says, "Who shall bring any charge against God's elect? It is God who justifies. Who is to condemn? Christ Jesus is the one who died—more than that, who was raised—who is at the right hand of God, who indeed is interceding for us" (Romans 8:33–34).

Christ's presence in heaven guarantees that those who are His will not fall under the judgment of God. There is no legal loophole by which God is able to get out of His pledge to save those who have believed on His beloved Son. He can't, and He won't.

Even as you read this book, if you are a believer in Christ, you already have taken up residency in heaven. We are "in Christ," and Christ is at the right hand of God the Father. We cannot be thrown out of heaven unless Christ Himself were to be thrown out. If we have really believed (what this means will be discussed in the next chapter), we can be sure that we will spend eternity with God.

But couldn't something happen that would cut us off from Christ? For us skeptics, Paul now lists all those things that will attempt to drive a wedge between us and God. Just when we seem to be free of guilt, Satan will want to make us doubt God's love. Or we may have a tragedy in our family, and the first thing that crosses our mind is, *If God loves us, why this?* There are times when we are deprived and times when we might be persecuted for our faith in Christ. And when the economy goes belly up and we lose everything we have worked for, it is easy to conclude that God really doesn't care for us after all.

Listen to how Paul raises these issues and then answers them:

> Who shall separate us from the love of Christ? Shall tribulation, or distress, or persecution, or famine, or nakedness, or danger, or sword? As it is written, "For your sake we are being killed all the day long; we are regarded as sheep to be slaughtered." No, in all these things we are more than conquerors through him who loved us. For I am sure that neither death nor life, nor angels nor rulers, nor things present nor things to come, nor powers, nor height nor depth, nor anything else in all creation, will be able to separate us from the love of God in Christ Jesus our Lord. (ROMANS 8:35–39)

What can separate us from the love of Christ? Death can't do it; life with all of its hassles can't do it; angels can't; Satan can't; present calamities can't; future catastrophes can't; political authorities can't; nor can anything that has been overlooked in this list!

Christ Our Shepherd

When Paul wrote, "As it is written, 'For your sake we are being killed all the day long; we are regarded as sheep to be slaughtered'" (verse 36), he was quoting Psalm 44:22. Although God's people are often mistreated, maligned, and misunderstood, the Shepherd does not abandon them. Even if they should be slaughtered, this Shepherd preserves them throughout eternity.

Paul's point, of course, is that despite the harsh treatment they receive, God's sheep are still God's sheep. He will never forget or abandon them. Nor will He disown them, for they are precious in His sight.

Christ confirmed the shepherd's commitment to His sheep in the strongest terms. "My sheep hear my voice, and I know them, and they follow me. I give them eternal life, and they will never perish, and no one will snatch them out of my hand. My Father, who has given them to me, is greater than all, and no one is able to snatch them out of the Father's hand" (John 10:27–29). The security of the sheep is the Father and Son's highest priority.

Just imagine a shepherd who has been given, say, a hundred sheep in the morning and returns with ninety-four in the evening! He'd be ridiculed to his face for losing sheep entrusted to his care. He might protest that the sheep were stubborn, or that they followed false paths and did not want to be brought back into the sheepfold. Even so, his reputation would be tarnished. Shepherds have full responsibility for sheep, no matter how irascible the sheep might be.

The sheep (that's those of us who believe on Christ) are a gift from the Father to the Son. We are in the Son's hands and in the hands of the Father too. Here are two pairs of hands that work in harmony—a double security for sheep who are prone to wander.

If you are still unconvinced, protesting that "Christ holds on to the hands of His own, but we can—if we wrest our hands away from Him—slip through His fingers," I reply that the matter is not quite that simple. We are one of His fingers (Ephesians 5:30)!

Believers have lined up with God's purposes. They have the assurance that if they have personally trusted the Shepherd, they are secure from here to eternity. God won't forsake them even in their rebellion.

This morning a note was on my desk telling of a born-again Christian who committed suicide. He walked outside and shot himself, leaving behind a grieving wife and shocked children. The reasons are unclear, except that he was weary of the emotional pain he suffered when he was abused as a child. Though he loved Christ, he thought he just couldn't take it anymore.

Of course no one knows the heart of a person except God. But I'm convinced that those who have trusted Christ are in heaven today even if they die with the sin of murder on their conscience. Even rebellious sheep are taken from earth to heaven.

The Son will not lose those whom the Father has entrusted to Him.

Children of the heav'nly Father
Safely in His bosom gather;
Nestling bird nor star in heaven
Such a refuge ne'er was given.

Neither life nor death shall ever
From the Lord His children sever;
Unto them His grace He showeth,
And their sorrows all He knoweth.

God, Ted Turner, and You

But what do we make of Ted Turner, who said he was saved seven or eight times but felt better when he lost his faith? What do we make of all those who turn away from the truth they once knew? These are difficult questions, and we must treat them carefully, for only God sees the human heart.

Of course, the fact that God has a place reserved for us in heaven could lead some to misuse this assurance. But the new birth gives us a love for God, a desire to live for Him rather than ourselves. Our motivation is to be a servant of Christ, not a servant of the Devil.

Suppose a young woman becomes engaged to a man. She knows that he is trustworthy. He will keep his word to marry her. Does she then use this promise as an excuse to sleep with other men, knowing that her fiancé will marry her no matter what? Of course not! She loves her suitor. His commitment to marry her makes her love him more. Secure in his love, she wants to please him in everything.

Just so, those whom God has reconciled to Himself desire to please Him. Realistically, we have to admit that grace can be misused; yes, even abused. A true believer may actually turn from the faith; and if so, the Father will discipline

His child for disobedience. Indeed, such discipline is proof of sonship (see Hebrews 12:6–8). That discipline might not always be effective, for sometimes God's children can be stubborn, but it will be administered. God won't abandon His children who misbehave.

But—and this is important—we also have to remember that many people who think they have trusted Christ as their Savior have not. They might never have been one of God's sheep, though they have heard about the Shepherd all of their lives and know some of His sheep. Later, they turn away from something they never really had; they deny a faith they only thought was theirs.

Let's listen as Ted Turner continues to explain his understanding of why he rejects the work of Christ for himself.

> If you really accept the Bible for what it says, the New Testament at any rate, the way it is generally interpreted, then everyone is going to hell. This idea of sin is horrible and disgusting. Christ had to come down here and suffer and die on the cross so that with his blood our sins could be washed away . . . weird, man! I'm telling you! Nobody has to die on the cross and have a blood sacrifice the way these ancient religions did down here in the pyramids of Mexico where they cut out virgins' hearts.[2]

Just a couple of observations. First, Turner obviously believes that a blood sacrifice is not necessary to take away sins. But whether such a sacrifice is needed is not really for us to decide. If the Bible is a reliable revelation from God, as all the evidence attests, then whether Christ had to die on the cross to save us from our sins is not really our call. We don't make the rules by which God operates.

Second, to equate the sacrifice of Christ to the cutting

out of the hearts of virgins in pagan religions is to turn away blindly from the chasm that exists between Christ and other religious teachers and beliefs. There is an infinite difference between Christianity, which demands a divine-human sacrifice, and paganism, where sinners kill other sinners in a futile attempt to take away their sins. Even pagans know that a sacrifice is needed to take away sins, but Christianity alone gives the reason that the sacrifice of Christ is the only one that God accepts.

Turner's words are those of a man who has never understood the basics of the Christian faith. He might have prayed prayers, heard the gospel, even made a decision, but the seed of God's Word never took root in his heart. He must have thought that one becomes a Christian by trying to live a Christian life. When that led nowhere, as well it might, he jettisoned "faith." The Bible is filled with warnings to apostates who turn away from the faith they claim to have once embraced.

In Canada a crew of men sold evergreens to a neighborhood and then showed up to plant them. Despite repeated watering, the small trees began to wither, stubbornly refusing to grow. Exasperated, one resident dug up one of the trees and discovered he could have pulled it out of the ground with one hand. These men, frauds that they were, had just taken evergreen branches and stuck them in the ground!

Christ has a word for the Ted Turners of this world. When the Pharisees were offended by some of the harsh remarks He made to them, He answered simply, "Every plant that my heavenly Father has not planted will be rooted up" (Matthew 15:13). If we have not been "planted by God," our commitment to Christ is not only shallow, but a mirage. The decisions we make pass away; what God does abides. In this life, the wheat and the tares grow up together, sometimes indistinguishable from one another. But at the time of the harvest, they shall be separated. God knows those who are His.

What kind of faith saves?

Bishop Munsey tells a parable of a man who, while walking along, suddenly fell off the edge of a cliff. As he hurtled down, he was able to reach out and grab a limb jutting out of the rock. He grasped it and hung suspended over the jagged rocks below.

The story goes that an angel appeared, and the man pleaded for the angel to save him. The angel responded, "Do you believe that I *can* save you?" The man saw the strong arms of the angel and said, "Yes, I believe that you are able to save me!"

The angel then asked, "Do you believe that I *will* save you?" The man saw the smile on the angel's face and replied, "Yes, I believe you will save me!"

Then the angel said, "If you believe that I *can* save you and if you believe that I *will* save you, *let go!*"

That "letting go" is faith. We quit clinging to our baptism, our good deeds, our own efforts to please God. We turn from our own sinfulness and transfer our trust to Christ. When we rely on Him to save us, He does. "Truly, truly, I say to you, whoever hears my word and believes him who sent me has eternal life. He does not come into judgment, but has passed from death to life" (John 5:24). That's a promise you can count on.

We've learned that there are many people who have not believed on Christ but only *think* they have, and that there are also many who have believed but are not sure of it. They wonder: Have I *really* believed?

On what does assurance rest? How do we really know that we will spend eternity with God?

These questions will be discussed in the next chapter.

CHAPTER 6

SAVED FOR SURE

In Michelangelo's painting of the final judgment, the expressions on the faces of those who are about to be judged reflect uncertainty and fear. No one in the fresco except the Virgin Mary knows his or her fate.

What expression would be on our faces if we knew that, say, in exactly one hour, we would be face-to-face with God? Samuel Johnson observed, "Nothing focuses the mind like the knowledge that one is to be hanged!" No matter how much confidence we profess, we all have our apprehensions about crossing the boundary into the unknown.

Yet, despite our anxieties, we can have a settled conviction that God will accept us without hesitation or reservation. He does not play games with us, keeping us off-balance, spiritually speaking. A loving Father would want His children to know that they belong to Him. Death, though mysterious, need not terrify us.

Here is a promise we can claim: "Since therefore the children share in flesh and blood, he himself likewise partook of the same things, that through death he might destroy the one who has the power of death, that is, the devil, and deliver all those who through fear of death were subject to lifelong slavery" (Hebrews 2:14–15). Christ came to free us from the terrors of death!

Paul compares death to the sting of a bee. "O death, where is your victory? O death, where is your sting?" (1 Corinthians 15:55). After a bee has stung its victim, it cannot sting again, regardless of how menacing its sound as it approaches a bare arm. Just so, death exhausted itself in Christ. Its sting has been removed. It can only frighten, not destroy.

In the previous chapter I gave reasons for God's bringing His children safely home. But now we come to the crucial question: How can we have the assurance that we are one of God's children? It is wonderful to believe that those who are saved are secure forever, but the pressing question now is *How can we know that we're included in that special number?*

We'll identify true faith more easily after we have contrasted it with some counterfeits. Just stay with me.

A Faith That Will Not Save

When Paul wrote to the church at Corinth he reminded them that he always determined to know nothing among them "except Jesus Christ and him crucified." He did this, he said, "so that your faith might not rest in the wisdom of men but in the power of God" (1 Corinthians 2:2, 5). He feared lest their faith was on a wrong foundation.

The characteristics of true faith will become clearer if we contrast it with some popular notions that fall short of a faith that actually saves. The difference is between the wisdom of men and the power of God.

First, there is the "I believe in Christ and . . ." kind of faith. Mutual funds, as you know, spread the risk of your financial investment. Your money purchases shares in a number of different companies so that if one goes bankrupt, the others will make up for it, and in the end your investment will be safe.

That's the way some people think of their faith in Christ. They believe in Him, but they also believe that baptism helps to save them, as do the Eucharist, church attendance, and good works. If one of those doesn't get them into heaven, another will. Or, perhaps when added together, all those will accumulate enough merit to lead one to God.

In a restaurant, a woman stopped to greet a friend of mine, and we struck up a conversation about religion in general and Christianity in particular. In the course of the discussion I asked her, "Why do you think God will let you into heaven?"

She replied, "My husband and I earned twelve hundred dollars in a bake sale, which we gave to charity." When I asked whether she had anything else to offer God, she mentioned a number of other good things she had done.

"And what if God demands more?" I persisted. She replied that she would depend on the grace of God for the rest.

At this point our mutual friend told this story:

A man came to the pearly gates of heaven and was asked by Saint Peter why he should be admitted into heaven.

The man replied, "My parents had me baptized."

Peter replied, "That's worth five points."

"I went to church every week."

"That's worth twenty points."

"I went to confession twice a year."

"That's worth ten points."

"I had an honest business."

"That's five points."

With this, the man became fearful, for he could think of no other merit he had accumulated. Simple arithmetic told him that he had only forty of the one hundred points needed. But, fortunately, he remembered a sermon he had heard on grace, so he answered, "I'm depending on the grace of God."

To which Peter replied, "You are lucky—the grace of God is worth sixty points!"

Of course a theologian might want to correct the story a bit and say that even the other forty points were God's grace, since He gives us the strength to do good deeds. Even so, in the story salvation is seen as a cooperative effort between man and God. It is based on the supposition that we can contribute toward the miracle we so desperately need.

As politely as possible, I tried to help this dear woman realize that those who distribute their faith between Christ and other works and rituals insult Him. They have not yet grasped that Christ alone is qualified to make us acceptable to God. They are like the Pharisee who trusted in God *and* in himself for salvation. For that error he left the temple without having been justified.

When I asked the woman if she was *sure* that she had done enough to enter heaven, she had to confess that, no, she was not sure that she would make it. And with good reason. Because she thinks salvation is partly of God's grace and partly of her own deeds, she can never be certain that she has lived up to her part of the bargain.

I challenged her to go for broke. I told her that there was a faith that could actually save her. It was the kind of faith that would lead to assurance and could take her safely all the way to heaven. More about that later.

Then there is the "I believe in Christ in a general sense . . ." kind of faith. Such a person might even believe that Christ died for sinners, but he or she does not accept this gift personally. There can be a change of mind without a conviction within the heart.

Just as deceptive is an "I went forward in a meeting and prayed a prayer . . ." kind of faith. This faith confuses an outward sign with an inward miracle. I've already warned about the dangers of associating genuine salvation with walking forward in a meeting or signing a decision card. When I was about ten years old, I was too shy to walk in front of several hundred people while an invitation hymn was being sung. So I suffered through those moments thinking I could never be saved. I was thinking, *I have to go forward to be saved. I guess I'll just go to hell!*

Somehow we just don't think God has done anything in our hearts until we have contributed to it. We want to at least raise our hand, walk down an aisle, or perform some other religious ritual. Those who confuse faith in Christ with such routines often backslide—and with good reason! They think they are saved because they have done something! And yet the transfer of trust might not have been made.

If you are inclined to believe that your own performance helps purchase your salvation, I have a question for you: *What makes you think that your good works could possibly mean more to God than the merits of His Son, whom He so deeply loves?* The good news is that Christ died saying, "It is finished." That expression really means "Paid in full."

To grasp this comes to the heart of a faith that saves.

The Faith That Saves

The faith that saves is based on a conviction, a settled belief in some facts. "Now faith is the assurance of things hoped for, the conviction of things not seen" (Hebrews 11:1). That word *assurance* can also mean confidence. Faith, then, is a *conviction,* a sense of assurance that something is true. And if we are convinced of the right things, we will be saved.

Notice how the apostle John connects the assurance of salvation with an inner witness or conviction within the heart:

> If we receive the testimony of men, the testimony of God is greater, for this is the testimony of God that he has borne concerning his Son. Whoever believes in the Son of God has the testimony in himself. Whoever does not believe God has made him a liar, because he has not believed in the testimony that God has borne concerning his Son. And this is the testimony, that God gave us eternal life, and this life is in his Son. Whoever has the Son has life; whoever does not have the Son of God does not have life. I write these things to you who believe in the name of the Son of God that you may know that you have eternal life. (1JOHN 5:9–13)

What are the characteristics of saving faith? What kind of faith gives us such assurance that we "know we have eternal life"?

A Faith Directed to Christ Alone

Saving faith means that I accept Christ as my substitute, my sin-bearer. I cherish and believe Christ's promises that He will give eternal life to those who believe. Calvin defined it as "the firm and certain knowledge of God's benevolence toward us, founded upon the truth of the freely given promise of Christ, both revealed to our minds and sealed upon our hearts by the Holy Spirit."[1] This is a faith that is given to us by God, an understanding that Christ did all that is necessary to declare us forever righteous before God.

The faith that saves is a personal affirmation of belief. The apostle Paul put it this way: "If you confess with your mouth that Jesus is Lord and believe in your heart that God raised him from the dead, you will be saved. For with the heart one believes and is justified, and with the mouth one confesses and is saved. For the Scripture says, 'Everyone who believes in him will not be put to shame.'" (Romans 10:9–11). This is a trust of the heart, not just the nodding approval of the mind.

R. T. Kendall correctly writes, "We are saved because we are persuaded that Jesus Christ is the Son of God, the God-man, and that He paid our debt by His shed blood on the cross. . . . If we are not persuaded that Christ has paid our debt there can be no assurance of saving faith, hence no assurance of salvation."[2]

Don't miss this: We must believe that Christ did all that is necessary and ever will be necessary for us to stand in the sight of God. If we have such faith, we will have assurance; we will know that we have eternal life.

Obviously, the more deeply we believe that Christ did all that is necessary for us, the greater our assurance. We might begin with a small faith (Christ said that faith the size of a mustard seed was all that is required), and within time it will grow.

Whether our faith be little or much, it must be directed to Christ *alone*, for God accepts only those who accept His

117

Son. And the more surely we are persuaded that His merit was completely accepted by God the Father, the more confident we will be that we are saved, and saved forever.

No wonder the figures in Michelangelo's painting of final judgment have consternation on their faces! In medieval times, the people, for the most part, were not taught that Christ paid the full debt of sin for all who believe. They were told that salvation was a cooperative effort between man and God. Churchgoers were discouraged from thinking that salvation was a gift; rather, they were expected to merit the merit of Christ. They had to add to His work through their own works and sufferings. Obviously, with that kind of theology, no one was ever sure that he had done enough. Those who said they had assurance were accused of being presumptuous.

Contrast this with Charles Spurgeon, a preacher in London in the last century, who is quoted as saying that he could swing above the flames of hell hanging on to a flax stalk and not fear damnation, provided he was trusting Christ alone for his salvation! That's not presumption—it is simply believing the promises of Christ no matter what. The difference is whether Christ did it all or we must help Him out.

Salvation is a matter of trusting a qualified Savior. It embraces Christ's work as sufficient. It transfers confidence from ourselves to Someone who actually has the credentials to meet God's high standard. Even better, it is a faith that believes that God's standard has already been met for those who believe. By Christ's death we are reconciled to God; by His resurrection we are assured that His sacrifice for us was accepted. For those who believe, it's a done deal!

Suppose someone says, "I can't be a Christian because I can't live the Christian lifestyle." Such a person still has not understood the good news. We do not have to live a Christian life in order to help Christ save us. He does the changing; He does whatever is needed to fit us for heaven above and to live on the earth below. He does not expect us to change ourselves first. He requires only that we see our sinfulness and our need for Christ's righteousness.

When at the age of fourteen I realized that I did not have to walk forward in a meeting to be saved, I accepted Christ personally; I understood Him to be my sin-bearer. From that moment I have had the settled conviction that I am saved—and saved forever. I learned that God can work anywhere and at any time. To be saved is not just something we decide to do (though it is a decision); nor is it merely the assent of the mind (though it is that too). True faith is a persuasion of the heart. It is a conviction that is wrought within us by the Holy Spirit. It is nothing less than a gift of God.

Let me say it once more: *If you are persuaded that Christ did all that is necessary and all that ever will be necessary to bring you to God, you not only will be saved, but know it!*

Today you and I should be able to say with Paul, "I am not ashamed, for I know whom I have believed, and I am convinced that he is able to guard until that Day what has been entrusted to me" (2 Timothy 1:12). If we were to ask Paul where this deep conviction originated, he would reply, "Faith comes from hearing, and hearing through the word of Christ" (Romans 10:17).

If you, my friend, are convinced in your heart that Christ paid your debt, and you are resting your eternal soul on Christ and nothing else, you too are saved—and saved forever. That is good news in a day of depressing headlines and an uncertain economy.

A Faith Confirmed by the Holy Spirit

The new birth, as we have learned, is not something we do but something that God does in us. We receive a new nature, but also the Holy Spirit takes up residence within us.

Listen to the words of Paul: "The Spirit himself bears witness with our spirit that we are children of God, and if children, then heirs—heirs of God and fellow heirs with Christ, provided we suffer with him in order that we may also be glorified with him" (Romans 8:16–17). The Spirit gives us an inner witness that we are indeed children of God. There is a sense of "belongingness," an inner conviction that, at long last, we have been reconciled to God. We begin to think of ourselves differently; for we are under new management.

God works directly in the hearts of those who are His. He does not do this through means of grace that are carried out by men, but He works in combination with the faith that has been planted within the heart. The church does not have the power to include or to exclude men from God's grace.

We can't repeat too often that salvation is God's work. We are saved directly by God and not by men acting in His behalf. The sacraments are symbols of what God does, but in themselves they are not the means of salvation. A soul can be saved without baptism, the Eucharist, and other rituals. In fact, a soul is saved *only apart from the rituals that men can perform.*

That explains why John can say, "Whoever believes in the Son of God has the testimony in himself" (1 John 5:10). The church cannot do this for us; God does this particular work quite apart from His ministers. If you believe that Christ paid your debt for both now and forever, you will have this inner witness that you are God's child.

We can all learn a lesson from John Wesley, an English eighteenth-century evangelist who came to America to convert the native people. But he returned to England with an overwhelming conviction that he had a sinful heart that had never been reborn. He wrote, "I have learned what I least of all suspected, that I, who went to America to convert the Indians, was never myself converted to God!"

Wesley envied the faith of his friends, who spoke of their confidence that they had come to know God, a faith that brought joy and peace. Wesley would have given his last drop of blood to have that kind of faith for himself. When he was told that it was a gift given to those who wanted it, he determined he would seek it.

On May 24, 1738, he quite unwillingly attended a meeting on Aldersgate Street, where a man was reading aloud from Luther's preface to the book of Romans. Wesley writes, "About a quarter before nine, while he was describing the change which God works in the heart through faith in Christ, I felt my heart strangely warmed. I felt that I did trust in Christ, Christ alone for my salvation: And an assurance was given me that He had taken away my sins, even mine, and saved me from the law of sin and death."

That is how personal faith in Christ must become to have the assurance that the miracle of the new birth has happened within us. Once such trust was in Wesley's heart, the assurance was there too. Notice the words, "I felt I did trust Christ, Christ alone. . . . And an assurance was given me that He had taken away my sins, even mine . . ."

Trust in Christ alone saves. That trust, thanks to the power of the Holy Spirit, leads to assurance.

A Faith That Bears Spiritual Fruit

I have gone to great lengths to show that we are not saved by good works but that, once we are saved by Christ's grace, we are expected to live a life of good works (see Ephesians 2:10). The inner transformation of life wrought by the Holy Spirit brings about fruit in the life of a Christian.

Our works are now pleasing to God because we as individuals have been made pleasing to God through the perfect merits of Christ. The works we did before we were justified were worthless, even a stumbling block, in our quest for God. The works that follow justification are made acceptable to God because we are now His children and serve Him with love and gratitude. Christ now makes our imperfect works perfect in God's sight.

After our conversion, we see God differently. Rather than thinking of Him as an impersonal, distant being, we will now speak to Him as a heavenly Father. We will also see sin differently. Rather than something to be tolerated and perhaps even enjoyed, we now see it as something that offends God.

What role do good works play in our assurance of salvation? They confirm our decision, but they cannot become the basis of our assurance. They provide a secondary kind of test, either encouraging us to gain a stronger assurance or, conversely, if there is no change of heart, giving us good reason to question our salvation. But personal assurance is first and foremost rooted in our faith in Christ.

If someone tells me that he has accepted Christ as his Savior yet lives the same selfish, sin-oriented life as before, I have reason to think that he might just be self-deceived. After all, as this book has shown, the work of God in the heart is deep and lasting. Not only should we question someone's salvation if his life is unchanged, but he should question it too.

On the other hand, if someone's faith has borne fruit, if there has been a transformation of life, then we have reason to think that his faith in Christ might be genuine. We can encourage him but should stop short of pronouncing him "saved."

We need to trust the Holy Spirit to give him the conviction that leads to assurance. Because we cannot see what is in the human heart, we can only point the way, but we cannot tell a person he has arrived. Remember: Many churchgoers who claim to be Christians aren't, though they think they are.

Until he was thirty-four, a friend of mine, reared in an evangelical church, believed he was a Christian. Others also thought of him as a fine Christian, the kind of person whose presence changed the attitude of those around him. People stopped their swearing when he walked into the room; no shady deals were concocted within his hearing. And yet, through a series of circumstances, he was led to deep conviction of sin and later was converted. I was interested to hear him say, "I didn't know that I was unsaved until the morning I got saved!"

I cannot impart assurance to you, nor can I judge you if you tell me that you have been persuaded in your heart that Christ has taken your penalty of sin away. If you doubt, I can counsel you to look at Christ, study His perfect works, and lay hold of His marvelous promises.

As a pastor I have counseled those who seek God but lack assurance of their salvation. One man read his Bible a few hours each day trying to gain assurance. Another went on a retreat to "seek God." As long as these men looked to their works, they never thought they had enough to "prove" they were saved. In both cases I had every reason to believe that they were indeed born again. (Who else would be so concerned about assurance except someone in whose life God had already done a great work?) But my responsibility was not to impart assurance but to counsel them to look to Christ and embrace His completed work for themselves.

Obviously, if we look to our works, we will never have enough by which we can say, "I now know for sure that I am saved, now and forever." Furthermore, we can't be sure that the good works will continue in the future. Some Christians have walked away from God for years, giving little outward evidence of conversion.

Suppose you were on a plane and asked a fellow passenger, "Why should God accept you into heaven?" and he were to reply, "Because I am a good person, I give money to charity and do volunteer work in a hospital, and live an honest life." You would, I hope, have every reason to doubt whether he was indeed a Christian, for as we have been at pains to prove, no one is ever saved by good works.

If it is idolatry to try to be saved by good works, it most assuredly is misleading to say that our primary basis of assurance is good works! To quote Calvin once more, "If men begin to judge whether they are regenerate by good works nothing will ever be more uncertain or more evil."[3] When we look at ourselves, we have only reason to despair. It is impossible to derive perfect assurance from our imperfect works. We are saved by looking to Christ's "good works" and not our own. Thanks to Him, we can have the inner certainty that He has stood in our place and paid our debt.

A new convert can have assurance if he is convinced that Christ bore his sin and did all that needs to be done on his behalf. Such a faith will be confirmed by the inner witness of the Spirit. The new convert's future works (or lack of them) can challenge the genuineness of his faith, but if he has believed God's promises for himself, he can even now rest in their certainty. The hymn is right:

The vilest offender who truly believes,
That moment from Jesus a pardon receives.

His faith should not be in the evidence for faith but in the promise of Christ.

Doubts must be taken seriously, and doubt must be resolved biblically. Remember, there are people who do not believe the gospel but just think they do. And there are those who think they do not believe the gospel but actually do!

More about that in the next chapter.

A Faith That Grows

A couple at a conference asked me to give my counsel to the wife, who had occasional bouts of fear that she was not a Christian. Meanwhile, she had led Bible studies, had introduced others to faith in Christ, and gave every indication that she was indeed born again. I told her a story that helped her understand how our faith can grow.

There was a man, the story goes, who wanted to cross a small lake in winter but feared that the ice could not hold him. To make it less likely that he would fall through, he distributed his weight by crawling, rather than walking, on top of the ice. Suddenly he looked up and saw a team of horses coming toward him on the lake! With that, he stood up and began to walk on the ice with confidence.

"That's what I'm doing!" this doubting woman said. "I am crawling on the ice while others have the confidence to walk or even skate!" To which I replied, "Yes, and remember: The ice under your feet is just as thick as it is under the rest of us!" She was encouraged to stand up and walk, spiritually speaking; she needed to know that Christ was just as strong for her as He is for anyone else.

To quote that old cliché, "We might tremble on the rock, but the rock beneath us never trembles!" The faith by which we receive Christ might be hesitant and trembling. But the amount of faith is not as important as the object of faith. We can come to Christ with our doubts and with our misgivings, and He will help us. We come believing that He is our only hope; we come trusting His promise to accept us.

We do not have to have a perfect faith to receive Christ. As we grow in our faith we will come to what the author of Hebrews calls a "full assurance of faith" (10:22); that is, we will grow in our confidence and ability to trust God. With the study of the Bible and strength that comes from fellowship with God's people, we will continue our pilgrimage en route to the heavenly city with a growing certainty.

Some who crawl today will walk tomorrow.

Is Christ Enough?

While sitting in my study at the Moody Church, I received a phone call from a woman who was weeping, insisting that she speak with me.

Here is her story. She lived in a nursing home in Chicago, and each morning the Christian women there would sit together to listen to Christian radio. That particular morning they heard a message in which the minister stressed that assurance of salvation was based on good works. He stated that a true Christian might backslide once or twice but that he would always return in fellowship with Christ. Without these evidences, there could be no assurance. Salvation comes by looking to Christ, the minister said, but after that our assurance comes by "checking our fruit."

The woman wept as she told me that, although she had accepted Christ as her Savior at the age of nineteen and had even led her daughter to faith in Christ, she now felt that the preacher had told her that she was unsaved.

"Why do you say this?" I asked.

"Well, according to him, if you backslide more than three times, you are not a Christian. My Lord knows how many times I have failed Him! I backslid many times! The preacher gave the impression that unless you are almost perfect, you are not saved!"

"What are you trusting for your salvation?" I asked.

"Well, the blood of Christ—there is nothing else." Then she added, "I cannot take steel wool to my heart and scrub it—I must trust the blood of Christ."

"The blood of Christ is *enough*," I told her.

"Are you sure?"

"Yes. I'm sure!"

By now she had stopped her weeping. I prayed with her on the telephone, and later she said, "As soon as I hang up, I'm going to tell the other women here in the room that the blood of Christ is enough!"

The book of Exodus records the clash of the Israelites and Pharaoh, who would not let them leave Egypt. God commanded Moses, you will recall, to tell the Israelites to put blood on the doorposts of their houses on the night of the Passover to keep the angel of death from entering their homes. I can imagine a frightened firstborn child asking his father, "Are you sure we will be safe?" The father could take him outside and show him the blood. "Yes, we will be safe."

In another home, a firstborn son might have been a notorious sinner. He might have been worse than one of the Egyptian sons who lived across the street. But there was no need to argue whose sin was greater. It was the blood on the doorpost that mattered.

Another firstborn might have been emotionally troubled with indecision and doubt. A skeptic might have knocked on the door, taunting him, reminding him that the houses of the Egyptians and the houses of the Israelites looked very much alike. If judgment came to one it would come to the other.

But the son of the Israelite need not have argued about the matter. All that he needed to do was to point to the blood on the door and remind his accuser that God had promised, "When I see the blood, I will pass over you" (Exodus 12:13). In every case, it was not the extent of the sin, the shape of the house, or the emotional stability of the inhabitants that mattered. The difference was the blood.

Blessed are those who are confident that the blood of Christ, the sacrifice He made for sinners on the cross, is enough! To grasp that promise is to receive assurance.

If God is satisfied with the death of Christ, we should be too. And when we are, we no longer owe God any righteousness. The song has it right:

> *I need no other argument,*
> *I need no other plea,*
> *It is enough that Jesus died,*
> *And that He died for me.*

Such assurance produces a spirit of repentance—a willingness to turn from ourselves and our sins to Christ, whom we now love. Our lives are changed because the chasm between us and God has been bridged.

We are saved and saved forever.

And yet if you doubt, the next chapter is for you!

CHAPTER 7

FOR DOUBTERS ONLY

God moves in a mysterious way
His wonders to perform;
He plants His footsteps in the sea
And rides upon the storm.

These words of William Cowper are widely known. What is not so widely known is that the evening he composed this poem, he tried to commit suicide. Although he wrote many poems that extolled the goodness and mercy of God, he believed that he himself was damned.

Cowper's mother died when he was six, and he was sent away to a boarding school. Early in life he felt the sting of rejection, the feeling that he was worthless, fit only to be rejected by God and men. No one craved God's acceptance as much as he; no one was more convinced that he would never experience it.

His first suicide attempt occurred in his thirties. He tried to drink laudanum, an opium solution he thought would put him into permanent sleep, but in the end, he could not bring himself to drink it. Later, he tried to commit suicide by cutting himself with a pen knife—that broke. Next he tried to hang himself, but the garter snapped and he slumped onto the floor. He wrote of that incident, "Though I had failed in my design, yet I had all the guilt of that to answer for; a sense of God's wrath and a deep despair of escaping it."

Cowper was convinced that he had committed the unpardonable sin. In his despair he wrote a poem titled "Lines Written During a Period of Insanity." He judged himself to be "damn'd below Judas." He described periods of horrible darkness, pain, and wild, incoherent thoughts. His sense of sin and expectation of punishment were overwhelming.

He was taken to live in a house for lunatics, where he suffered from terrible visions and voices. Through wise counsel, he improved somewhat and even planned to marry. But later he suffered his second attack of full-blown insanity.

John Newton, the author of the hymn "Amazing Grace," invited Cowper into his home. There, Cowper—now suffering from paranoia—believed his food was poisoned. Again he tried suicide, thinking he heard God's voice condemning him to eternal punishment for his past failures in trying to end his life. He wrote about God's grace, yet believed that he himself was excluded from it.

Newton tried to reason Cowper out of his despair, but to no avail. Yet, though his battles with depression grew even more intense, Cowper continued to write poetry, extolling the wonders of the gospel. He wrote ballads for use in William Wilberforce's campaign against slavery, and he honored God's sovereignty over the affairs of men.

Finally, after another bout with insanity, he wrote no more hymns. Though he believed he was damned by God through a providential decree, he clung to the hope that God might one day relent and change His mind. His last six years were spent haunted by horrific dreams at night and depression during the day. He died believing he was doomed to hell.

We wish this story had a happy ending. It would have been wonderful indeed if Cowper had come to peaceful assurance just prior to his death. We could wish he had experienced the peace he longed for. He did not. He who understood God's grace wavered as he grasped for it himself.[1]

Cowper's friends had no doubt that he was a Christian, primarily because of his steadfast perseverance, honesty, and deep desire to do God's will, whatever the cost. In other words, this was an instance in which good works testified to saving grace, and it is an example of how we can see the work of God in the life of a believer, even if he or she cannot.

Who but a person in whom God did a mighty work would so passionately desire to be included in the circle of God's mercy? Who but a believer would write about the grace of God, even when he felt he was not included in the circle of those who were blessed? Who but a believer would defend God's right to judge men, even when he thought that he himself would be the object of such judgment?

Of course we cannot be sure, for only God knows the human heart. But it is certainly possible that Cowper was a believer, for as we have seen elsewhere in this book, there are many people who are saved but lack personal assurance.

There is no despair so deep, no depression so dark, as the belief that one cannot, for whatever reason, be saved. It is my hope that by the time you have finished reading this chapter, you will be saved and *know* it. And if you already know it, I pray that your assurance will be greater still.

A man faced heart surgery with confidence, believing that he would make it through the operation successfully. Yet he fretted the night before, fearful of what would happen when he went under the doctor's knife.

"I thought you were sure that everything will be all right," his wife tried to reassure him.

"I am sure that everything will be all right," he replied. "But it's just that I'm not *sure* that I'm *sure!*"

Yes, we might be sure that we will go to heaven when we die. But being sure that we are sure is the problem!

We have said earlier that some people who doubt their salvation should do so. They have good reason to be unsure: they have never had the faith that saves. For them, doubt is helpful, for it might lead them to examine their faith. Doubt, if properly used, can be the servant of truth. Of course, the perpetual doubt of the skeptic who holds Christ at arms' length leads to damnation. But the doubt of the honest seeker can lead to assurance. We must analyze our doubts and learn from them.

WHY SOME DOUBT

Why do some true believers doubt?

Uncertainty Regarding the Time of Their Conversion

Most Christians can give the day and the hour when they came to saving faith in Christ. Others, particularly those who were brought up in Christian homes, may have had personal faith in Christ at such an early age that they do not remember when they crossed the line and were "born again."

"I'm not saved, but my parents tell me that I am!" the

young woman said to me. "I don't even remember when I accepted Christ as my Savior." She needed this bit of counsel: It is possible to know that the sun is shining even if we do not know the time of the sunrise!

The question is not whether we can remember the day or the hour in the past, but whether our faith is in Christ in the present. Are we now persuaded that Christ met all of our obligations for us when He died on the cross? And if not, rather than analyze the past, why not accept Christ as our personal sin-bearer now? We cannot revisit the past, but we can acknowledge our faith in Christ in the present.

Contributing to this lack of assurance is the teaching that we must "accept Jesus into our hearts," an expression that is not found in the Bible. I just read an account of someone who "accepted Christ as his Savior" three times a year! I, for one, prayed a prayer to "accept Jesus" every night for months when I was a child and yet lacked assurance. Every evening before I went to bed, I prayed the prayer again, but in my mind nothing happened. I thought myself doomed.

Some questions we should ask are: Why do we have to "accept Jesus into our heart"? What difference will He make when this happens? How will having Jesus in our heart rectify our relationship with God? How will we know it has happened? The expression is confusing.

The gospel is not primarily Christ in my heart (although it is that) but Christ as my *sin-bearer*. It was when I understood that Christ had died for me and must be received by faith, not feelings, that I had the assurance that I had been accepted by God. When we speak of Christ as the One who died and took our penalty, then faith has an objective basis.

Faulty Teaching

If you were taught that the possibility that you will be saved tomorrow does not exist until tomorrow comes; if you believe that you can lose your salvation whenever you cease to believe or fall into sin, then assurance is beyond reach.

That is why I tried to establish in an earlier chapter the doctrine of the security of the believer. If we are not sure that our relationship with God is eternally secure, it is very difficult to grow in the Christian life. We must have the confidence that if we have truly believed, we shall not be lost.

The Power of Guilt

I receive many letters from people who think they have committed the unpardonable sin. A small voice seems to say to them, "If you were a Christian you would not have done that . . . you would not have behaved this way!"

These doubters must remember that it is possible for Christians to do terrible things. When this happens, God does discipline those who are His, but He does not cast them off. In fact, their own sense of guilt might play a part in God's discipline in restoring them to fellowship with God.

Guilt is used by God only until his children repent. After that there is false guilt, which is exploited by Satan, the "accuser of the brethren." He enjoys engendering doubt in believers.

C. S. Lewis, in *The Screwtape Letters,* has the senior demon give instructions to his nephew about how to cause Christians to lose their confidence in God. He says the best way to do that is to get them to stop thinking about God and instead think about their state of mind. They must, at all costs, be preoccupied with their feelings and doubts; they must be made to wallow in uncertainties so that they will be discouraged.

As for the "unpardonable sin," it is committed only by unbelievers who harden their hearts against God. Those who seek God's forgiveness, no matter how great their sin, can be assured of mercy. That is why it is often said that those who are troubled about whether they have committed the unpardonable sin almost certainly have not done so.

Those who *have* committed this sin have seared their conscience and have no qualms about their rebellion. They have no desire to seek God for forgiveness. They probably would never read this book!

Confusion between Faith and Feelings

Some people think that saving faith entails an instantaneous spiritual experience that will flood them with overwhelming peace and joy. Sometimes that does happen, but often it does not. We must remember that faith, not feelings, is the basis for our assurance.

Martin Luther was once asked if he felt saved. He replied, "No I don't feel saved, but my confidence in Christ's promise is greater than my doubts!" And that, at the end of the day, is the basis of assurance—the belief that Christ was not lying to us when He said that we could believe on Him and be saved.

The Effect of Personal Rebellion

We have all met Christians who doubt because they have turned away from what they know to be right. Understandably, the Holy Spirit is grieved because of their sin, and peace from God eludes them. Recently I spoke to a homosexual who believes he accepted Christ at the age of twenty, only to plunge into a life of wanton immorality. He became so angry with God that he even asked God to remove from his mind the verses of Scripture he had learned. For ten years he quenched the prompting of the Holy Spirit.

However, in recent months he has repented and has "come clean." He has left the homosexual lifestyle and speaks openly about God's deliverance from this "mountain of guilt," as he called it. He also tells of the wonderful joy of assurance—the knowledge that he belongs to God forever. That assurance was lost during his days of rebellion. Whether or not he was a child of God during those days of heedless carnality (who of us knows for sure?), he lost fellowship with his Father. Assurance comes to our hearts most strongly when our faith is living.

The Chronic Doubter

Finally, there are those who, like Cowper, have become chronic doubters. They wallow in introspection and find it practically impossible to look away from themselves to Christ. They are unable to grasp the wonder of God's grace and cannot see that what Christ did can be applied to them. For whatever reason, they see themselves as sinners too vile to save.

And yet they believe. They cling to Christ and throw themselves upon His mercy. They trust, but they are not persuaded; they hope, though they are not assured. The inner confidence eludes them. These are the William Cowpers of this world.

Why are they saved? Because they accept the premise that if they are to be saved at all, they will be saved by God's grace through Christ. Their faith wavers, but it is directed toward the right person. Whatever else might be said about Cowper, he was under no illusions that he could be saved through living a good life and cooperating with God in salvation. Much better to believe in grace with a trembling heart than to believe in works with steady confidence.

Such doubters also often give evidence of being saved because of an implanted desire to please Christ. Though they believe they have been rejected by God, their greatest longing is that He be honored. This is further evidence of the work of God within them. Just as Moses, who did not know that his face shone when he came down from the mountain, though the people did (Exodus 34:29–30), so we often see the life of Christ in the believer even when he or she does not. The marks of grace are often found in the lives of these troubled souls even while they lack the assurance of such grace.

These doubters must be contrasted with volitional doubters, those who choose to not believe. We have all met unbelievers who fold their hands over their chests, sit back in their chairs, assume an air of superiority, and confidently say, "I dare you to convince me!" They are closed to faith.

Cowper was not a volitional doubter. He did not choose to not believe. He longed to believe but felt he could not. Although he held to the grace of God with a trembling hand, I believe he grasped the treasure nevertheless. For such, there is mercy.

There is a great deal of difference between a weak faith and a wrong faith. We might not believe the truths of the gospel as firmly as, say, the apostle Peter did. Yet, as Luther pointed out,

> two persons may hold glasses of wine in their hands; the hand of one trembles, the other does not. Two persons may hold a purse full of money: one with a weak hand, the other with a strong hand. Whether the hand is strong or weak, it neither increases nor decreases the contents of the purse. So the only difference between me and St. Peter is that he holds the treasure more firmly.[2]

Even a weak faith saves if it is directed to Christ alone. But a wrong faith leads to destruction, even if it is held with unwavering confidence. Those who cling to their good deeds or to a false savior will be damned, no matter how strong their trust. It is, after all, Christ alone who saves.

HELP FOR DOUBTERS

Here are some principles that will help us personally to resolve our doubts or give us the direction we need to help others who struggle with assurance.

Identify the Cause of Doubt

If, as someone has said, it is true that "he who has never doubted has never believed," doubts must be considered as healthy if they prod us in the direction of faith.

Properly interpreted, doubt should lead to probing, questioning, and testing of ideas. Alister McGrath put it this way: Suppose you want to see the stars or catch a glimpse of the Milky Way. You can't do this in broad daylight. You have to wait until it is dark. The stars don't need darkness to exist, but we need darkness in order to see them. We can be told about the existence of the stars, but only in the night do we see them. Just so, it is often in the darkness that we see God.

It is interesting that those who have experienced the severest doubts often emerge with the strongest faith. We should, as much as possible, create an atmosphere where doubts can be openly expressed. Many a child raised in a Christian home has grown up with the notion that to doubt is to disbelieve, and to disbelieve is to be damned.

Obviously, God wants to bring us through our doubts to the light of assurance. But the starting point is to voice our doubts, to talk about the barriers that hinder us from belief.

Some people struggle with factual doubt. They question the reliability of the Bible and the basis for the Christian faith. These people need instruction in apologetics, the rationality of the Christian faith. Many books have been written that give a defense of Christianity over against other options. Of course, we cannot prove Christianity with mathematical certainty. If that were possible, there would be no need for faith. But we can give reasons that are powerful enough for an honest doubter, but not a dishonest one.

There is no formula for dealing with doubters. "We come into the world with question marks in our heads," someone has said. Each person comes with his own questions, apprehensions, and reasons not to believe. We cannot bring a person to faith in Christ, for only the Holy Spirit can do that. We can, however, clear away misconceptions, answer questions, and encourage people to give the gospel a hearing.

Doubts must be taken seriously. Remember that some people think they believe the gospel but don't; whereas others, like Cowper, might have doubts and yet do believe.

Magnify the Grace of God

For those who doubt because of the greatness of their sin or the fear that they are beyond God's mercy, we should not minimize their sin. Be thankful when people see their sins for what they are.

Those who are troubled by an oversensitive conscience often are told, "Your sin is not that bad—there are many people who have done things far worse than you." That may be true, and even be of small comfort, but the doubter is not impressed. He sees his sin as being a giant mountain, a barrier that is too great for God to overcome.

What do we say to a child molester who must daily live with the knowledge that he has ruined, perhaps permanently, the lives of others? Recently a man in prison for rape wrote to me, asking how he could be freed from the guilt of the past. I did not minimize his sin, but I did magnify grace! I explained why the only place to face such a burden of sin is in the presence *of Jesus Christ*. He is the friend of sinners.

On August 21, 1544, Martin Luther wrote a letter to one of his faithful and trusted coworkers, George Spalatin, who had given a friend some advice that he later regarded as sinful. Because of the harm he thought his suggestion would bring, Spalatin was immersed in grief and guilt. He would not be consoled.

Luther wrote to him. He did not minimize the sin but saw Christ as sufficient for great sinners.

> My faithful request and admonition is that you join our company and associate with us, who are real, great and hard-boiled sinners. You must by no means make Christ to seem paltry and trifling to us, as though He could be our Helper only when we want to be rid from imaginary, minimal and childish sins. No, no! That would not be good for us. He must rather be a Savior and Redeemer from real, great, grievous and damnable transgressions and iniquities, yea, from the very greatest and most shocking sins; to be brief, from all sins added together in a grand total. . . . You will have to get used to the belief that Christ is a real Savior and you a real sinner. For God is neither jesting nor dealing in imaginary affairs, but He was greatly and most assuredly in earnest when He sent His own Son into the world and sacrificed Him for our sakes.

Christ did not come to save only sinners who were reared in Christian homes, sinners whose greatest crime is to have angrily bent a golf club on a tree stump! No, He came to save big sinners, child molesters, rapists. Christ was not just a Savior for "respectable" sinners. He is a real Savior for real sinners.

Satan always wants us to see our sin as greater than God's grace. We must never forget that the grace that is in *God's* heart is greater than the sin that is in our past. God anticipated our sinfulness and is well able to clear the account of anyone who trusts His Son.

Teach the Fatherhood of God

Recently I spoke to a young man whose father was a strict disciplinarian, a man who was never pleased with his son's performance. Is it any wonder that this young man struggled with assurance, no matter how long and consistently he called on God? If the human love we experience is always conditional, if we have felt the deep hurt of rejection, we tend to think that God is just like the one who turned his back on us.

I am certainly not qualified to diagnose Cowper's spiritual struggles, but I would like to suggest that the root of his doubts originated in the rejection he felt as a child. Like many abused children, he felt helpless, unworthy of God's love and personal attention.

I have had more than one person tell me, "I had an earthly father who abused me. How can I trust my heavenly Father?" God wants to bring us through such times of doubt and develop confidence in Him despite our past.

We have to help people see that God is not like a man. Once He makes a promise to His people, He can be counted on to fulfill it. He does not delight in having children who are constantly doubting their paternity.

Cowper also wrestled with a theological problem that he did not correctly resolve. He grew up in an era when the doctrine of election was stressed, namely, the idea that God is the One who chooses who will be saved and leaves the rest to be damned. Cowper felt that he was not worthy to be classified as belonging to the chosen. He thought that, for whatever reason, election excluded him from the wonders of God's love.

Apparently he did not understand that we can find out whether we are one of the chosen! We can do this by coming to Christ and receiving His love and grace. If we do this, it is proof that God is at work drawing us to Himself. Notice how Christ combines God's sovereign work of election with the assurance that those who come to Him will be received. "All that the Father gives me will come to me, and whoever comes to me I will never cast out" (John 6:37). Cowper could have taken comfort from the fact that the gospel is offered to all.

No one who wishes to receive God's grace in Christ will ever be excluded. Indeed, "everyone who calls on the name of the Lord will be saved" (Romans 10:13). If only Cowper had grasped that grace was available for him since he desired to believe. As the preacher Spurgeon said with considerable insight, "He who worries about not being among the elect, probably is one of the elect!"

Receive Encouragement from Others

Often people who experience doubt are encouraged to know that others, often great men of the past, have doubted. It is not just the Cowpers of the world who have struggled with belief. Some biblical heroes have done so too.

John the Baptist, that great preacher of righteousness, was

thrown into a dungeon for telling King Herod that he had an illegal marriage. The suffering turned John the prophet into John the doubter.

Why the doubts? First, he was suffering from injustice. His crime was speaking the truth to a king who needed to hear what God thought of his lifestyle. It is always difficult for us to reconcile God's love for us with a feeling of betrayal when we are wrongly accused. Our sense of fairness cries out for retribution. This is the soil in which our doubts grow.

Second, John was in isolation, solitary confinement. He did have some visitors, but nothing is more demoralizing than to survive when we cannot be strengthened by those who could stand with us in our need.

Third, and most important, his imprisonment seemed to be a breach of God's promise. He interpreted some Old Testament passages to teach that the Messiah would deliver the Israelites from the heavy-handed political occupation of Rome. The prisons would be opened, the enemy vanquished, and the nation of Israel freed.

Just the other day I inadvertently tore the flap from an envelope I hoped to mail. To find the missing piece, I went through my wastebasket, searching for the flap that would match the torn envelope. Just so, John could not find the missing piece. Reality did not square with the promises.

So John sent a group of disciples to Christ, asking Him candidly, "Are you the one who is to come, or should we expect someone else?" (Matthew 11:3 NIV). He was being as polite as he could be, but the question could not have been more pointed or plaintive. He was wondering whether the Christ had been mistakenly identified.

Christ did not chide John for wavering. Nor did He preach a sermon about the evils of unbelief. He pointed John to the Scriptures. First, He said, in effect, that prophecy *was* being fulfilled: "Go back and report to John what you hear and see: The blind receive sight, the lame walk, those who have leprosy are cleansed, the deaf hear, the dead are raised, and the good news is proclaimed to the poor. Blessed is anyone who does not stumble on account of me" (Matthew 11:4–6 NIV).

Yes, some Scriptures *were* being fulfilled, even if others were not. John, like most of his peers, did not realize that there would be two comings of the Messiah, separated by hundreds of years. Yes, Christ *will* return to bring about the political deliverance the Old Testament promised, but that was not to happen now. John was insisting on present fulfillment of a promise that was to be fulfilled in the future.

Second, Christ added, "Blessed is anyone who does not stumble on account of me" (verse 6 NIV). Christ was saying that those who would believe even when He was not fulfilling their expectations would be blessed. Yes, there were reasons why some might stumble because of Him, but those who believed, even when disappointed, would be blessed.

It is interesting that it was in the context of his doubt that Christ proclaimed the greatness of John the Baptist: "Truly, I say to you, among those born of women there has arisen no one greater than John the Baptist. Yet the one who is least in the kingdom of heaven is greater than he" (Matthew 11:11). F. B. Meyer says of this, "The Master seems to say, heaven judges, not by a passing mood but by the general tenor of a man's life." With that, John is beheaded and passes from this life to the next.

And what shall we say of the disciple Thomas? He had a streak of pessimism, the sense that in the end nothing would come out quite right. It happened that Thomas was absent the day Christ appeared to the other disciples in the upper room. When the disciples saw Thomas, they shouted, "We have seen the Lord!" Thomas should have believed, for he had the report of these ten credible witnesses. What is more, he had known Christ and was privy to the miracles He had performed.

But Thomas replied, "Unless I see in his hands the mark of the nails, and place my finger into the mark of the nails, and place my hand into his side, I will never believe" (John 20:25). Eight days later Christ graciously gave Thomas his request. Thomas had the honesty to admit the truth when the evidence was convincing. He exclaimed, "My Lord and my God!"

Let me encourage you by saying that your name might just be in the Bible. Christ said to Thomas, "Have you believed because you have seen me? Blessed are those who have not seen and yet have believed" (verse 29). We could paraphrase it, "Blessed are you, Tom, Ruth, or Marie, for, though you have not seen, you have believed!"

Who but a doubting Cowper could write of God:

> *Behind a frowning providence*
> *He hides a smiling face.*

His life should be an encouragement to all who doubt.

Faith, Doubt, and Assurance

Several years ago I interviewed a young minister who later died of a rare, fast-growing brain tumor. The doctors had told him he had only a few months to live, so he did all he could to prepare his peers for the future success of his ministry.

"When the electricity goes off," he told me, "you can walk around in the darkness of your house because you lived in it when it was light." Then he added, "I want to walk with God in the light so that when the darkness comes, I will know my way around." Months later, he died with a spirit of acceptance, knowing that even in the darkness he could trust the faithfulness of God. The better we know God in the light, the better we will be prepared for the dark.

We can grow in our faith if we remember these principles.

First, *faith does not exclude doubt.* Whether John the Baptist, Job, or Peter, who walked on the water, these believed despite their doubts. The father of the son stricken by convulsions (Mark 9:20) reflected the ambivalence of us all when he cried, "Lord, I believe; help thou mine unbelief" (verse 24 KJV).

Luther said, "Faith is the free surrender and a joyous wager on the unseen, untried and unknown goodness of God." Someday our faith will become sight. Until then, we might tremble on the rock of God's promises, even though the rock beneath us remains unshaken.

Second, *doubts might lead to certainties.* A seventeenth-century philosopher said, "If a man will begin with certainties he will end in doubts; but if he is content to begin with doubts, he will end in certainties." Or perhaps we should change that and say that doubts should end with certainties. Doubt can be used by God to deepen our faith by showing us how far we yet have to progress in our Christian experience. Our faithlessness, says Paul, in no way changes God's faithfulness (see 2 Timothy 2:13).

New believers often have an overwhelming sense of God's presence. He seems as near to them as breath itself. With time, those feelings dissipate so that we might learn to believe His bare word, even without the spiritual ecstasy we once experienced.

Doubts make our faith even more precious to God. The faith by which we believe in Christ is a gift of God, granted to those whom God has chosen for eternal life. But growth in faith is the constant theme of the New Testament. It is precisely because we are so prone to doubt that "the tested genuineness of your faith—more precious than gold that perishes though it is tested by fire—may be found to result in praise and glory and honor at the revelation of Jesus Christ" (1 Peter 1:7). Our doubts might, in the end, purify our faith.

Third, *admitting our doubts to others, and particularly to God, is essential*. God already knows our doubts, of course, but allowing us to admit them is His way of helping us in our need. For example, in Psalm 13 David remembers the times when he felt close to God, and that helps him to overcome his fear that God has forsaken him.

> *How long, O LORD? Will you forget me forever?*
> *How long will you hide your face from me? How long*
> *must I take counsel in my soul*
> *and have sorrow in my heart all the day?*
> *How long shall my enemy be exalted over me?*
> *Consider and answer me, O LORD my God;*
> *light up my eyes, lest I sleep the sleep of death,*
> *lest my enemy say, "I have prevailed over him,"*
> *lest my foes rejoice because I am shaken.*
> *But I have trusted in your steadfast love;*
> *my heart shall rejoice in your salvation.*
> *I will sing to the LORD,*
> *because he has dealt bountifully with me.*

In Bunyan's famous allegory *The Pilgrim's Progress*, the men Christian and Hopeful disobey their instructions when they leave the path toward the Celestial City and climb over a giant fence. There they encounter a terrifying storm. They are caught by Giant Despair and thrust into the dungeon called Doubting Castle. Here they languish until Christian realizes he has the key of God's promises that will bring release and restoration. And so it is. Assurance cannot come by looking at our good deeds but by looking to the promises of Christ.

Suppose the sun is shining outside, but you are in a darkened room. The shutter in front of you is preventing the sun from bringing light within. You are not being asked to generate the light and heat of the sun. That has already been done. Your only task, the one you *must* do, is to open the shutter and come to Christ with the helpless recognition that He alone is able to save you.

If Cowper was a believer, as we have reason to believe, he lacked assurance because he simply could not see the grace of God. Though most Christians have more faith than doubts, Cowper had more doubts than faith. Thanks be, the object of his wavering faith was Christ. Better to have little faith in Christ than solid faith in our good works or other means of grace. Too bad he could not throw the shutter open!

One day a man in great distress called me to say that he was terrified that he was not a Christian, believing that he was eternally damned and simply unable to believe. This modern-day Cowper kept grace at arm's length, insisting that he had "tried to believe" but found it impossible.

He thought he had to resolve all of his doubts before he could come to Christ. I explained that he could come to Christ as he was, doubts and all. Whatever little faith he had must be put in the only One who is able to save him.

But when I asked him to pray with me, he hung up, saying, "I'm not ready to come to Christ." I don't know why he was unwilling to come to Christ with his doubts. I should think that someone who was troubled about his eternal soul would be glad to come with his needs.

Could it be that the real reason was that he simply did not want to believe, despite his despair? Despite his confessed desire to be saved, he appeared to be a volitional doubter, a man who for all his emotional guilt nevertheless chose not to believe. And if he does not believe, he will not be saved.

Another man called me with the same kind of troubled spirit. He had sold his soul to the Devil and now felt he needed to honor his promise. He even doubted whether Christ was actually stronger than Satan and could therefore deliver him from his bondage.

I urged him to come to Christ, just as he was, doubts and all. To come with little faith is better than to not come at all. To come hesitantly is better than turning away with wistful sorrow.

I quoted the words I share with all doubters, a beautiful stanza of Charlotte Elliot's famous hymn:

Just as I am, though tossed about
With many a conflict, many a doubt;
Fightings within and fears without,
O Lamb of God, I come, I come!

The young man came to Christ with his doubts, accepting Christ as his sin-bearer. Though he since has had many struggles with the Enemy, he discovered by faith that he had been accepted by God.

Unbelief will damn us; doubts do not. God receives honest doubters; He does not accept dishonest ones.

CHAPTER 8

YES...BUT

If you have followed the discussion so far, you probably
have many questions. Accepting God's grace is never easy,
especially if you have been brought up with the notion that
we are expected to earn our salvation. Or maybe you were
told that eternal life is a free gift, but we are in constant danger of losing it if we don't perform.

Here are some of the most common questions I have
been asked whenever I speak on the topic of salvation.

Question:
What about those passages that seem to teach that baptism is necessary for salvation?

151

Answer:
Although there are those who teach that without this ritual no one will ever be saved, our salvation is not dependent upon baptism.

Let us always remember that the Bible is consistent with itself. More than one hundred times we are told that faith in Christ establishes our relationship with God. If baptism were necessary, why would Paul say to the church in Corinth, "I thank God that I baptized none of you except Crispus and Gaius, so that no one may say that you were baptized in my name. (I did baptize also the household of Stephanas. Beyond that, I do not know whether I baptized anyone else.) For Christ did not send me to baptize but to preach the gospel, and not with words of eloquent wisdom, lest the cross of Christ be emptied of its power" (1 Corinthians 1:14–17).

The apostle makes two points. First, although baptism is important, he wasn't called to baptize but to "preach the gospel." Second, it is clear that Paul distinguishes baptism and the gospel. Baptism does not save, but the gospel does. When Paul describes the gospel in 1 Corinthians 15:1–8, he does not mention baptism.

In addition to John 3:5, which was discussed in chapter 4 of this book, two other passages are often thought to teach that baptism is necessary for salvation. The first of these is Acts 2:38. On the day of Pentecost, Peter said, "Repent and be baptized every one of you in the name of Jesus Christ for the forgiveness of your sins, and you will receive the gift of the Holy Spirit."

The mention of both baptism and repentance in the same verse does not mean that both are necessary for the forgiveness of sins. I might say, "Take your keys and coat and start

152

the car," but that does not mean that taking your coat is necessary to starting the car, even though it is mentioned along with taking the keys.

The Greek grammar of Acts 2:38 confirms this interpretation. The phrase "and be baptized . . . in the name of Jesus Christ" is actually a parenthesis, and it is singular, which sets it off from the rest of the sentence. The command to repent is plural, and so is the phrase "for the forgiveness of your sins." "Repent . . . for the forgiveness of your sins" is the central point. Notice also that in Acts 10:43, Peter mentions faith as the *only* requirement to receive the forgiveness of sins.

A second passage that some believe teaches baptism as the way of salvation was written by Peter: "Baptism, which corresponds to this, now saves you, not as a removal of dirt from the body but as an appeal to God for a good conscience, through the resurrection of Jesus Christ" (1 Peter 3:21).

Peter makes a parallel between the waters that appear in the story of Noah and the ritual of baptism. Water did not save Noah at all but was actually an instrument of judgment. The ark saved him by bringing him "safely through the water" (verse 20).

Peter goes on to explain that water does not save *us,* either. Baptism saves, he says, but it is not the physical act of the washing that does it ("not the removal of dirt from the body") but rather "an appeal to God for a good conscience, through the resurrection of Jesus Christ" (verse 21).

What saves? The appeal of a good conscience before God. That word *appeal* can be translated "answer." The people at that time were required to make a statement of faith before being baptized, and this saved them from a guilty conscience.

Many people in Peter's day were afraid to confess Christ publicly for fear of being persecuted. Those who *did* publicly testify had made an appeal for a "good conscience."

To summarize the parallel: Water didn't save Noah, but he was brought safely through the water because of his faith in God. Nor does water save the person who is baptized, but his confession at the time of baptism saves him from a timid conscience.

Question:
There are some passages, for example Hebrews 6, that seem to teach that a believer can fall away into sin and be lost forever. How should these passages be interpreted?
Answer:
True believers cannot fall away to eternal damnation.

Since whole books have been written about these matters, I will respond to only one of the controversial passages.

In Hebrews 6, the author wrote that in the case of those who have begun the Christian life and then have fallen away, "it is impossible... to restore them again to repentance" since "they are crucifying once again the Son of God to their own harm and holding him up to contempt" (verses 4–6).

We have to admit that the author is talking about true Christians in this passage, for his description of these people is clear (see Hebrews 6:1–3). Not all commentators agree with this interpretation, but, if you read the context, it makes the best sense.

Yes, believers can "fall away." But does that mean to be lost in hell forever? The context makes clear that this is not what the writer had in mind. He used the same expression "fall away" for the Israelites who fell in the desert (3:17; cf. verse 12). Their "falling away" did not determine their eternal destiny but resulted in earthly chastisement and loss of temporal blessings.

The book of Hebrews was written to those who were tempted to revert to the Old Testament sacrificial system. They were beginning to doubt whether Christ was fully sufficient, whether He did in fact replace the rituals and sacrifices required by the law. To have such doubts indicated unbelief and hardness of heart. To return to the Old Testament sacrifices was to crucify "once again the Son of God to their own harm and holding him up to contempt" (Hebrews 6:6).

The point is that so long as they were returning to the Old Testament sacrifices, they could not be brought back to repentance. Understandably, they could not be restored to fellowship with God *while* they were offering lambs on the altar ("since they again crucify to themselves the Son of God" NASB; "crucify. . .the son of God afresh" KJV). But if they ceased such practices, there is no reason to suggest that they could not be restored. Yes, believers can fall away, but not to eternal damnation.

Question:

What about passages such as Revelation 3:5, where we read that those who overcome will not have their names erased from the book of life? Doesn't this imply that some people's names will be blotted out?

Answer:

No, it does not.

First, we should notice that the passage is a promise that Christ will *not* blot out the names of the faithful. Of course there is the implication that under certain circumstances He would blot out a name, but that is making an unnecessary assumption.

Bible scholars say that expressing a positive promise by using a negative is a *litotes*, that is, a figure of speech in which one thing is strongly affirmed by negating its opposite.

A good example of this is seen in John 6:37, where Jesus says, "All those the Father gives me will come to me, and whoever comes to me I will never drive away" (NIV). What Jesus means is that He will welcome those who come to Him. Far from casting them out, He will keep them and preserve them. We should not interpret this passage to mean that under certain circumstances He *does* cast out those whom the Father has given Him.

Similarly, it makes no more sense to ask under what condition Christ would blot a name from the Book of Life than to ask under what condition He might drive away those who come to Him. None of those who belong to Christ will be blotted out.

Question:

What about those passages that teach that if we deny Christ He will deny us? Does this not show that unless we live up to our end of the bargain we will lose our salvation?

Answer:

Most Christians do not deny Christ, at least not permanently. That is why there have been so many martyrs throughout the history of the Christian church. But if a true believer should deny Christ, that does not mean that he will lose his salvation. Christ will never deny that a child is His, although He may well deny a child a place of honor in the kingdom.

God gives His people the grace to stand for Him even in the midst of much opposition. However, some Bible teachers have pushed this point to an extreme and interpret such passages to teach that no true believer ever denies Christ. They hold that all believers may have occasional lapses but will always progress toward a deeper commitment to Christ. So, the argument goes, if you really deny Christ you were never truly saved.

I respectfully disagree. History has shown that many true Christians denied Christ during times of persecution. And if we were honest, we too can deny Him through our silence or maybe even through our words, as Peter did in the presence of a servant girl the night before the crucifixion (see John 18:15, 25–27). Most of the time Christians bounce back from such failures, but I think we would be naïve to think that no true believer has ever lived and died in a state of denial of Christ.

I think, however, that we are too quick to assume that Christ's denial of those who deny Him means that they will be eternally lost. In fact, the very context of 2 Timothy 2:11–13 speaks of God's faithfulness toward us in the midst of our failure. We read, "The saying is trustworthy, for: If we have died with him, we will also live with him; if we endure, we will also reign with him; if we deny him, he also will deny us; if we are faithless, he remains faithful—for he cannot deny himself."

Obviously Paul believed that we Christians could become "faithless," though that would not alter God's faithfulness toward us. A failure to endure would mean, rather, that we cannot reign with Him, because such a privilege is given only to those who are faithful in this life.

So a failure to endure is a form of denial, and, appropriately, if we deny Him, He will deny us. He would not deny that we are His children (for He is faithful to His promises), but He will deny us a special reward and place of honor in the kingdom. This is illustrated by the servant in Luke

19:22–24, who did not hear the "well done," nor was he allowed to reign with Christ, though his soul was saved. Yes, in the end, everyone in heaven will be fulfilled, but some will be given a more prominent position than others.

We also read that Christ will be ashamed of us if we are ashamed of him (Mark 8:38). This does not refer to a loss of eternal life but to a loss of honor and recognition in the presence of Christ. That explains why John says we should live in such a way that we will not be ashamed before him at his coming (1 John 2:28; see also Mark 8:38). Shame is always experienced in direct proportion to sensitivity to sin. When we are transformed and see sin for what it really is, when we "know fully even as I have been fully known" (see 1 Corinthians 13:12), we might be ashamed indeed.

Question:
Doesn't the doctrine of eternal security lead to a wanton lifestyle? If people know that they are saved eternally, will they have no motivation to keep their relationship with God current?

Answer:
There is always the possibility that we will misuse grace. However, the believer has been regenerated by the Holy Spirit and has received a radical transformation. Believers who do misuse grace will experience God's discipline.

Paul had to warn the believers in Galatia that they were not to misuse their freedom. Grace is vulnerable to misuse. However, two things must be borne in mind.

First, those who have been regenerated by the Holy Spirit have experienced a radical transformation. The Holy Spirit changes the inner desires and disposition of those who believe so that they are given a new appetite and a new spiritual motivation.

Of course, there might be backsliding and struggles with sin, for believers are, as Luther has said, "simultaneously saint and sinner." But there is a change in our affections. We now love God, whereas before we regarded Him with indifference.

Second, when we become one of God's children, He begins to discipline us for disobedience. God does not let His children "get by" with their rebellion. Sometimes the discipline is through circumstances; sometimes it is by internal despair.

I am told that a Christian woman once said to her pastor, "Well, for the Christian, sin is different than it is for the non-Christian." To which the pastor replied, "You are right; for the Christian it is more serious!"

Question:
Did not James say that we are justified by works and not faith only? Why are you so insistent that we are justified by faith alone?
Answer:
Both Paul and James taught that Abraham was justified by faith alone.

Some people think that James taught that Abraham was justified by faith *and* works because he wrote, "Was not Abraham our father justified by works when he offered up his son Isaac on the altar? You see that faith was active along with his works, and faith was completed by his works" (James 2:21–22). They contrast this with Paul, who said, "If Abraham was justified by works, he has something to boast about, but not before God" (Romans 4:2).

James is consistent with Paul because the two of them

are using the word *justification* with different meanings. Paul is talking about our justification in the sight of God; James is speaking about our justification in the sight of others. He uses the word *justification* in the sense I might if I asked, "Can you justify your belief in God?"

We know that James had this meaning of justification in mind because of the difference in time between two important events in Abraham's life. In Genesis 15:6, God renews the covenant with him, and Abraham "believed the LORD, and he counted it to him as righteousness." This is the justification of which Paul speaks.

Years later, when Abraham was willing to offer Isaac on the altar, his original faith was vindicated. That, says James, is when he was "justified by works." This was the fulfillment of his original faith.

As a result of Abraham's obedience in the test regarding Isaac (see Genesis 22), he could now be called a "friend of God" (James 2:23; cf. 2 Chronicles 20:7; Isaiah 41:8). Future generations saw his act as a proof that indeed he loved God above everything else. Had he not obeyed God in his willingness to offer Isaac on the altar, he still would have been justified by faith before God (see Genesis 14, 15, 16, and 17). But by passing the test of obedience in Genesis 22, his faith was vindicated and he attained special recognition among men.

We must bear in mind that the word *justification* is often used in the sense of *vindication* in other contexts (for example, in Matthew 12:37). We ourselves use the word *justify* in other contexts, just as did the biblical writers.

A Final Appeal

Sometimes nursery rhymes are more than just a bit of doggerel:

Humpty Dumpty sat on a wall
Humpty Dumpty had a great fall
All the King's horses and
all the King's men
Couldn't put Humpty together again

This poem might have been written to describe a politician in England, but it is a parable about us. We have had a great fall; the evidence is all around us. We simply cannot put ourselves back together again. Much less can we reconcile ourselves with God. Only Christ can put our lives back together by spanning the chasm that exists between us and God.

Many good people will be in hell because they put faith in their goodness. Others will die believing that they had sinned too greatly to be saved. No wonder "the way is broad that leads to destruction, and there are many who enter through it" (Matthew 7:13 NASB).

The question is neither the greatness of our sin nor the long list of good things we have done; the question is whether we have placed our trust in Christ alone, persuaded that He has done all that is necessary and ever will be necessary for us to be welcomed by God.

An old man stood to his feet in a church service and said, "It has taken me fifty-two years to learn three things."

The congregation hushed, hoping to discover in three minutes what had taken this man so long to learn.

"First," he began, "I learned that I cannot save myself. Second, I learned that God did not expect me to save myself."

Then he lowered his voice and added, "And the third thing I've learned is that God, through Christ, has done it all!"

And so it is. For those who are willing to entrust their

eternal souls into Christ's care, for them, God has done it all.

I have written a prayer that I would encourage you to pray, though I must caution you that it is not the prayer itself that will save you. Only Christ can do that. What's important is that this prayer be simply the desire that is in your heart. If you pray it in faith, Christ will save you. Christ will respond to the faith in your heart. Don't back away, for He has promised that He will receive all who come to Him.

> O God,
> I know that I have sinned and that I cannot save myself.
> I thank You that Christ died to reconcile me to You. At
> this moment I accept Him as my sin-bearer. I affirm
> that His death was for me; I receive His sacrifice in my
> behalf. I receive from You at this moment what I do not
> have.
>
> I take the gift of eternal life, which You have promised
> to those who believe. As best I can, I now transfer all of
> my trust to Christ.
>
> Thank You for hearing this prayer in the name of Jesus
> Christ the Lord.
> Amen.

NOTES

Chapter 2: Why Grace Is So Amazing

1. John Newton, *Out of the Depths* (reprint; Chicago: Moody Press, Moody Literature Ministry, n.d.), 81–82.
2. John Calloway, *Chicago Tonight*, April 22, 1994.
3. Aleksandr Solzhenitsyn, *Christianity Today*, February 7, 1994.

Chapter 4: The Miracle We Need

1. Words and music by John W. Peterson. Copyright 1948, renewed by John W. Peterson Music Co. All rights reserved. Used by permission.

Chapter 5: Held in God's Hands

1. Ted Turner, in *The Humanist*, January/February 1991, 13.
2. Ibid.

Chapter 6: Saved for Sure

1. John Calvin, *The Institutes of the Christian Religion*, ed. Tony Lane and Hilary Osborne (Grand Rapids: Baker, 1987), 144.
2. R. T. Kendall, "The Ground of Assurance," *Westminster Record*, Winter 1988, 26.
3. John Calvin, quoted in Kendall, "The Ground of Assurance," 29.

Chapter 7: For Doubters Only

1. Virginia Stem Owens, "The Dark Side of Grace," *Christianity Today*, 19 July 1993, 32–33.
2. Martin Luther, *What Luther Says: An Anthology*, ed. Ewald M. Plass (St. Louis: Concordia), 1:487.

ONE MINUTE AFTER YOU DIE

Portions adapted from Salt & Light Pocket Guides:
    © 1992 *Coming to Grips with Death & Dying*
    © 1992 *Coming to Grips with Heaven*
    © 1992 *Coming to Grips with Hell*

Unless otherwise indicated, Scripture quotations are from The Holy Bible, English Standard Version® (ESV®), copyright © 2001 by Crossway, a publishing ministry of Good News Publishers. Used by permission. All rights reserved.

Scripture quotations marked NASB are taken from the *New American Standard Bible®*, Copyright © 1960, 1962, 1963, 1968, 1971, 1972, 1973, 1975, 1977, 1995 by The Lockman Foundation. Used by permission. (www.Lockman.org)

Scripture quotations marked KJV are taken from the King James Version.

Interior design: Erik M. Peterson
Cover design: Smartt Guys design
Cover image of supernova copyright © Masterfile / 679-02684646. All rights reserved.

ISBN: 978-0-8024-1411-3

CONTENTS

WELCOME TO ETERNITY

One minute after you slip behind the parted curtain, you will either be enjoying a personal welcome from Christ or catching your first glimpse of gloom as you have never known it. Either way, your future will be irrevocably fixed and eternally unchangeable.

"Every human being," says C. S. Lewis, "is in the process of becoming a noble being; noble beyond imagination. Or else, alas, a vile being beyond redemption." He exhorts us to remember that "the dullest and most uninteresting person you can talk to may one day be a creature which, if you saw it now, you would be strongly tempted to worship, or else a horror and a corruption such as you now meet, if at all, only in a nightmare. . . . There are no ordinary people . . . It is immortals whom we joke with, work with, marry, snub and exploit—immortal horrors or everlasting splendors."[1]

Those who find themselves in heaven will be surrounded with friends whom they have known on earth. Friendships, once rudely interrupted by death, will continue where they left off. Every description of heaven they have ever heard will pale in the light of reality. All this, forever.

Others—indeed many others—will be shrouded in darkness, a region of deprivation and unending regret. There, with their memories and feelings fully intact, images of their life on earth will return to haunt them. They will think back to their friends, family, and relatives; they will brood over opportunities they squandered and intuitively know that their future is both hopeless and unending. For them, death will be far worse than they imagined.

And so while relatives and friends plan your funeral—deciding on a casket, a burial plot, and who the pallbearers shall be—you will be more alive than you have ever been. You will either see God on His throne surrounded by angels and redeemed humanity, or you will feel an indescribable weight of guilt and abandonment. There is no destination midway between these two extremes; just gladness or gloom.

Nor will it be possible to transfer from one region to another. No matter how endless the ages, no matter how heartfelt the cries, no matter how intense the suffering, your travel plans are limited to your present abode. Those who find themselves in the lower gloomy regions shall never enter the gates that lead to endless light and ecstasy. They will discover that the beautiful words spoken in their eulogy bear no resemblance to the reality that now confronts them. If only their friends could see them now!

I'm told that there is a cemetery in Indiana that has an old tombstone bearing this epitaph:

> *Pause, stranger, when you pass me by*
> *As you are now, so once was I*
> *As I am now, so you will be*
> *So prepare for death and follow me*

An unknown passerby read those words and underneath scratched this reply:

> *To follow you I'm not content*
> *Until I know which way you went*

Some time ago I conducted two very different funerals. The first was that of a Christian woman who had distinguished herself by a life of sacrificial service for Christ. The triumph of the family was striking; there was irrepressible joy mixed with the sorrow.

The second was that of an apparent unbeliever who was killed in a highway accident. The grief of the relatives was marked by desperation and hopelessness. They refused to be comforted.

You and I shall follow these two people to the grave. Unless Christ should return in our lifetime, we all shall pass through that iron gate described by Hamlet as "the undiscover'd country from whose bourn / No traveller returns" (III.i. 79–80).

Thinking about our final destination gives us perspective. Visualize a measuring tape extending from earth to the farthest star. Our stay here is but a hairline, almost invisible to the length of the tape. Strictly speaking, no distance can be compared to eternity. No matter how endless we visualize eternity to be, our conception is never endless enough.

Every one of us wants to make wise investments, to get the "biggest bang for our buck," as the saying goes. The best investments are those that are safe and permanent; if we are wise, we will spend our time preparing for that which lasts forever. What is life but preparation for eternity?

I once read a tragic story about people enjoying themselves on the top stories of a tall apartment building, not knowing that there was a fire burning on the lower floors. Just so, many are enjoying life, comfortably ignoring the fact that their death is not only inevitable, but much nearer than they think. Though there are many uncertainties in our lives, we can count on this: Whatever we strive for in this world must of necessity be temporary. Indeed, this world and all we have accumulated will eventually be burned up.

The other day I was browsing in the travel section of a bookstore. Potential travelers were buying maps and guidebooks on Hawaii and Europe. Some were purchasing booklets to help them learn some phrases of a foreign language. No doubt they had saved their money, blocked out their vacation schedules, and purchased airline tickets. All that just for a two-week journey.

I wondered how many of them were giving at least that much attention to their final destination. I wondered how many were reading the guidebook, studying the map, and trying to learn the language of heaven. Europe and Hawaii seemed so much more real than the unseen realm of the dead. And yet, even as they planned their vacations, they were en route to a more distant destination.

The purpose of this book is to study what the Bible has

to say about the life beyond. Many who read it will be comforted; others will be disturbed; and everyone, I hope, will be instructed. I claim no special revelation, just a desire to accurately explain what the Bible has to say.

I pray God will help me make heaven so inviting that those who are ready to enter will scarcely be able to wait. I pray also, that I shall make hell so fearsome that those who are not ready to die shall quickly come to trust the only One who can shield them from "the wrath to come."

Death, our enemy, can be our friend when God gives us the final call. We can be glad He has given us a shaft of light to illumine the darkness. Death is not a hopeless plunge into the vast unknown.

So, what can we expect one minute after we die?

CHAPTER 1

ATTEMPTING TO PEEK BEHIND THE CURTAIN

Channeling | Reincarnation | Near-Death Experiences

During the last few months of her struggle with cancer, Jacquelyn Helton kept a diary. Her thoughts and feelings would become a legacy for her husband, Tom, and her eighteen-month-old daughter, Jennifer.

In her diary she wonders what death would be like? What clothes should she wear for burial? She thinks of her daughter. Who will love her? Put her to sleep? In her writings, she tells Jennifer that when it hurts, she should remember that her mother would have cared. Then she thinks of her husband and the needs he will have after she is gone.

Finally she cries out, "What is the matter with you, God?

My family is not a bunch of Boy Scouts who can figure all these things out for themselves—you're some kind of idiot to pull something like this!"

Denial, anger, fear, depression, and helpless resignation—all of these feelings erupt in the souls of those who face death. No matter that death is common to the human race; each person must face this ultimate ignominy individually. No one can endure this moment for us. Friends and family can walk only as far as the curtain; the dying one must disappear behind the veil alone.

Understandably, Jacquelyn was apprehensive as she faced the closed partition. She thought about the mystery that lay back of the shrouded veil. She wished for some insight, some glimpse into the future that would assure her that she did not have to be afraid. Yet neither her curiosity nor her desire to live kept her from slipping through the curtain and going into the night alone. Will she find herself fully conscious in some dark cavern seeking companionship but finding none?

Tom Howard says that when we face death we are like a hen before a cobra, incapable of doing anything at all in the presence of the very thing that seems to call for the most drastic and decisive action. "There is, in fact, nothing we can do," he writes. "Say what we will, dance how we will, we will soon enough be a heap of ruined feathers and bones, indistinguishable from the rest of the ruins that lie about. It will not appear to matter in the slightest whether we met the enemy with equanimity, shrieks, or a trumped-up gaiety, there we will be."[1]

Naturally, we would like to know in advance what we can expect on the other side. Human nature being what it is, we grasp for some clue, some hint we might glean from those who are about to cross the boundary. We are particularly anxious to hear a good word, the assurance that all will be well. When television actor Michael Landon, a star on the classic television shows *Bonanza* and *Little House on the Prairie,* lay on his deathbed, he confided to friends that he saw a "bright white light" that eased his fears and made him look forward to what awaited him on the other side. He died calmly, anticipating what he called "quite an experience."

Reincarnation, altered states of consciousness, and glad reunions in a metaphysical place such as heaven are popular themes at the box office. Larry Gordon, chief executive of Largo Entertainment, says, "People are looking for something that makes them feel good. We all want to believe that death isn't so bad."[2] Dozens of movies portray the enchantment of the life beyond. One advertised, "There is at least one laugh on the other side."

Fear of death has been supplanted by blissful feelings about a hereafter where everyone ends happily reunited. There is no judgment, no careful review of one's life. To be sure, death has mystery, we are told, but is not to be dreaded. Given this positive assessment of the Great Beyond, we should not be surprised that some people want to hasten their arrival at this destination.

How legitimate are reported glimpses from behind the parted curtain? Many are convinced that the immortality of the soul is now confirmed by paranormal experiences that can have no other explanation but that the soul survives the death of the body. We might agree that the soul does survive the death of the body, but how much reliable information can be transmitted back to earth by those who tell us what they have seen and heard from the other side?

Let us evaluate three different kinds of evidence that are

sometimes used to assure us that all will be well as we make our own exits through the mysterious veil.

CHANNELING

Some people claim to have talks with the dead. In his book *The Other Side*, Bishop James A. Pike described in detail how he made contact with his son, who had committed suicide. Using a spirit medium, the bishop had what he believed to be several extensive conversations with the boy.

"I failed the test, I can't face you, can't face life," Pike's son reportedly said. "I'm confused. . . . I am not in purgatory, but something like Hell, here, . . . yet nobody blames me here."[3] Jesus, the boy said, was an example but not a Savior.

A surprise was the alleged appearance in spirit of a friend, Paul Tillich, a well-known German-American theologian who had died several months before. Pike was caught off guard when he discerned his deceased friend's German accent passing through the lips of the medium (or channeler).

How should this evidence be interpreted? Liberal theologian that he was, Pike did not realize that demons impersonate the dead to create the illusion that the living can communicate with the dead. These spirits have astonishing knowledge of the dead person's life since they carefully observe individuals while they are living. Through the power of deception, they can mimic a deceased person's voice, personality, and even appearance. The King James Version actually translates the word *medium* as those who have "familiar spirits" (Leviticus 19:31; 20:6, 27; Deuteronomy 18:11), suggesting the familiarity some demons have with individuals.

Sometimes the story of Samuel and Saul is used to justify communication with the dead. In this remarkable instance,

Samuel was apparently brought back from the dead, but not by the witch of Endor. God Himself seems to have done this miracle; only such a surprising act can explain the medium's terror (1 Samuel 28:3–25).

We must remember that the voice of Samuel did not speak through the lips of this medium. Samuel and Saul spoke to one another directly because of this surprising miracle. What is more, the Almighty was displeased with Saul's desperate attempt to consult the dead prophet. No wonder Saul heard a prophecy of judgment that he and his sons would die the very next day—a prophecy that was fulfilled. Attempting to talk with the dead is consistently condemned by God (Deuteronomy 18:11–12).

So you can be quite sure that no one has ever talked to your dead uncle, cousin, or grandmother. There are, however, spirits that impersonate the dead. Their trickery is compounded because they may actually talk about love, the value of religion, or make favorable references to Christ. And of course they know enough about the one who has died to deceive the unwary.

This ability of demonic spirits to masquerade as the personality of the dead helps us understand haunted houses. While I was staying in a hotel near Calgary, a local newspaper carried a story saying that there were at least two ghosts in the beautiful building. One of the employees showed us a marble staircase where one of these ghosts lived (verified by the testimony of employees). A new bride had stumbled down the stairs years ago and hit her head, resulting in her death. We were told that her spirit now lives on the stairs, appearing with some regularity.

How do we explain this phenomenon? When a person who is inhabited by evil spirits dies, these demons need to relocate. Often they choose to stay in the place where the death took place (this seems particularly true in the case of violent deaths, such as murder or suicide). They will take the name and characteristics of the deceased person and make occasional appearances under these pretenses. Such entities (as they are frequently called today) are evil spirits who often pose as "friendly ghosts."

To try to contact the dead is to invite fellowship with hosts of darkness pretending to be helpful angels of light. Isaiah the prophet warned the people that to consult a medium was to turn one's back on God. "When they say to you, 'Consult the mediums and the spiritists who whisper and mutter,' should not a people consult their God? Should they consult the dead on behalf of the living? To the law and to the testimony! If they do not speak according to this word, it is because they have no dawn [light]" (Isaiah 8:19–20 NASB).

The point, of course, is that all information about life after death that comes from spiritists or channelers is unreliable. Those who turn to the occult world for knowledge of death are misled. Yes, there is life after death, but we cannot learn the details from demons, whose chief delight is to confuse and deceive. No wonder the theology allegedly given by Pike's son was so convoluted.

We have no right to try to peek behind the curtain by communicating with those on the other side. Once the curtain has opened to admit a fellow traveler, it closes and we must not try to peek behind the veil.

REINCARNATION

Another form of occultism that purports to give information about life after death is reincarnation. This doctrine teaches that we just keep being recycled; death is nothing more than a transition from one body to another. Thus, we can eliminate the fear of death by proclaiming that it does not exist. Some people even claim that through contacts in the spirit world, they have discovered that they had a previous existence. One celebrity announced she has been a princess in Atlantis, an Inca in Peru, and even was a child raised by elephants.

A woman I met on a plane told me that as a child she had detailed knowledge of a house in Vermont that she had never visited. Later, as an adult, she visited the house, and the details coincided with her visions. She was then convinced she had lived there during the eighteenth century. I pointed out that there is no such thing as a transmigration of souls, but there is a transmigration of demons. She was getting knowledge about an eighteenth-century family from evil spirits.

"But," she protested, "I have nothing to do with evil spirits; I communicate only with good ones!"

"How do you tell the difference between good spirits and evil ones?" I asked.

"I communicate only with those spirits that come to me clothed in light."

I reminded her of 2 Corinthians 11:13–14, "For such men are false apostles, deceitful workmen, disguising themselves as apostles of Christ. And no wonder, for even Satan disguises himself as an angel of light." Yes, light indeed!

Her experiences and similar ones do not prove reincarnation, but rather confirm that people of all ages can become the victims of demonic influence. There is evidence that even children sometimes inherit the demonically induced traits of their parents or ancestors. This would explain why some children, a few months old, have reportedly babbled blasphemies and obscenities they could never have personally learned in their short lifetimes.

Occultism, of whatever variety, is not a reliable source of information regarding what happens after death. It proves only the existence of a spirit world, a world of deception and dark intelligence. God considers all forms of occultism an abomination (Leviticus 19:31; Deuteronomy 18:9–12; Isaiah 8:19–20; 1 Corinthians 10:14–22).

No self-proclaimed guru is qualified to tell us about eternity. No one can prove that he or she has had the experience of being recycled from another existence. The curtain opens when we go in, but once it is firmly closed, it will not open to let us return.

NEAR-DEATH EXPERIENCES

Some people claim to have died and returned to their bodies to give us information on the life beyond. Raymond Moody, in *Life After Life*,[4] recorded the interviews of many who were near death but were successfully resuscitated. Their stories, for the most part, had many similar elements: the patient would hear himself being pronounced dead; he would be out of his body, watching the doctors work over his corpse. While in this state, he would meet relatives or friends who had died and then encounter a "being of light." When he knows that he must return to his body, he does so reluctantly because the experience of love and peace has engulfed him.

Melvin Morse, in *Closer to the Light*, recounts the stories of children who have had near-death experiences. Again, their stories are remarkably similar, and in almost all instances very positive. Typical is the account of a sixteen-year-old boy who was rushed to the hospital with a very severe kidney problem. While in the admitting room, he slumped over in his chair. A nurse searched for his pulse but found none. Thankfully, he was eventually resuscitated. Later he told of a supernatural experience:

> I reached a certain point in the tunnel where lights suddenly began flashing all around me. They made me certain that I was in some kind of tunnel, and the way I moved past them, I knew I was going hundreds of miles an hour.
>
> At this point I also noticed that there was somebody with me. He was about seven feet tall and wore a long white gown with a simple belt tied at the waist. His hair was golden, and although he didn't say anything, I wasn't afraid because I could feel him radiating peace and love.
>
> No, he wasn't the Christ, but I knew that he was sent from Christ. It was probably one of his angels or someone else sent to transport me to Heaven.[5]

Betty Eadie, in *Embraced by the Light*,[6] gives a fantastic account of her visit to the "other side." She claims to have seen Christ and thus even dedicated her book to him: "To the Light, my Lord and Savior Jesus Christ, to whom I owe all that I have. He is the 'staff' that I lean on; without Him I would fail." Yet it becomes clear that the Christ she tells us about is not the Jesus of the New Testament.

Eadie's Jesus is a benevolent being of light that surrounded her in such a way that she could not tell where her "light" stopped and his began. Jesus, she tells us, is separate from the Father and would do nothing to offend her. There was no reason to regret past deeds, for we as humans are not sinful creatures; indeed, human "spirit beings" assisted the heavenly Father at creation. Thankfully, the world is not filled with tragedy as we suppose, and in the presence of

Christ, Eadie concluded, "I knew that I was worthy to embrace Him."[7]

What do these experiences prove? Apparently, they do confirm that at death the soul separates from the body. A few patients not only looked back and saw doctors hover around their body, but could see what was going on in other places in the hospital. This, it seems, is impossible unless the soul had actually left the body and could review earth from a different perspective.

We have reason to believe that a person may see Christ in the twilight zone between life and death. Before Stephen was stoned God gave him a glimpse into heaven. Stephen said, "Behold, I see the heavens opened, and the Son of Man standing at the right hand of God" (Acts 7:56). This experience was unique in that it happened before Stephen died, not at death. Here was positive encouragement that heaven was waiting to receive him!

The apostle Paul had a similar experience, though some think that he actually died when he was caught up into paradise, where he heard "things that cannot be told, which man may not utter" (2 Corinthians 12:4). Since he said it happened fourteen years before writing these words to the church at Corinth, there is at least some evidence that the event coincided with his experience at Lystra, where he was stoned and dragged out of the city presumed dead (Acts 14:19–20). If he did die and then revived, this account could be classified as a near-death experience, or perhaps even a "revived from death" experience.

If Stephen saw our Lord before he died, and if Paul died and was caught up into paradise, it is just possible that other believers might also have such a vision. Reports of seeing Christ or relatives long dead might have some validity. We should not expect such experiences, but they could happen.

The problem, of course, is that we cannot accept without scrutiny what people claim to have seen behind the curtain. Near-death experiences may or may not reflect the true conditions of life beyond death. They must be carefully evaluated to see whether they conform to the biblical picture of the hereafter. Also, the prior beliefs of those who report what they have seen and heard are essential in evaluating what was experienced.

Remember—and this is important—Satan would try to duplicate the same positive experiences for unbelievers that God gave to Stephen and Paul. The Great Deceiver wants to have people think that one's relationship with Jesus Christ has no bearing on the beauty and bliss that awaits everyone. If it is true that angels await those who have been made righteous by Christ, it is understandable that demonic spirits would await those who enter eternity without God's forgiveness and acceptance.

We know that at least some positive near-death experiences are demonic, for they sharply contradict the teaching of the Bible. First, some like Betty Eadie tell us that the Jesus they met assured them that everyone will have an equally blissful welcome into the life beyond. Second, we are told that there is no judgment, no rigorous examination of a person's life. Several of the people explicitly mention that the "being of Light" they met gives everyone an unconditional welcome.

One woman reported that when she crossed the line between life and death she met Christ, who took her for a walk. He explained that all the religions of the world were paths to the same destination. There was a Buddhist path, a Hindu path, an Islamic path, and of course, a Christian path. But, like spokes in a wheel, all of them led to the central hub of heaven. In other words, everyone will be saved. This has always been Satan's most believable lie.

As for the widely reported experiences of seeing light, we should remember that since God is light, it is understandable that Satan duplicates light of his own. We cannot emphasize too strongly that he wishes to disguise himself as an "angel of light" (2 Corinthians 11:14). And of course, many unsuspecting souls simply assume that this "being" who radiates light is kind and benevolent; in an age of "feel-good" religion they can't imagine that it is anyone else but Christ.

Although positive near-death experiences are widely reported, I must point out that other research indicates that many have dark and foreboding experiences. In *The Edge of Death* by Philip Swihart,[8] and *Beyond Death's Door* by Maurice Rawlings,[9] there are accounts of those who tell terrifying stories of the life beyond. Some have seen a lake of fire or abysmal darkness, along with tormented persons—all of whom are awaiting judgment. These reports, the authors contend, are more accurate because they were gained through interviews almost immediately following near-death and resuscitation. These dark experiences, the writers say, are often lost to the memory after a short period of time.

We cannot overstate the deception perpetuated by the "religion of the resuscitated," who report only the utopian idea that death leads to a higher degree of consciousness for all people regardless of their religion or beliefs. We must remember that all near-death reports are from those who might have died clinically but have not experienced biological or irreversible death. None has been resurrected. Whether the experience is positive or negative, it must always be evaluated by a more reliable authority.

Personally, I am much more concerned about what I will

experience after death than what I will experience when I am near death. It's not the transition but the destination that really counts. Thus, to discover what really lies on the other side, we must find a more credible map, a more certain authority than people who go only to the threshold of the life beyond and give us their reports.

We will do much better if we trust someone who was actually dead, not someone who was just near death. Christ, as we shall see, is the only One who is qualified to tell us what we can expect on the other side. He was dead—so dead that His body became cold and was put into a tomb. Three days later He was raised from the dead with a glorified body. Here is someone whose opinion can be trusted. To John this risen Christ said, "Fear not, I am the first and the last, and the living one. I died, and behold I am alive forevermore, and I have the keys of Death and Hades" (Revelation 1:17–18).

Reliable information does not come to us by trying to peer behind the partially open curtain. God alone knows what really lies on the other side of the veil. And that is why we can do no better than study what the Bible has to say about the Great Beyond.

We begin with the Old Testament, where the first glimpses of the regions of death come into view. This will prepare us for the much clearer revelation given in the New Testament. Though we have no right to peer behind the curtain and report what we have found, we can gratefully accept all that God has shown to us in His Word.

What follows in the next chapters of this book is His revelation, not our observation. God parts the curtain so that we can glimpse inside.

Let us find out what is there.

CHAPTER 2

THE DESCENT INTO GLOOM

Sheol | Hades | Purgatory

One day I received a call from a distraught family who wanted a minister to do a quick funeral. I say "quick" because they asked me to speak for only a few minutes. "We don't want anything religious," the son told me, "and nothing you do will be too short."

I asked him why it was so important for the funeral to be brief. He told me his family was not religious; his father, who had died suddenly, had never attended church. They did not even believe in God; the only reason I was called was because a relative thought a minister should be present.

I made a deal with him. Yes, I would be brief; but I would

have to tell the guests what I believed about death in general and Christ in particular. He reluctantly agreed.

If there is one word that characterized that funeral, it was *hopelessness*. Here was a man who had apparently made millions of dollars in the shipping industry, but now he was dead, and his body was to be cremated on that very day, after a rather long eulogy but a very short sermon.

What did he experience one minute after he died? Of course I can't be this man's judge. Only God knows whether or not he had come to trust Christ as his Savior, even in the closing minutes of his life. But, for the purposes of illustration, we can assume that he died as an unbeliever, just as his son had said. If so, what was this man experiencing even as we gathered in the funeral parlor to honor his memory? What would we have seen if we could have looked beyond the elegant casket?

To give a complete answer to this question, we must embark on a quick tour of the Old Testament teaching regarding the afterlife and then take a further step into the New Testament. When we are finished, we will have a fairly good understanding of what was happening to this man in the region of death, even as his family was frantically seeking for a minister to make his funeral appropriately religious. What we will discover is both mysterious and frightening.

Death, we must remember, is the consequence of Adam's and Eve's disobedience in the garden of Eden. God had warned them that if they ate the forbidden fruit they would die. And die they did. They died spiritually in that they were separated from God and tried to hide from Him. They also began to die physically, as their bodies began the journey to the grave. And if Adam and Eve had not been redeemed by God, they would have died eternally, which is the third form of death. From the original disobedience in Eden, death in all of its forms began its trek throughout the world.

The Old Testament goes on to unfold God's revelation of the afterlife. Of course, those writers didn't understand as much as we do, having the light of the New Testament, but clearly they knew that the soul survived the life of the body. In fact, a belief in the consciousness in the afterlife was so universally accepted by all cultures that the biblical writers simply assumed it was so. All that they did was clarify what God had already revealed through natural revelation.

Let's take a tour of the data.

THE SHEOL OF THE OLD TESTAMENT

The most important word in the Old Testament that speaks of the afterlife is the Hebrew word *sheol*, which occurs sixty-five times in the Old Testament. In the King James Version of the Bible it is translated "hell" thirty-one times, "grave" thirty-one times, and "pit" three times. This inconsistency in translation has caused some to be confused regarding what sheol really means.

First, we must remember that elsewhere in the Bible, sheol is clearly distinguished from hell (I'll comment more on this later). And second, just because it is sometimes translated "grave," this does not mean that it refers only to the literal grave. Some people who believe that it refers to the grave and nothing more assume that when we die, we just die like a dog; i.e., since our bodies have died, our existence has ended.

Not so. Of course, sheol can be translated "grave" in some contexts, because the word includes the concept of the grave. But what seems clear is that the writers of the Old Testament believed that to go to sheol was not only to go to the grave but also to experience a conscious afterlife.

There is a Hebrew word that can only be translated "grave"—*kever*—but the writers often preferred the word sheol because it encompassed the region of departed spirits who were conscious, either in bliss or torment. The word sheol never means just a physical grave.

For the purpose of greater clarity, more recent translations of the Bible sometimes do not attempt to use an English equivalent to translate sheol. They simply let the Hebrew word stand as it is. For example, in the very first use of the word in the Old Testament, the New American Standard Bible quotes Jacob as saying, "Surely I will go down to Sheol in mourning for my son" (Genesis 37:35).

So here are some facts we should know in order to understand what the Old Testament means by the word sheol.[1]

First, there is a clear distinction between the grave, where the body rests, and sheol, where the spirits of the dead gather. Although graves are usually in shallow earth or even above the earth, sheol is always thought of as down under, somewhere in a hollow part of the earth. Isaiah writes that when the king is overthrown, "Sheol from beneath is excited over you to meet you when you come; it arouses for you the spirits of the dead, all the leaders of the earth; it raises all the kings of the nations from their thrones" (Isaiah 14:9 NASB; see also verse 10). Sheol is not impersonal; it is a place of activity.

Second, sheol is often spoken of as a shadowy place of darkness, a place that is not a part of this existence. Another prophet, Ezekiel, says that Tyre will be "[brought] down with those who go down to the pit, to the people of old, and I will make you to dwell in the world below, among ruins from of old, with those who go down to the pit [sheol], so that you will not be inhabited; but I will set beauty in the land of the living" (Ezekiel 26:20).

Job speaks of the inhabitants of sheol as in pain. "The dead tremble under the waters and their inhabitants. Sheol is naked before God, and Abaddon has no covering" (Job 26:5–6).

Third, after death one can be united with his ancestors in sheol. Jacob went down into sheol and was "gathered to his people" (Genesis 49:33). Abraham was assured by the Lord that he would go down to his fathers in peace (Genesis 15:15). Some have interpreted this as simply a reference to the fact that the bones of a particular family were often buried together. But the clear implication is that there would be a reunion of some kind in the world beyond.

That the word *sheol* refers to the realm of departed spirits seems unmistakable. What seems equally clear is that those who entered this region did not all have the same experience. For some, it was a region of gloom; but for others, it was a place where they would dwell with God.

Asaph, the author of many of the psalms, wrote, "Nevertheless, I am continually with you; you hold my right hand. You guide me with your counsel, and afterward you will receive me to glory. Whom have I in heaven but you? And there is nothing on earth that I desire besides you" (Psalm 73:23–25). He expected to see the glory of God at death; indeed, he speaks about heaven.

Fourth, there are hints in the Old Testament that sheol has different regions. Both the wicked and the righteous are said to go to sheol. Jacob went into sheol, but so did rebellious people, such as Korah and Dathan. This explains why there is a "lower region." The Lord says, "For a fire is kindled in My anger, and burns to the lowest part of Sheol, and consumes the earth with its yield, and sets on fire the foundations of the mountains" (Deuteronomy 32:22 NASB).

The reason there are two different realms in sheol is best explained by remembering that sheol has two different kinds of inhabitants. "This is the way of those who are foolish. . . . As sheep they are appointed for Sheol; death shall be their shepherd; and the upright shall rule over them in the morning, and their form shall be for Sheol to consume so that they have no habitation. But God will redeem my soul from the power of Sheol, for He will receive me" (Psalm 49:13–15 NASB). Other Old Testament passages make a similar contrast (Job 24:19; Psalms 9:17; 16:10; 31:17; 55:15).

Perhaps one of the clearest expressions of immortality in the Old Testament comes from the book of Daniel. "Many of those who sleep in the dust of the earth shall awake, some to everlasting life, and some to shame and everlasting contempt" (Daniel 12:2). Daniel not only believed that there were two classes of people who would live either in bliss or contempt, but that their bodies would also arise someday. This is an explicit reference to the New Testament doctrine of the resurrection of the body.

The Old Testament makes a sharp distinction between the wicked and the righteous, with the clear implication that they have separate destinies in the afterlife. Though this division of sheol is not expressly stated, later rabbis clearly taught that sheol has two compartments.

Sheol, then, is a general term for the nether world, the region of departed spirits. As the scholar B. B. Warfield wrote, "Israel from the beginning of its recorded history cherished the most settled conviction of the persistence of the soul in life after death. . . . The body is laid in the grave and the soul departs for sheol." Here the righteous and the wicked enter, though when they arrive, they do not have the same experience.

If the door to the afterlife is open but a crack in the Old Testament, it is thrown wide open in the New. Here we have detailed descriptions of both the righteous and the unbelievers after death. Based on this information, we are better able to answer the question of what we can expect one minute after we have breathed our last.

HADES IN THE NEW TESTAMENT

We have learned that the Hebrew word *sheol* is used for the realm of the dead in the Old Testament. The New Testament, however, was written in Greek, and there we find sheol translated by the Greek word *hades*. In fact, when the whole of the Old Testament was translated into Greek before the time of Christ, sheol was always translated "hades." Similarly, when the New Testament quotes Old Testament texts, sheol is always translated "hades"; they are one and the same.

The New Testament pulls back the curtain so that we can see into hades (or sheol) with more clarity. As we might expect, just like sheol, the word hades is never used of the grave, but always refers to the world of departed spirits. Here we are given some very specific details about what hades is like, both for those who die as believers as well as those who die as unbelievers. At least some of the mystery disappears as God parts the curtain for us.

Christ accepted the rabbis' understanding that sheol, or hades, had two compartments. To emphasize to the greedy Pharisees how the fortunes of rich people might someday be reversed in the world to come, he told a story that takes us behind the veil that separates the dead from the living.

Remember the context. A rich man who habitually dressed in purple and fine linen and lived in splendor every day died and his soul was taken to hades. A beggar named Lazarus who lay at the rich man's gate also died and was carried into Abraham's bosom (the blissful region of hades). Now the description of the hereafter begins:

> In Hades [the Greek translation of the Old Testament *sheol*], being in torment, he lifted up his eyes and saw Abraham far off and Lazarus at his side. And he called out, "Father Abraham, have mercy on me, and send Lazarus to dip the end of his finger in water and cool my tongue, for I am in anguish in this flame." But Abraham said, "Child, remember that you in your lifetime received your good things, and Lazarus in like manner bad things; but now he is comforted here, and you are in anguish. And besides all this, between us and you a great chasm has been fixed, in order that those who would pass from here to you may not be able, and none may cross from there to us." (LUKE 16:23–26)

It would be a mistake to think that this tormented man ended in hades because he was rich! Elsewhere in the New Testament we are clearly taught that our riches or lack of them do not dictate our eternal destiny. Remember, Christ told this story to jolt greedy Pharisees into the realization that their riches cannot save them; poor people might be better off in the life to come. (Exactly what determines where we will spend eternity will be discussed later in this book.)

Christ described the radically different destinies of a believer and unbeliever. For our purposes, let us focus on the fate of the rich man, trying to understand his predicament while his family was still enjoying the creature comforts of earth. Though we can be quite sure his family didn't know it, he was in acute distress.

My mind goes back to the shipping magnate at whose funeral I spoke in Chicago. Both he and the rich man in the parable—and millions like them—have discovered too late that their worldly influence could not save them; nor could their wealth and reputation extricate them from this bind. Instead of victors, they were now victims; rather than bragging about their freedom, they now had to confess their enslavement.

First, the man in hades was fully conscious immediately after death. Memory, speaking, pain, and bliss—all of these were a part of his experience. The rich man said, "Father Abraham, have mercy on me, and send Lazarus to dip the end of his finger in water and cool my tongue, for I am in anguish in this flame" (verse 24). In hades, an alcoholic will thirst for a drop of liquor, but none will be given to him. The drug addict will crave a shot of heroin, but will not receive it. The immoral man will burn with sexual desire, but never be satisfied.

Perpetually burning lusts never subside, and the tortured conscience aches but is never sedated. There will be increased desire with decreased satisfaction. In Proverbs, we read of the insatiable desires of both the nether world and a man's lusts: "Sheol and Abaddon are never satisfied, and never satisfied are the eyes of man" (Proverbs 27:20).

So while we listened attentively to the obituary read in that funeral home in Chicago, the one whose memory was respectfully honored was in pain; he had smoldering needs that were unmet. He had inflamed desires that were neither satisfied nor quenched.

Second, the eternal destiny of this man was irrevocably fixed. "Between us and you a great chasm has been fixed, in order that those who would pass from here to you may not be able, and none may cross from there to us" (Luke 16:26). Whereas the relatives on earth can leave the funeral home, go out for dinner, and plan a vacation, their friend in hades is confined, without any possibility of escape.

As M. R. DeHaan put it, "Once we have passed through the door of death we can't pick up our suitcase and move out because we don't like the accommodations." In hades, then, there is monotony; here is the isolation of boredom and triviality. No challenges can be undertaken; no goals set; no pleasures sampled.

While I was preaching that short sermon, the man whose body lay in that beautiful casket was fully aware that he was hemmed in; his future was no longer under his control. He had an overwhelming realization that his destiny was irrevocably fixed. And as we shall see, in the future his predicament will yet become worse, never better.

Third, this man knew himself well enough to know that what he was experiencing was fair and just. In hades his entire life was present to him; his transfer into the nether world did not diminish, but only heightened, his self-awareness. He begged Abraham to send Lazarus back to his father's house to warn them, "so that they will not also come to this place of torment" (verse 28 NASB).

We have reason to think that this man believed that what was happening to him was just for two reasons. First, he says nothing about how unfair it is for him to be there. He complains about the pain, but he does not complain about injustice. Second, and more important, he knew exactly what his brothers would have to do if they were to avoid his own fate! If they would repent, they would be kept from joining him in misery.

Incredibly, the man suddenly became interested in missions! He asked Abraham to warn his five brothers that they might not come to the same place of torment. And when Abraham said no, because they had Moses and the Prophets, this man replied, "No, father Abraham, but if someone goes to them from the dead, they will repent" (verse 30).

Unforgiven sin, the rich man knew, led quite logically to a place of agony. And if his brothers were to escape his distress, they would have to do something about their predicament while they were alive on earth. With heightened perception and a better understanding, he could see that his relationship with the Almighty should have been his highest priority.

We might think this man would have preferred to have his brothers join him in hades for the sake of companionship. But he was more than willing to never see them again if only he knew that they would be on the other side of the gulf where Lazarus and Abraham were meeting for the first time. Apparently, even in hades there is compassion, a natural human concern about the fate of those who are loved.

Abraham's answer is instructive. "If they do not hear Moses and the Prophets, neither will they be convinced if someone should rise from the dead" (verse 31).

How true! When Christ told this story, He had not yet been put to death and resurrected. Yet He taught that His resurrection was the only sign that He would give to the world. But today, even though the evidence for His resurrection is overwhelming, many men and women still do not believe. As the saying goes, "A man convinced against his will is of the same opinion still."

I think back to the rich man buried in Chicago. He too had a keen memory; he thought of the family he had left behind. While I was scouring about looking for a parking space at the funeral home and discussing the service with his weeping widow and self-assured son, the man whose death brought us together was thinking fondly of his children. He thought back to how he had treated his wife; he remembered those with whom he had done business.

The beautiful words said at his eulogy, had he heard them, would have brought him shame. The shallow opinions of men now rose to mock him. He, too, I'm sure, had the plaintive hope that his family would repent so that they might not have to join him! If only he, and not his son, had been able to tell me what to say at his funeral!

Fourth, let us not forget that the rich man of Luke 16 was not yet in hell, but hades. Because the King James Version often translated both *sheol* and *hades* as *hell*, this has needlessly confused two different kinds of regions. The Bible seems clear that no one is yet in hell today. Someday, hades will be thrown into hell, but that has as yet not happened (Revelation 20:14).

Peter has just finished expounding on the judgment of disobedient angels, then adds, "The Lord knows how to rescue the godly from trials, and to keep the unrighteous under punishment until the day of judgment" (2 Peter 2:9). The tense of the verb attests that the punishment is ongoing, though the final judgment is yet future.

What about the believer, Lazarus? He was in that region of sheol, or hades, which is called here "Abraham's bosom." But after the ascension of Christ believers are said to go directly into heaven. In other words, the two regions of hades no longer exist side by side; there is reason to believe that Abraham's bosom is in heaven today.

So if you die and your spirit goes to heaven, I believe you will not be able to see those who are suffering in hades as Lazarus did. Perhaps at the ascension, Christ took those who were in Abraham's bosom (located near those who suffered in hades) to heaven with him. So Abraham's bosom, paradise, and heaven all refer to the same abode, namely the place of bliss in the presence of God. As Paul says, "To be absent from the body and to be at home with the Lord" (2 Corinthians 5:8 NASB).

Hades, as far as we know, now has only one region, and that is where unbelievers enter. I believe it is still an abode for departed spirits, a temporary intermediate state where those who have not received God's forgiveness must wait until further notice. When they hear their names called, the news that awaits them will not be encouraging.

THE PURGATORY OF MEDIEVAL THEOLOGY

Hades is not purgatory. We've learned that those who are in hades have no possibility of entering heaven. In contrast, purgatory is believed to have an exit. After the soul is purified by the sufferings of purgatory, we are told that it goes to God. Purgatory might be defined as a temporary place where those who have died as penitents are purified from sin by punishment.

The doctrine of purgatory is not found in the Bible but was accepted as a tradition in medieval times because of a faulty doctrine of salvation. The belief was that nobody (or almost nobody) was righteous enough to enter into heaven at death; thus there must be a place where men and women are purged from their sins to prepare them for heavenly perfections. Purgatory, the theory went, might last for a few years or millions of years (depending on the level of righteousness one had attained), but eventually it would come to an end and the penitent could enter heaven.

Thanks be, purgatory is unnecessary. As we shall see in a future chapter, when Christ's righteousness is credited to us, we can go directly to heaven. The apostle Paul, you might recall, wrote, "We are of good courage, and we would rather be away from the body and at home with the Lord" (2 Corinthians 5:8). The good news is that we can have the same confidence.

One day on a talk show a woman called with this question: "My father, though religious, died without believing in Christ as his Savior. Is there something I can do to get him out of where I think he probably went?"

I replied, "I have some good news and some bad news. First, the bad news: no, there is nothing you can do to change the eternal destiny of your father. The good news is that whatever God does will be just . . . not one single fact will be overlooked in judging your father's fate . . . there is no possibility that the information will be misinterpreted or the penalty unfairly administered." (This will be more fully discussed in the chapter on hell.)

So far we have learned that death has two faces: to the unbeliever the very thought of death is terrifying, or at least it should be. But for those who have made their peace with God, death is a blessing. Death is a means of redemption, a doorway into a blissful eternity. Just what that means will be clarified in future chapters.

When the curtain parts for us, nothing can keep us from answering the summons. One minute after we die we will be either elated or terrified. And it will be too late to reroute our travel plans.

But now we turn to a much brighter side of death.

CHAPTER 3

THE ASCENT INTO GLORY

**A Departure | A Restful Sleep |
A Collapsing Tent | A Sailing Ship |
A Permanent Home | Good Grief**

The doctor has just told you news that you thought could only be true about someone else. Your worst suspicions regarding that lump have been confirmed: you have a rare form of cancer, which almost certainly is terminal. The surgeon tells you that you have at most a year to live.

Where do you turn for comfort? To your family and friends, yes; you need them more now than ever. They sit in stunned silence when you give them the news, and they assure you of their prayers and love. You know you will not have to walk through these dark days alone.

Of course you also turn to God. You have come to know

Christ personally and have lived your life with single-minded devotion to Him and His agenda. You know the promises of God by memory. In a sense, you have been prepared for this hour ever since you transferred your trust to a qualified Savior, perhaps years ago.

No doubt you will vacillate between despair and hope, denial and determination. Perhaps you will have more concern for those you leave behind than you do for yourself. Not a one of us can predict how we might react when it is our turn to hear the dreadful news.

And yet the Bible presents an entirely different picture of death that should give us hope. After Adam and Eve sinned, they died spiritually as well as physically. Sending them out of the garden, far from being an act of cruelty, was actually proof of God's kindness. We read, "'he might stretch out his hand, and take also from the tree of life, and eat, and live forever'—therefore the Lord God sent him out from the garden of Eden, to cultivate the ground from which he was taken" (Genesis 3:22–23 NASB).

If Adam and Eve had eaten of the other special tree of the garden—the Tree of Life—they would have been immortalized in their sinful condition. They never would have qualified for the heaven that God wanted them to enjoy. Imagine living forever as sinners, with no possibility of redemption and permanent transformation. Although they would never have had to face the finality of death, they would have been condemned to a pitiful existence.

Thus God prevented Adam and Eve from eternal sinfulness by giving them the gift of death, the ability to exit this life and arrive safely in the wondrous life to come. Death, though it would appear to be man's greatest enemy, would in the end, prove to be his greatest friend. Only through death can we go to God (unless, of course, we are still living when Christ returns).

That is why Paul classified death as one of the possessions of the Christian. "All things are yours, whether Paul or Apollos or Cephas or the world or life or death or the present or the future—all are yours, and you are Christ's, and Christ is God's (1 Corinthians 3:21–23). We should not be surprised that death is listed as one of the gifts that belongs to us. Only death can give us the gift of eternity.

When persecutions came to the Christian church during the heady days of the Roman Empire, the believers realized that the pagans could take many things from them: wealth, food, friends, and health, to name a few. But they could not rid Christians of the gift of death that would escort them into the presence of God. Indeed, God often used the pagans to give His children that special present without which no man can see the Lord.

Think of how powerless death actually is! Rather than rid us of our wealth, it introduces us to "riches eternal." In exchange for poor health, death gives us a right to the Tree of Life that is for "the healing of the nations" (Revelation 22:2). Death might temporarily take our friends from us, but only to introduce us to that land in which there are no good-byes.

That is why Christ could say, "And do not fear those who kill the body but cannot kill the soul. Rather fear him who can destroy both soul and body in hell" (Matthew 10:28). The body might temporarily be the possession of cancer or evil men, but these enemies cannot prevent the soul from going to God. When the executioners have done their worst, God will be shown to have done His best.

Just drive up to the Drake Hotel in Chicago and a valet will park your car and a doorman will open the door to let you in. Similarly, death is the means by which our bodies are put to rest while our spirits are escorted through the gates of heaven. Death itself brings us to the gate, but then it is opened by One who says, "He who is holy, who is true, who has the key of David, who opens and no one will shut, and who shuts and no one opens" (Revelation 3:7 NASB). If the Drake prides itself in twenty-four-hour doorman service, would the Good Shepherd do any less?

Christ came, wrote the author of Hebrews, that "through death he might destroy the one who has the power of death, that is, the devil, and deliver all those who through fear of death were subject to lifelong slavery" (Hebrews 2:14–15). Satan does not have the power of death in the sense that he determines the day that a believer dies. But he has used the fear of death to keep Christians in bondage, unable to approach the curtain with a tranquility borne of the "full assurance of faith."

In the next chapters I shall discuss more specifically what we can expect when the curtain parts for those who are at peace with God through Christ. For now, I want to provide comfort by describing five figures of speech that help us understand how death is viewed in the New Testament. For those who are prepared, the journey need not be feared.

Death in the New Testament is transformed from a monster to a minister. What at first seems to box us in, frees us to go to God. Here are some words of comfort that will help us soften the blow.

A DEPARTURE

Jesus, whose courage in the face of death is a model for us, referred to His death as a departure, an exodus. There on the Mount of Transfiguration Moses and Elijah appeared with Christ and "spoke of his departure, which he was about to accomplish at Jerusalem" (Luke 9:31). That word *departure* in Greek is *exodus*, from which we get our word *exit*. The second book of the Old Testament is called Exodus because it gives the details regarding the exit of the children of Israel from Egypt.

Just as Moses led his people out of slavery, so now Christ passed through His own Red Sea, routing the enemies and preparing to lead His people to the Promised Land. His exodus is proof that He can safely conduct us all the way from earth to heaven.

There was nothing fearful about taking the journey from Egypt to Canaan; the people simply had to follow Moses, the servant of God. Once they had gone through the Red Sea, Canaan lay on the other side. If you have a qualified leader, you can enjoy the journey.

Neither is it fearful for us to make our final exodus, for we are following our leader, who has gone on ahead. When the curtain parts, we shall not only find Him on the other side but discover that He is the One who led us toward the curtain in the first place.

Just before His death, Christ told the disciples He was going where they could not come. Peter, who did not like what he heard, wanted to follow Christ everywhere. But Christ's response was, "Where I am going you cannot follow me now, but you will follow afterward" (John 13:36).

Yes, now that He has died and been raised to heaven, we all shall follow Him. What gives us courage is the knowledge that He does not ask us to go where He Himself has not gone. He who made a successful exit will make our exit successful also. Christ paid our debt on the cross, and the resurrection was our receipt. His resurrection was the "proof of purchase."

A little girl was asked whether she feared walking through the cemetery. She replied, "No, I'm not afraid, for my home is on the other side!" An exodus need never be feared if it is the route to a better land.

A RESTFUL SLEEP

When Christ entered the home of the ruler of the synagogue, He comforted the crowd by saying that the ruler's daughter was not dead, but sleeping (Luke 8:52). On another occasion, when He began His trip to Bethany He said to the disciples, "Our friend Lazarus has fallen asleep, but I go to awaken him" (John 11:11).

Paul used the same figure of speech when he taught that some believers would not see death but would be caught up to meet Christ. "Behold! I tell you a mystery. We shall not all sleep, but we shall all be changed" (1 Corinthians 15:51). Not everyone shall die; some will live until the return of Christ. Death, then, is spoken of as a restful sleep.

As you are probably aware, there are those who teach "soul sleep," that is, the belief that no one is conscious at death because the soul sleeps until the resurrection of the body. Although this view has had some able defenders, it suffers from the difficulty of having to reinterpret many clear passages of Scripture in order to make this doctrine fit.

Moses certainly did not "sleep" until the day of resurrection but was fully conscious when He appeared on the Mount of Transfiguration. To say, as some do, that he already was resurrected, is to make an assumption that is not found in the Bible. We should be content with the fact that though he died and was buried by God, he was not unconscious but able to converse with Christ. When Stephen was about to die, he did not ask the grave to receive him, but said, "Lord Jesus, receive my spirit" (Acts 7:59). Clearly he was not looking forward to an unconscious existence, but awaited the immediate bliss of heaven and fellowship with Christ.

Then there is the story of the dying thief, to whom Christ said, "Truly, I say to you, today you will be with me in Paradise" (Luke 23:43). Ignoring both the rules of grammar and syntax, those who believe in soul sleep say that the word *today* refers only to the time that Christ spoke the words. They interpret Christ's words to say, "Truly, I say to you today, you shall be with me in paradise." So, the argument goes, the thief was not going to paradise on that day; it was just that Christ made a promise to him on that day!

The problem is that Greek scholars agree that this rearranging of the words is "grammatically senseless."[1] It was already rather obvious that Christ was speaking to the thief on that day (could Christ have been speaking to him yesterday or tomorrow?). Clearly, Christ was comforting the thief by telling him that they would yet meet in paradise before the end of that very day. To force any other meaning on the text because of a preconceived idea that the soul sleeps is a disservice to the plain sense of Scripture.

Paul certainly expected to be with Christ when he died. He writes that he has a great desire "to depart and be with Christ, for that is far better" (Philippians 1:23). Paul does not long for death so that his soul can sleep; he longs for death because he knows he will be with Christ, which is far better. Again he writes that his preference is to "be away from the body and at home with the Lord" (2 Corinthians 5:8). There is no fair way to interpret this except to understand that he expected to be with Christ immediately after he died.

Sleep is used as a picture of death in the New Testament because the body sleeps until the day of resurrection, not the soul. Sleep is used as a picture of death because it is a means of rejuvenation. We look forward to sleep when we feel exhausted and our work is done. Furthermore, we do not fear falling asleep, for we have the assurance that we shall awaken in the morning; we have proved a thousand times that daylight will come.

Just last night I arrived home from a speaking engagement at 2:30 a.m. I was so exhausted my last recollection was putting my head on the pillow. I longed for the sleep that came quickly and peacefully. This morning I am refreshed, able to continue the work I had begun days ago. Sleep is a welcome experience for those who need not fear the morning.

The difference, of course, is that we have never had the experience of death, so we aren't sure exactly what it will be like to awaken in eternity. But of this we can be certain: Those who die in the Lord need not fear the unknown, for they fall asleep to awaken in the arms of God.

It is difficult to fall asleep when you are not tired. Just so, those of us who enjoy good health, a fulfilling vocation, and a wholesome family life do not look forward to "falling asleep in Jesus." But the day will come when it will no longer be our choice; we will have to obey our summons. If we should live long enough to be weary of life, falling asleep will be more inviting. Indeed, many of the saints looked forward with increasing joy to the day of their final rest.

The book of Revelation describes those who follow the beast [Antichrist] as those who "have no rest, day or night"

(Revelation 14:11); but as for those who belong to the Lord, "Blessed are the dead who die in the Lord from now on. . . that they may rest from their labors, for their deeds follow them" (verse 13). Believers find their death to be the joyous rest of fulfillment. And their deeds follow after them, never to be lost in the annals of eternity. Like a pebble thrown into a pool whose ripples continue in ever-widening circles, so the deeds of the godly will reverberate for all of eternity. Blessed are the dead who die in the Lord!

"As for me, I shall behold your face in righteousness; when I awake, I shall be satisfied with your likeness" (Psalm 17:15).

Rest at last!

A COLLAPSING TENT

Paul spoke of death as the dismantling of a tent. "For we know that if the tent that is our earthly home is destroyed, we have a building from God, a house not made with hands, eternal in the heavens" (2 Corinthians 5:1).

Our present body is like a tent where our spirit dwells; it is a temporary structure. Tents deteriorate in the face of changing weather and storms. If used regularly, they often need repairs. A tattered tent is a sign that we will soon have to move. Death takes us from the tent to the palace; it is changing our address from earth to heaven.

You've met camping enthusiasts who want to camp out most of the year. They can do that, of course, until the rains come or the snow begins to fly. The more uncomfortable they become, the more willing they are to move into a house. Thus the persecuted and infirm long for heaven, while those who are healthy and fulfilled wish to postpone death indefinitely. But the time will come when even the strongest among us will have to leave the tent behind.

Some people act as if they intend to live in this body forever, not realizing that it is about to collapse around them. A tent reminds us that we are only pilgrims here on earth, en route to our final home. Someone has said that we should not drive in our stakes too deeply, for we are leaving in the morning!

A SAILING SHIP

Paul also speaks of death as the sailing of a ship. In a passage already quoted, he wrote, "I am hard pressed between the two. My desire is to depart and be with Christ, for that is far better" (Philippians 1:23). That word *depart* was used for the loosing of an anchor. A. T. Robertson translates it, "To weigh anchor and put out to sea."

Thanks to Christ, Paul was ready to embark on this special journey that would take him to his heavenly destination. Christ had already successfully navigated to the other side and was waiting with a host of Paul's friends. Of course, he had some friends on this side too; that's why he added, "But to remain in the flesh is more necessary on your account" (verse 24).

Paul's bags were packed. But for now the Captain said, "Wait!" A few years later, Paul was closer to leaving earth's shore. Again he spoke of death as his departure: "For I am already being poured out as a drink offering, and the time of my departure has come" (2 Timothy 4:6). The signal for him to push off was imminent. He said good-bye, but only for the time being. He would not return to Timothy, but Timothy would soon cross over and they would meet again.

The author of Hebrews picks up on the same imagery

and says that we can flee to Christ to lay hold of the hope set before us. He adds, "We have this as a sure and steadfast anchor of the soul, a hope that enters into the inner place behind the curtain, where Jesus has gone as a forerunner on our behalf" (Hebrews 6:19–20). That means that we do not cast our anchor on anything within ourselves. We seek our security neither in feelings nor experiences. Our anchor is fastened to Christ, who is within the Holy of Holies where He resides now that His blood bought our salvation.

Philip Mauro suggests that the picture here is that of the forerunner used in ancient times to help a vessel enter the harbor safely. He would jump from the ship, wade to the harbor, and fasten the strong rope of the ship to a rock along the shore. Then, by means of a winch, the vessel was brought in.

Just so, our forerunner has gone to heaven, where He stands ready to guide us safely into the Holy of Holies. We are fastened to a rock that cannot be moved. Let the storms tear our sails to shreds; let the floors creak; let the gusts of wind attempt to blow us off course; let the tides overwhelm us; we shall arrive safely into the port. Each day we are pulled a notch closer to the harbor by the One who proved He is more powerful than death.

> *We have an anchor that keeps the soul*
> *Steadfast and sure while the billows roll,*
> *Fastened to the Rock which cannot move,*
> *Grounded firm and deep in the Saviour's love.*

John Drummond tells the story of a sea captain who was asked to visit a dying man in a hospital. When the captain reached the sick man's room, he noticed decorated flags of different colors surrounding his bed. As they talked, the captain learned that both of them had actually served on the same ship many years earlier.

"What do these flags mean?" the captain wondered.

"Have you forgotten the symbols?" the dying man asked. "These flags mean that the ship is ready to sail and is awaiting orders," he reminded the captain.

Our flags must always be flying, for we know neither the day nor the hour of our departure. Some are given more notice than others, but all must go when the celestial clock strikes.

Thankfully, we can be ready to embark on the last leg of our voyage. Christ leads His own safely into the harbor.

A PERMANENT HOME

In a sense, to speak of heaven as our home is not a figure of speech; heaven is our home. Jesus, you will recall, spoke of leaving His disciples to build a mansion for them in the world beyond.

> In my Father's house are many rooms. If it were not so, would I have told you that I go to prepare a place for you? And if I go and prepare a place for you, I will come again and will take you to myself, that where I am you may be also. (JOHN 14:2–3)

The King James translation "many mansions" elicits the vision of a sprawling home with a fifty-acre front yard and limousines parked in the driveway. But that word *abode* really means "dwelling place," a place that we can call home.

We should not think that Christ has been working for two thousand years getting heaven ready for us. It has been facetiously suggested that since Christ was a carpenter on earth, He has been exercising His trade in glory, working to finish the rooms for our arrival.

As God, He didn't have to get a head start. He can create our future home in a moment of time. Christ's point is simply that just as a mother prepares for the arrival of her son who has been at sea, so Christ awaits our arrival in heaven. Heaven is called home, for it is where we belong.

Paul wrote that in this world we are "at home" in the body, but in the world to come we will be "at home" with the Lord (2 Corinthians 5:6–8). And he left no doubt as to which home he prefers. "Yes, we are of good courage, and we would rather be away from the body and at home with the Lord" (verse 8). Understandably, he preferred the mansion to the tent.

After I left home I never feared returning. In fact, I often was so lonely in college I could hardly wait until Christmas break so that I could join my parents and siblings to get caught up on our friendship. There sitting around the table, I found love, acceptance, and comfort when I needed it. Home sweet home.

Why should we fear death if it is the route to our final home? Jesus assures us that there is nothing to fear; in fact, the knowledge that we shall die gives us the courage and hope to live triumphantly in this world!

Most of us find comfort in being told that we are going to go on living; Paul was comforted when he was told that he soon would be dying! He kept referring to death as that which was "far better."

The fact that we don't view death with optimism just might be because we think of death as taking us from our home rather than bringing us to our home! Unlike Paul, we have become so attached to our tent that we just don't want to move.

The old song says it best:

This world is not my home,
I'm just a pass'n through.
My treasures are laid up
Somewhere beyond the blue.

To die is to go home to heaven; to live is to exist in a foreign country on earth. Someday we'll understand this distinction much better; for now the future is ours by faith.

In the Old Testament there is a beautiful story of a man who apparently was taken to heaven without dying. "Enoch walked with God, and he was not, for God took him" (Genesis 5:24). A little girl who described what she had learned in Sunday school said to her mother, "One day Enoch and God took a long walk together until Enoch said it was getting late. And the Lord said, 'We are now closer to my home than we are to yours . . . Why don't you just come to my home tonight?'"

When we are closer to heaven than earth, we'll just keep walking all the way to God's home. Home is where we belong.

GOOD GRIEF

Though we are comforted by these images, we still find that death can terrify us. Paul asks, "O death, where is your victory? O death, where is your sting?" (1 Corinthians 15:55). A bee can only sting a man once. Although the insect can still frighten us when the stinger is gone, it can do no damage. Because Christ removed death's sting, it can now only threaten; it cannot make good on its threats.

Will we have grace to face our exit victoriously? I have

not had to face my own imminent death; I can't predict how I might react if I were told that I have a terminal disease.

I, for one, would like to have dying grace long before I need it! But the famous English preacher Charles Haddon Spurgeon says that death is the last enemy to be destroyed, and we should leave him to the last. He adds:

> Brother, you do not want dying grace till dying moments. What would be the good of dying grace while you are yet alive? A boat will only be needful when you reach a river. Ask for living grace, and glorify Christ thereby, and then you shall have dying grace when the time comes.
> Your enemy is going to be destroyed but not today. . . .
> Leave the final shock of arms till the last adversary advances, and meanwhile hold your place in the conflict. God will in due time help you to overcome your last enemy, but meanwhile see to it that you overcome the world, the flesh and the devil.

Some believers who thought they could not face death discovered they had the strength to die gracefully when their time came. The same God who guides us on earth will escort us all the way to heaven. "You guide me with your counsel, and afterward you will receive me to glory" (Psalm 73:24).

When Corrie ten Boom was a girl, her first experience with death came after visiting the home of a neighbor who had just died. When she thought of the fact that her parents would die someday, her father comforted her by asking, "When I go to Amsterdam, when do I give you your ticket?"

"Just before we get on the train."

"Exactly. Just so your heavenly Father will give you exactly what you need when we die—He'll give it to you just when you need it."

Dying grace does not mean that we will be free from sorrow, whether at our own impending death or the death of someone we love. Some Christians have mistakenly thought that grief demonstrates a lack of faith. Thus they have felt it necessary to maintain strength rather than deal honestly with a painful loss.

Good grief is grief that enables us to make the transition to a new phase of existence. The widow must learn to live alone; the parents must bear the loneliness brought on by the death of a child. Grief that deals honestly with the pain is a part of the healing process. Christ wept at the tomb of Lazarus and agonized with "loud cries and tears" in Gethsemane at His own impending death (Hebrews 5:7).

Sorrow and grief are to be expected. If we feel the pain of loneliness when a friend of ours moves from Chicago to Atlanta, why should we not experience genuine grief when a friend leaves us for heaven? Dozens of passages in the Old and New Testaments tell how the saints mourned. When Stephen, the first Christian martyr, was stoned we read, "Devout men buried Stephen and made great lamentation over him" (Acts 8:2).

Joe Bayly, who had three sons who died, wrote of his own experience, "Death wounds us, but wounds are meant to heal. And given time they will. But we must want to be healed. We cannot be like the child who keeps picking the scab from the cut."[2] As Christians, we live with the tension between what is "already ours" and the "not yet" of our experience. Paul said believers should look forward to Christ's return "that you may not grieve as others do who have no hope" (1 Thessalonians 4:13). Grief was expected, but it is different from the grief of the world. There is a difference between tears of hope and tears of hopelessness.

Let those of us who wish to comfort the sorrowing remember that words can have a hollow ring for those who are overwhelmed with grief. Let us by our presence "weep with those who weep" (Romans 12:15). We must say we care much louder with our actions than with our words. Our presence and our tears can say more than words could ever communicate.

Donald Grey Barnhouse, on the way home from the funeral of his first wife, was trying to think of some way of comforting his children. Just then a huge moving van passed by their car and its shadow swept over them. Instantly, Barnhouse asked, "Children, would you rather be run over by a truck or by its shadow?" The children replied, "Of course we'd prefer the shadow!"

To which Barnhouse replied, "Two thousand years ago the truck of death ran over the Lord Jesus . . . now only the shadow of death can run over us!"

> Yea, though I walk through the
>   valley of the shadow of death,
> I will fear no evil:
> for thou art with me.
>   (Psalm 23:4 KJV)

Death is the chariot our heavenly Father sends to bring us to Himself.

CHAPTER 4

WELCOME!
YOU HAVE ARRIVED!

**Your Personality | Your Intermediate State |
Your Resurrection Body | The Death of Infants |
Our Enemy, Our Friend**

When my friend Del Fahsenfeld was battling a rare brain tumor, the doctors assured him in April that he would be dead before Christmas. When I interviewed him, he told me that he wanted to follow God so fully while he still had strength that when weakness came he would be able to endure his suffering with confidence. When you come home at night, he said, "you can manage to get around the house in the darkness because you have been there so often in the light."

When Del died in November of that year, those who were with him reported that he died well. For him, the darkness of death was as the light. He was prepared for that final hour; the Christ he had known for so many years led him through the curtain all the way to the other side.

What can we expect one minute after we die?

While relatives sorrow on earth, you will find yourself in new surroundings which just now are beyond our imagination. Most probably, you will have seen angels who have been assigned the responsibility of escorting you to your destination, just as the angels who carried Lazarus into "Abraham's bosom."

Back in January 1956, five young missionaries were speared to death in the jungles of Ecuador. The offenders have now become Christians and have told Steve Saint, the son of one of the martyrs, that they heard and saw what they now believe to be angels while the killings were taking place. A woman hiding at a distance also saw these beings above the trees and didn't know what kind of music it was until she heard a Christian choir on records.[1]

Though such a revelation of angels is rare, this incident is a reminder that these heavenly beings who watch us on earth await us in heaven. Of course our greatest desire is to see Christ, who will be on hand to welcome us, but angels will be on hand too.

Since we are Christ's sheep, He calls us by name, perhaps standing even as He did for Stephen (Acts 7:55). We look into His eyes and see compassion, love, and understanding. Though we are unworthy, we know His welcome is genuine. We see the nail prints in His hands, and this triggers memories that make us fall on our faces in worship. Were it not for His tender hand helping us to our feet, we'd be unable to stand up.

So much is different, yet you are quite the same. You have

entered heaven without a break in consciousness. Back on earth our friends will bury our body, but they cannot bury us. Personhood survives the death of the body. Just before Stephen died, he said, "Lord, receive my spirit." He did not say, "Receive my body." Death, someone has said, "is powerful business," for you just keep living somewhere else without undue interruption.

YOUR PERSONALITY CONTINUES

We are accustomed to talk about the differences there will be when we make our transition from earth to heaven. But there are some similarities too. Given the fact that our personalities continue, we can expect continuity. Heaven is the earthly life of the believer glorified and perfected.

Personal Knowledge Continues

One minute after we die, our minds, our memories, will be clearer than ever before. In chapter 2 we were reminded of Jesus' story of the rich man who went to hades with his memory intact. He knew his family on earth, pleading, "I have five brothers." Death does not change what we know; our personalities will just go on with the same information we have stored in our minds today.

Think back to your background: your parents, brothers, sisters, family reunions. Of course, you will remember all of this and more in heaven. Do you actually think you might know less in heaven than you do on earth? Unthinkable!

Once in heaven we will soon get to meet a host of others, some known to us in this life or through the pages of church history, others nameless in this world but equally honored in the world to come. On the Mount of Transfiguration, three of the disciples met Moses and Elijah. So far as we know, there was no need for introductions; no need for name tags. In heaven there will be intuitive knowledge, for our minds will be redeemed from the limitations sin imposed upon them.

Of course, we will not know everything, for such knowledge belongs only to God. But we shall "know fully," even as we are "fully known" (1 Corinthians 13:12). In heaven, we will know just like we do on earth, except more so. Only our desire to sin will no longer be a part of our being.

Personal Love Continues

Again we are reminded of the rich man who was concerned about his brothers, lest they come to the same place of torment. He not only knew who his brothers were, but he was concerned about them. He loved them so much that he was willing to never see them again if only they would not join him in this place of torment. He would endure isolation if they experienced consolation.

Of course, dear widow, your husband who is in heaven continues to love you as he did on earth. Today he loves you with a fonder, sweeter, purer love. It is a love purified by God. Your child loves you; so do your mother and father. There is no more a break in love than there is in continuity of thought. Death breaks ties on earth but renews them in heaven.

Christ made clear that we will not marry in heaven nor be given in marriage. But that does not mean that we will be sexless. In heaven we will retain our female or male gender. Your mother will be still known as your mother in heaven; your son or daughter will be known as a member of your earthly family. I like what Chet Bitterman said after his missionary son was killed by guerrillas. "We have eight children. And they all are living: one's in heaven and seven are on earth."

Our love for God will also be intensified. Here, at last, without distractions, God can be loved, for faith has given way to sight. We will keep loving whatever we loved on earth, apart from sin. In heaven, our affections will be like they were on earth, except more so.

There is no evidence that those in heaven can actually see us on earth, though that might be possible. It is more likely that they can ask for regular updates on how we are doing. I cannot imagine that such a request would be denied.

When her grandfather died, a seven-year-old girl at the Moody Church asked her father, "Can we ask Jesus to get a message to Grampa?" He was caught somewhat by surprise but realized that there was nothing in his theology that would cause him to say no. So he responded, "Yes, that might be possible; let's tell Jesus what we want Grampa to know."

We might not be sure whether Jesus gave the message to her grampa, but we must agree that this little girl's theology was much better than that of millions of other people in the world. She knew that although we might pray to Jesus to get a message to her grampa, we don't pray to her grampa to get a message to Jesus!

We must warn, however, that those who are in heaven cannot communicate with us. In the first chapter I emphasized that the Bible strictly forbids any attempt to communicate with those who have died. We must be satisfied that they are more knowledgeable than we and that someday we will be with them. God has told us all we need to know in this life; we need to entrust our loved ones into His loving care for the life to come.

If those in heaven could talk with us, what would they say? They would urge us to be faithful; they would tell us that if we only knew how generous God is, we would do all we could to please Him. "For I consider that the sufferings of this present time are not worth comparing with the glory that is to be revealed to us" (Romans 8:18). They would tell us to live on earth with heaven in mind.

Personal Feelings Continue

Think of your purest joy on earth; then multiply that many times and you might catch a glimpse of heaven's euphoria. Even in the Old Testament, David knew enough to write, "In your presence there is fullness of joy; at your right hand are pleasures forevermore" (Psalm 16:11). Heaven is the perfecting of the highest moments of our present Christian experience.

What about sorrow? Yes, there will be sorrow until God Himself "will wipe away every tear from their eyes (Revelation 7:17; 21:4). When we think of the opportunities we squandered, when we consider how imperfectly we loved Christ on earth, we will grieve. Such sorrow will vanish, but for the moment the reality of what could have been will dawn upon us.

If we still question whether the departed spirits experience the same emotions as we, let us read these words:

> When he opened the fifth seal, I saw under the altar the souls of those who had been slain for the word of God and for the witness they had borne. They cried out with a loud voice, "O Sovereign Lord, holy and true, how long before you will judge and avenge our blood on those who dwell on the earth?" (REVELATION 6:9–10)

Knowledge, love, feelings, a desire for justice—all of these are the present experience of those who have gone ahead of us to heaven. Remember that the entire personality simply carries over into the life beyond. Heaven has its differences, but it is populated with your friends, who are still the people who once dwelt on the earth. They are still your friends!

Personal Activities Continue

Yes, in heaven we will rest, but it is not the rest of inactivity. We will most probably continue many of the same kinds of projects we knew on earth. Artists will do art as never before; the scientist just might be invited to continue his or her exploration of God's magnificent creation. The musicians will do music; all of us will continue to learn.

We are, says Maclaren, saplings here, but we shall be transported into our heavenly soil to grow in God's light. Here our abilities are in blossom; there they shall burst forth with fruits of greater beauty. Our death is but the passing from one degree of loving service to another; the difference is like that of the unborn child and the one who has entered into the experiences of a new life. Our love for God will continue, but awakened with new purity and purposefulness.

The famous Puritan writer Jonathan Edwards believed that the saints in heaven would begin by contemplating God's providential care of the church on earth and then move on to other aspects of the divine plan, and thus "the ideas of the saints shall increase to eternity."

The "real you" will be there.

THE INTERMEDIATE STATE

The question on our minds is: What kind of body do the saints have in heaven now? Since the permanent, resurrection body is still future, what kind of an existence do believers have even now as you are reading this book?

227

Since the resurrection of the body is future, are the present saints in heaven disembodied spirits? Or do they have some kind of temporary "intermediate" body that will be discarded on the day of resurrection—the day when we shall receive our permanent, glorified bodies?

The point of disagreement is over Paul's words in 2 Corinthians 5:1, "For we know that if the tent that is our earthly home is destroyed, we have a building from God, a house not made with hands, eternal in the heavens." The question is: To what period in the future does he refer when he speaks of our having "a building from God . . . eternal in the heavens"? Do we have that building [a body] at death, or do we receive it at the future resurrection? Paul shrinks from the idea that his soul would live through a period of nakedness, a time when it would exist without a body.

One explanation is that God creates a body for these believers and that this explains how the redeemed in heaven can relate to Christ and to one another. Since departed believers can sing the praises of God and communicate with one another, it seems that they must have a body in which to do so. What is more, at the point of transition between life and death some have actually testified that they saw departed relatives awaiting their arrival. That points to the conclusion that the saints in heaven already have recognizable bodies.

On the Mount of Transfiguration, Moses and Elijah appeared in some kind of body, though neither yet has his permanent resurrection body. Admittedly, Elijah was taken up to heaven without dying and Moses was buried on Mount Nebo by God, but they also still await the resurrection. Yet there they were, talking, communicating, and evidently recognizable to Peter, James, and John.

The rich man who died and went to hades must have had

a body, since he was able to use human speech and wanted his tongue cooled. He had eyes to see and ears to hear. His body, of whatever kind, was sensitive to pain and was recognizable to Lazarus, who was on the other side of the great divide. Usually we think of spirits as unable to perform such functions.

However, we must ask ourselves: If the saints already have bodies in heaven (albeit temporary ones), why does Paul place such an emphasis on the resurrection in his writings? He clearly implies that the saints in heaven today are incomplete and in an unnatural state.

So a second plausible explanation might be that the souls of the departed dead may in some ways have the functions of a body. If that is the case, it would explain how they can communicate with one another and have a visible presence in heaven. These capabilities of the soul are implied in Revelation 6:9–10, which was quoted earlier. The souls that were beneath the altar had a voice with which they were able to cry up to God. And what is more, these souls were actually given white robes to wear as they waited for God to avenge them.

Admittedly the word *psychas* (translated "souls") has a broad meaning and can also be translated "lives," or "persons." But the word is often translated "soul" as distinguished from the body. If that is what John meant, it would give credence to the view that souls can take upon themselves shape and bodily characteristics. If that seems strange to us, it may well be that our concept of the soul is too limited.

We cannot be sure which of these views is correct. Of this much we may be certain: Believers go directly into the presence of Christ at death. They are conscious and in command of all of their faculties. As D. L. Moody said before he died, "Soon you will read in the papers that Moody is dead. . . .

Don't believe it . . . for in that moment I will be more alive than I have ever been."

We do not have to know exactly what kind of body we will have in order to have the assurance that our personalities will continue. We will be the same people we were on earth, will have the same thoughts, feelings, and desires. Though our struggles with sin will be over, we will be aware of who we really are. There will be no doubt in our minds that we have just moved from one place to another without an intermediate stop.

And yet we will await the final resurrection.

The Resurrection Body

The New Testament doctrine of the resurrection is an affirmation that we are a spiritual and physical unity and that God intends to put us back together again. Although the soul is separable from the body, such a separation is only temporary. If we are to live forever, we must be brought together as a united human being—body, soul, and spirit.

Some Christians assume that God will create new permanent bodies for us ex nihilo, that is, out of nothing. But if that were so, there would be no need for the doctrine of resurrection. In 1 Corinthians 15 Paul makes four contrasts between our present bodies and our future ones. "It is sown a perishable body, it is raised an imperishable body; it is sown in dishonor, it is raised in glory; it is sown in weakness, it is raised in power; it is sown a natural body, it is raised a spiritual body" (1 Corinthians 15:42–44 NASB).

First, we are sown a perishable body, but we will be raised imperishable. Like a seed sown in the ground, there is continuity between the acorn and the tree, between the kernel and the stalk. Not every particle that ever was a part of you has to be raised, and God just might add additional material to make up the deficiencies.

In heaven, no one will comment on your age or notice that the years are beginning to take their toll. You will look as young a billion years from now as you will a thousand years from now.

As Dr. Hinson wrote:

> *The stars shall live for a million years,*
> *A million years and a day.*
> *But God and I will live and love*
> *When the stars have passed away.*

Second, we are sown in dishonor, but raised in power. When a body is transported to a funeral home it is always covered by a sheet to shield gaping eyes from the ignominy of looking upon the corpse. Every dead body is a reminder of our dishonor, a reminder that we are but frail. But we shall be raised in power.

Third, we are sown in weakness, but raised in strength. The resurrection body is not subject to material forces. Remember how Christ came through closed doors after the resurrection. Keep in mind that the reason the angel rolled the stone from the tomb was not to let Christ out, but to let the disciples in!

Finally, we are sown a natural body, but we are raised a spiritual body. To say that we will have a "spiritual body" does not mean that we will just be spirits. Christ's glorified body was so human that He invited the disciples to touch Him and affirmed, "See my hands and my feet, that it is I myself. Touch me, and see. For a spirit does not have flesh and bones as you see that I have" (Luke 24:39).

There will be continuity with a difference. Our future body will be like Christ's resurrection body. "We know that when he appears we shall be like him, because we shall see him as he is" (1 John 3:2). Just think of the implications.

The continuity between Christ's earthly and heavenly body was clear to see—for example, the nail prints were in His hands. The disciples recognized Him instantly, and He even ate fish with them at the seashore. But there were also radical changes. He was able to travel from one place to another without physical effort and went through doors without opening them.

Evidently we too shall be able to travel effortlessly. Just as Christ could be in Galilee and then suddenly appear in Judea, so we shall be free from the limitations of terrestrial travel. That does not mean, of course, that we will be omnipresent, as God is; we will be limited to one place at one time. But travel will be swift and effortless.

And yet, to the delight of many people, we shall still eat, not because we are hungry, but because we will delight in the fellowship it affords. After the resurrection, Christ ate fish with His disciples on the shores of Galilee. And, of course, believers will be present at the marriage supper of the Lamb (Revelation 19:7).

THE DEATH OF INFANTS

A close friend lost a baby; little Grace Elizabeth died one day old. Since there is continuity between the earthly and heavenly body, will she be an infant forever?

A few years ago my wife and I were eagerly anticipating becoming grandparents, but God had other plans. Our granddaughter, Sarah, was stillborn. We have struggled, along with our daughter and son-in-law, wondering what God's purpose might be in our disappointment and grief.

Yes, I believe that our precious Sarah is in heaven, but we must be clear as to why we believe that she and other children will be there. Contrary to popular opinion, children will not be in heaven because they are innocent. Paul taught clearly that children are born under condemnation of Adam's sin (Romans 5:12). Indeed, it is because they are born sinners that they experience death.

Nor should we make a distinction between children who are baptized and those who are not, as if such a ritual can make one a child of God. The idea of infant baptism arose in North Africa years after the New Testament was written. Even if it can be justified theologically as a sign of the covenant (a debatable proposition), there is no evidence whatever that it can give to children the gift of eternal life.

If children are saved (and I believe they shall be), it can only be because God credits their sin to Christ; and because they are too young to believe, the requirement of personal faith is waived. We do not know at what age they are held personally accountable. It is impossible to suggest an age, since that may vary, depending on the child's capacity and mental development.

There are strong indications that children who die are with the Lord. David lost two sons for whom he grieved deeply. For Absalom, his rebellious son, he wept uncontrollably and refused comfort, for he was uncertain about the young man's destiny. But when the child born to Bathsheba died, he washed, anointed himself, and came into the house of the Lord to worship. He gave this explanation to those who asked about his behavior: "But now he is dead. Why should I fast? Can I bring him back again? I shall go to him, but he will not return to me" (2 Samuel 12:23).

Christ saw children as being in close proximity to God and the kingdom of heaven. "See that you do not despise one of these little ones. For I tell you that in heaven their angels always see the face of my Father who is in heaven" (Matthew 18:10). Children are close to the heart of God.

Will a baby always be a baby in heaven? James Vernon McGee has made the interesting suggestion that God will resurrect the infants as they are and that the mothers' arms that have ached for them will have the opportunity of holding their little ones. The father who never had the opportunity of holding that little hand will be given that privilege. Thus the children will grow up with their parents.

Whether that will be the case, we do not know. But of this we can be confident: A child in heaven will be complete. Either the child will look as he would have if he were full grown, or else his mental and physical capacities will be enhanced to give him full status among the redeemed. All handicaps are gone, for heaven is a place of perfection.

The death of an infant, however, causes all of us to struggle with the will and purpose of God. It seems strange that God would grant the gift of life and then cause it to be snuffed out before it could blossom into a stage of usefulness. But we can be sure that there is a purpose in such a life, even if it is not immediately discernible.

James Vernon McGee again says that when a shepherd seeks to lead his sheep to better grass up the winding, thorny mountain paths, he often finds that the sheep will not follow him. They fear the unknown ridges and the sharp rocks. The shepherd will then reach into the flock and take a little lamb on one arm and another on his other arm. Then he starts up the precipitous pathway. Soon the two mother sheep begin to follow, and afterward the entire flock. Thus they ascend the tortuous path to greener pastures.

So it is with the Good Shepherd. Sometimes He reaches into the flock and takes a lamb to Himself. He uses the experience to lead His people, to lift them to new heights of commitment as they follow the little lamb all the way home.

A little girl died in a hotel where she was staying with her father. Since her mother was already dead, just two followed the body to the cemetery—the father and the minister. The man grieved uncontrollably as he took the key and unlocked the casket to look upon the face of his child one last time. Then he closed the casket and handed the key to the keeper of the cemetery.

On the way back the minister quoted Revelation 1:17– 18 to the brokenhearted man. "'Fear not, I am the first and the last, and the living one. I died, and behold I am alive forevermore, and I have the keys of Death and Hades.'"

"You think the key to your little daughter's casket is in the hands of the keeper of the cemetery," the minister said. "But the key is in the hands of the Son of God, and He will come some morning and use it."

Bob Neudorf wrote "To My Baby":

> *Is it proper to cry*
> *For a baby too small*
> *For a coffin?*
> *Yes, I think it is.*
> *Does Jesus have*
> *My too-small baby*
> *In His tender arms?*
> *Yes, I think He does.*
> *There is so much I do not know*

About you—my child—
He, she? quiet or restless?
Will I recognize
Someone I knew so little about,
Yet loved so much?
Yes, I think I will.
Ah, sweet, small child
Can I say
That loving you is like loving God?
Loving—yet not seeing,
Holding—yet not touching,
Caressing—yet separated by the chasm of time.
No tombstone marks your sojourn,
And only God recorded your name.
The banquet was not canceled,
Just moved. Just moved.
Yet a tear remains
Where baby should have been.

The Alliance Witness,
16 September 1987, 14.
Used by permission.

When the great preacher Peter Marshall was taken by ambulance to a hospital in Washington, D.C., his wife, Catherine, said that at that moment she realized that "life consists not in duration, but in donation."

It is not how long you live but the contribution you make that matters. And yes, these little ones have made their contribution too—they have opened the hearts of their loved ones to the realization that we are all headed toward home.

OUR ENEMY, OUR FRIEND

Why is death such a blessing? Paul said, "Flesh and blood cannot inherit the kingdom of God, nor does the perishable inherit the imperishable" (1 Corinthians 15:50). The fact is that you and I can't go to heaven just as we are today. No matter how alert and primed, no matter how neatly we have showered and dressed, we are not fit for heaven. You can't have a decaying body in a permanent home.

Death rescues us from the endlessness of this existence; it is the means by which those who love God finally are brought to Him. Paul had no illusions as to whether heaven was better than earth. He was itching to depart and to be with Christ, which "is far better." Even our heroic attempts to live one day longer with respirators and other high-tech equipment would seem unnecessary if we could see what awaits us.

Only on this side of the curtain is death our enemy. Just beyond the curtain the monster turns out to be our friend. The label "Death" is still on the bottle, but the contents are "Life Eternal." Death is our friend because it reminds us that heaven is near. How near? As near as a heartbeat; as near as an auto accident; as near as a stray bullet; as near as a plane crash. If our eyes could see the spirit world, we might find that we are already at its gates.

Judson B. Palmer relates the story of the Reverend A. D. Sandborn, who preceded him as pastor in a church in Iowa. Reverend Sandborn called on a young Christian woman who was seriously ill. She was bolstered up in bed, almost in a sitting position, looking off in the distance. "Now just as soon as they open the gate I will go in," she whispered.

Then she sank upon her pillow in disappointment. "They have let Mamie go in ahead of me, but soon I will go in."

Moments later she again spoke, "They let Grampa in ahead of me, but next time I will go in for sure."

No one spoke to her and she said nothing more to anyone, and seemed to see nothing except the sights of the beautiful city. Reverend Sandborn then left the house because of the press of other duties.

Later in the day the pastor learned that the young woman had died that morning. He was so impressed with what she had said that he asked the family about the identity of Mamie and Grampa. Mamie was a little girl who had lived near them at one time but later moved to New York State. As for Grampa, he was a friend of the family and had moved somewhere in the Southwest.

Reverend Sandborn then wrote to the addresses given him to inquire about these two individuals. Much to his astonishment he discovered that both Mamie and Grampa had died the morning of September 16, the very hour that the young woman herself had passed into glory.

Death is not the end of the road; it is only a bend in the road. The road winds only through those paths through which Christ Himself has gone. This Travel Agent does not expect us to discover the trail for ourselves. Often we say that Christ will meet us on the other side. That is true, of course, but misleading. Let us never forget that He walks with us on this side of the curtain and then guides us through the opening. We will meet Him there, because we have met Him here.

The tomb is not an entrance to death, but to life. The sepulcher is not an empty vault, but the doorway to heaven. When we die, nothing in God dies, and His faithfulness endures. Little wonder the pagans said of the early church that they carried their dead as if in triumph!

Aristides, a first-century Greek, marveled at the extraordinary success of Christianity and wrote to a friend, "If any righteous man among the Christians passes from this world, they rejoice and offer thanks to God, and they escort his body with songs and thanksgiving as if he were setting out from one place to another nearby."

And so it is. At death believers set out from one place to another. There is reason for sorrowing but "not as those who have no hope." Such confidence makes the unbelievers take notice that Christians die differently.

Christ assures us, "Where I am, there you may be also" (John 14:3 NASB).

CHAPTER 5

LIVING IN THE NEW JERUSALEM

**The Size of the City | The Materials of the City |
Our New Occupation | Our New Family |
A New Order of Reality**

Y ou are lying in the hospital surrounded by friends who
have tiptoed in and out of your room for the last two
days. The doctor has not told you that your death is imminent, because you already know that the end is near. You have
had the courage to talk to your family about your funeral, and
you are relieved to know that you have done all you could to
prepare for this hour. Your bags are packed for the journey.

When you breathe your last, a doctor will come and verify
the death. Your family will leave the room, and a sheet will be
draped over your body, which will be carried to the temporary
morgue. While your family is making funeral arrangements,

you have already arrived at your permanent home.

We've already emphasized that we will make the transition into heaven without a break in consciousness. We will meet Christ and be introduced to the company of the redeemed. Those whom you did not know on earth are just as instantly known as those of your earthly friends who often joined you at your favorite restaurant. Your uncle asks about the well-being of some of his relatives, but the primary conversation is about the beauty of Christ, the wonder of God's love, and the undeserved grace that makes you a beneficiary of such blessings.

A little girl who had been looking at pictures of Christ in the evening dreamed about Him at night. In the morning she said, "Oh, He is a hundred times better than the pictures." Now that you see Him, you will agree, I'm sure, that He is much better than our most enchanting dreams.

At your leisure you explore your new home. This, after all, is where you will spend eternity, so it is worth a look. Christ assured the disciples that the place He was preparing had "many dwelling places." There would be plenty of room for all of the redeemed.

In the book of Revelation, we have the best description of the New Jerusalem, which is our permanent home. John writes,

> Then I saw a new heaven and a new earth, for the first heaven and the first earth had passed away, and the sea was no more. And I saw the holy city, new Jerusalem, coming down out of heaven from God, prepared as a bride adorned for her husband. (REVELATION 21:1–2)

This city is new—that is, re-created—just as our resurrected bodies are re-created from our earthly bodies. The previous heavens (the atmospheric heavens) and the earth, tainted by sin, will have been obliterated by fire to make room for the new order of creation (2 Peter 3:7–13). This new city came out of heaven because it is part of the heavenly realm.

Let's consider some features of this beautiful permanent home.

THE SIZE OF THE CITY

The dimensions are given as a cube, fifteen hundred miles square. "The city is laid out as a square, and its length is as great as the width; and he measured the city with the rod, fifteen hundred miles; its length and width and height are equal" (Revelation 21:16 NASB).

If we take that literally, heaven will be composed of 396,000 stories (at twenty feet per story) each having an area as big as one half the size of the United States! Divide that into separate condominiums, and you have plenty of room for all who have been redeemed by God since the beginning of time. The Old Testament saints—Abraham, Isaac, and Jacob—they will be there. Then we think of the New Testament apostles and all the redeemed throughout two thousand years of church history—heaven will be the home for all of them. Unfortunately, however, the majority of the world's population will likely not be there. Heaven, as Christ explained, is a special place for special people.

You need not fear that you will be lost in the crowd; nor need you fear being stuck on the thousandth floor when all of the activity is in the downstairs lounge. All you will need to do is to decide where you would like to be, and you will be there! Each occupant will receive individualized attention. The Good Shepherd who calls His own sheep by name will have a special place prepared for each of His lambs. As someone has said, there will be a crown awaiting us that no one else can wear, a dwelling place that no one else can enter.

THE MATERIALS OF THE CITY

The details can be written, though hardly imagined. In John Bunyan's *Pilgrim's Progress*, as Christian and Hopeful finally see the City of God, there was such beauty that they fell sick with happiness, crying out, "If you see my Beloved, tell Him I am sick with love." The city was so glorious that they could not yet look upon it directly but had to use an instrument made for that purpose. This, after all, is the dwelling place of God.

John wrote in the Revelation that the city had the glory of God. "Her brilliance was like a very costly stone, as a stone of crystal-clear jasper" (21:11 NASB). It is interesting that the city shares some features of the earthly Jerusalem, but we are more impressed with the contrasts. The New Jerusalem is a city of unimaginable beauty and brilliance.

First, there is a wall with twelve foundation stones that encompasses the city. "And the wall of the city had twelve foundations, and on them were the twelve names of the twelve apostles of the Lamb" (21:14).

As for the foundation stones on which the wall is built, each is adorned with a different kind of precious stone—the list is in 21:19–20. The jewels roughly parallel the twelve stones in the breastplate of the high priest (Exodus 28:17–20).

The height of the wall is given as seventy-two yards, not very high in comparison to the massive size of the city, but high enough, however, to provide security and to make sure that it is accessible only through proper entrances.

Second, we notice the twelve gates, each a single pearl (Revelation 21:12–21). That is a reminder that entrance into the city is restricted; only those who belong are admitted, and "nothing unclean will ever enter it, nor anyone who does what is detestable or false, but only those who are written in the Lamb's book of life" (verse 27).

John gives a further description of those who are outside the city walls. "Outside are the dogs and sorcerers and the sexually immoral and murderers and idolaters, and everyone who loves and practices falsehood" (22:15). There is a sentinel angel at each gate, evidently to make sure that only those who have their names written in the book are admitted.

The twelve gates are divided into four groups; thus three gates face each of the four directions. "There were three gates on the east and three gates on the north and three gates on the south and three gates on the west" (21:13 NASB). That is a reminder that the gospel is for all men, and all the tribes of the earth will be represented.

Notice that the saints of the Old Testament and the New are both included. The names of the twelve sons of Israel are written on the gates of the city, and the New Testament apostles have their names inscribed on the foundation stones. Thus the unity of the people of God throughout all ages is evident.

As for the street of the city, it was "pure gold, like transparent glass" (verse 21). It is illuminated by the glory of God, and the Lamb is the lamp. Now we can better understand why Bunyan said that the pilgrims must see the city through a special instrument. Its beauty is simply too much for us to comprehend. We need a transformed body and mind to behold it with unrestricted admiration.

When Christ said He was preparing a home for us with

many mansions, He did not imply, as some have suggested, that He needed plenty of time to do the building. God is able to create the heavenly Jerusalem in a moment of time. But Christ did emphasize that we would be with Him, and we know that His presence will be even more marvelous than our environment.

OUR NEW OCCUPATION

It has been estimated that there are at least forty thousand different occupations in the United States. Yet for all that, only a small percentage of the population is completely satisfied with their responsibilities. Personnel problems, the lack of adequate pay, and wearisome hours of routine tasks are only some of the reasons. Few people, if any, are truly satisfied.

But those problems will be behind us forever in heaven. Each job description will entail two primary responsibilities. First, there will be the worship of God; second, there will be the serving of the Most High in whatever capacity assigned to us.

The Worship of God

Let's try to capture the privilege of worship.

Heaven is first and foremost the dwelling place of God. It is true, of course, that God's presence is not limited to heaven, for He is omnipresent. Solomon perceptively commented, "Behold, heaven and the highest heaven cannot contain you; how much less this house that I have built!" (1 Kings 8:27).

Yet in heaven God is localized. John saw God seated upon a throne with twenty-four other thrones occupied by twenty-four elders who worship the King. "From the throne came flashes of lightning, and rumblings and peals of thunder" (Revelation 4:5). And what is the nature of the activity around that throne? There is uninhibited joy and spontaneous worship.

Needless to say, the saints on earth are imperfect. They are beset by quarrels, carnality, and doctrinal deviations. Read a book on church history and you will marvel that the church has survived these two thousand years.

Have you ever wondered what it would be like to belong to a perfect church? That is precisely what John saw when he peered into heaven. Free from the limitations of the flesh and the opposition of the devil, the perfect church is found singing the praises of Christ without self-consciousness or mixed motives.

Repeatedly John sees worship taking place in heaven. Even after the judgment of God is heaped upon unrepentant sinners, the saints join with other created beings to chant the praises of God:

> And from the throne came a voice saying,
> "Praise our God, all you his servants, you who fear him,
> small and great." Then I heard what seemed to be the
> voice of a great multitude, like the roar of many waters
> and like the sound of mighty peals of thunder, crying out,
> "Hallelujah! For the Lord our God the Almighty
> reigns." (REVELATION 19:5–6)

If we want to prepare for our final destination, we should begin to worship God here on earth. Our arrival in heaven will only be a continuation of what we have already begun. Praise is the language of heaven and the language of the faithful on earth.

Service to the Lord

Though worship shall occupy much of our time in heaven, we will also be assigned responsibilities commensurate with the faithfulness we displayed here on earth: "And his servants will worship him. They will see his face, and his name will be on their foreheads" (Revelation 22:3–4).

That word *servant* is found frequently in the book of Revelation, for it pictures a continuation of the relationship we even now have with Christ. However, the word *serve* that appears here is used primarily in the New Testament for service that is carried on within the temple or church (Matthew 4:10; Luke 2:37; Acts 24:14). Thus we shall serve Him in that special, intimate relationship available only to those who are included within the inner circle of the redeemed. David Gregg gives his impression of what that kind of work will be like:

> It is work as free from care and toil and fatigue as is the wing-stroke of the jubilant lark when it soars into the sunlight of a fresh, clear day and, spontaneously and for self-relief, pours out its thrilling carol. Work up there is a matter of self-relief, as well as a matter of obedience to the ruling will of God. It is work according to one's tastes and delight and ability. If tastes vary there, if abilities vary there, then occupations will vary there.[1]

What responsibilities will we have? Christ told a parable that taught that the faithful were given authority over cities. Most scholars believe that will be fulfilled during the millennial kingdom when we shall rule with Christ here on earth. But it is reasonable to assume that there is continuity between the earthly kingdom and the eternal heavenly kingdom. In other words, it may well be that our faithfulness (or unfaithfulness) on earth may have repercussions throughout eternity.

Yes, everyone in heaven will be happy and fulfilled. Everyone will be assigned a place in the administration of the vast heavenly kingdom. But just as there are varied responsibilities in the palace of an earthly king, so in heaven some will be given more prominent responsibilities than others.

Of this we may be certain: Heaven is not a place of inactivity or boredom. It is not, as a Sunday school pupil thought, an interminable worship service where we begin on page one of the hymnal and sing all the way through. God will have productive work for us to do. We will increase our knowledge of Him and His wondrous works. Will not Christ show us the Father that we might be forever satisfied? Will we not then learn to love the Lord our God in ways that we have never been able to do on earth?

We do not know, as some have speculated, whether we shall explore other worlds. Others have suggested that we shall be able to complete many projects begun on earth. Whatever our activity, we can be sure that our infinite heavenly Father will have infinite possibilities.

OUR NEW FAMILY

We have already learned that we will know our earthly family in heaven. But now our family will be expanded. Think of it this way: The intimacy you now enjoy with your family will include all the other saints who are present.

One day some of Christ's friends sent word that His mother and brothers were looking for Him. Christ responded, "Who are my mother and my brothers?" Looking about at those who were sitting around Him, He said, "Here are my mother and my brothers! For whoever does the will of God, he is my brother and sister and mother" (Mark 3:33–35).

Think of the implications. We will be just as close to Christ as we are to any member of our present family. Indeed, He is not ashamed to call us His brothers and sisters! There will be extended family with greater intimacy than we have known on earth.

Archbishop Richard Whately has an excellent description of the kind of friendship we can expect in heaven.

> I am convinced that the extension and perfection of friendship will constitute a great part of the future happiness of the blest. . . . A wish to see and personally know, for example, the apostle Paul, or John, is the most likely to arise in the noblest and purest mind. I should be sorry to think such a wish absurd and presumptuous, or unlikely ever to be gratified. The highest enjoyment doubtless to the blest will be the personal knowledge of their great and beloved Master. Yet I cannot but think that some part of their happiness will consist in an intimate knowledge of the greatest of His followers also; and of those of them in particular, whose peculiar qualities are, to each, the most peculiarly attractive.[2]

Think of the joys of such a family! And of the infinite time to become better acquainted.

A NEW ORDER OF REALITY

Fortunately, heaven will not have everything. In fact the apostle John lists in Revelation 7, 21, and 22 many different experiences and realities known on earth that will be absent there.

No More Sea (21:1)

Throughout the Bible, the word *sea* stands for the nations of the world, usually the rebellious nations. Heaven means that the strife between nations and the seething turmoil that accompanies those struggles will vanish. No broken treaties, no wars, no scandals.

No More Death (21:4)

The hearse will have made its last journey. Today we look at death as a thief that robs us of our earthly existence. It is simply the final act in the deterioration of the human body. As such it is almost universally feared; no one can escape its terrors. Even Christians who have conquered it in Christ may tremble at its fearsome onslaught. But death shall not enter heaven. No funeral services, no tombstones, no tearful good-byes.

No More Sorrow (21:4)

Read the newspaper, and sorrow is written on every page. An automobile accident takes the life of a young father; a child is raped by a madman; a flood in Bangladesh kills twenty thousand. No one can fathom the amount of emotional pain borne by the inhabitants of this world in any single moment. In heaven there will be uninterrupted joy and emotional tranquility.

No More Crying (7:17; 21:4)

No one could possibly calculate the buckets of tears that are shed every single moment in this hurting world. From the child crying because of the death of a parent to the woman weeping because of a failed marriage—multiply those tears by a million, and you will realize that we live in a crying world.

In heaven, He who wiped away our sins now wipes away our tears. This comment has raised the question of why there would be tears in heaven in the first place. And does the Lord come with a handkerchief and literally wipe away each tear? That is possible. But I think that John means more than that. He wants us to understand that God will give us an explanation for the sorrow we experienced on earth so that we will not have to cry anymore. If that were not so, then the tears might return after He has wiped them away. But being able to view the tearful events of earth from the perspective of heaven will dry up our tears forever.

The question is often asked how we can be happy in heaven if one or more of our relatives is in hell. Can a child, for example, enjoy the glories of eternity knowing that a father or a mother will always be absent from the celebration? Or can a godly mother serve and worship with joy knowing that her precious son will be in torment forever? That question has so vexed the minds of theologians that some have actually asserted that in heaven God will blank out a part of our memory. The child will not know that his parents are lost in hell; the mother will not remember that she had a son.

However, it is unlikely that we will know less in heaven than we do on earth. It is not characteristic of God to resolve a problem by expanding the sphere of human ignorance. That is especially true in heaven, where we will have better mental faculties than on earth. In heaven we shall be comforted, not because we know less than we did on earth but because we know more.

It is more likely that God will wipe away all tears by explaining His ultimate purposes. We will look at heaven and hell from His viewpoint and say that He did all things well. If God can be content knowing that unbelievers are in hell, so will we. I expect that all who are in heaven will live with the knowledge that justice was fully served and that God's plan was right. And with such an explanation and perspective, our emotions will mirror those of our heavenly Father. Jonathan Edwards said that heaven will have no pity for hell, not because the saints are unloving but because they are perfectly loving. They will see everything in conformity with God's love, justice, and glory. Thus with both head and heart we will worship the Lord without regret, sorrow, or misgivings about our Father's plan.

No More Pain (21:4)

Come with me as we walk down the corridor of a hospital. Here is a young mother dying of cancer; there is a man gasping for breath, trying to overcome the terror of a heart attack. In the next ward an abused child has just been admitted with burns inflicted by an angry father. For those and countless other emergencies scientists have prepared painkillers to help people make it through life, one day at a time.

In heaven, pain, which is the result of sin, is banished forever. No headaches, slipped discs, or surgery. And no more emotional pain because of rejection, separation, or abuse.

No Temple (21:22)

Some have been puzzled by that assertion because elsewhere John says that there is a temple in heaven (Revelation 11:19). Wilbur M. Smith points out that the apparent contradiction can be resolved when we realize that the temple and its angelic messengers "continue in action during the time of man's sin and the outpouring of the wrath of God, but after the old earth has disappeared, the temple has no longer any function."³ The worship in heaven is now carried on directly; God Himself is the shrine, the temple. The former patterns of worship give way to a new, unrestricted order.

No More Sun or Moon (7:16; 21:23; 22:5)

Those planets created by God to give light to the earth have outlived their purpose. God Himself is the light of heaven. "And the city has no need of sun or moon to shine on it, for the glory of God gives it light, and its lamp is the Lamb" (21:23; see also 7:16). Again we read, "And night will be no more. They will need no light of lamp or sun, for the Lord God will be their light, and they will reign forever and ever" (22:5).

That means that the holy city is interpenetrated with light. Joseph Seiss explains it this way:

> That shining is not from any material combustion, not from any consumption of fuel that needs to be replaced as one supply burns out; for it is the uncreated light of Him who is light, dispensed by and through the Lamb as the everlasting Lamp, to the home, and hearts, and understandings of His glorified saints.⁴

No Abominations (21:27)

The nations shall bring the honor and glory of God into the city, but we read, "Nothing unclean will ever enter it, nor anyone who does what is detestable or false, but only those who are written in the Lamb's book of life" (21:27). John lists others who will be excluded: immoral people, murderers, idolaters, and the like (21:8; 22:15).

No More Hunger, Thirst, or Heat (7:16)

Those burdens borne by the multitudes of this present world will vanish forever. In their place will be the Tree of Life and the beauty of the paradise of God.

Those things that cast such a pall of gloom over the earth today will be replaced by indescribable happiness in the presence of Divine Glory.

> *Face to face with Christ my Savior,*
> *Face to face—what will it be—*
> *When with rapture I behold Him,*
> *Jesus Christ Who died for me?*
> *Only faintly now I see Him,*
> *With the darkling veil between;*
> *But a blessed day is coming,*
> *When His glory shall be seen.*
> *Face to face I shall behold Him,*
> *Far beyond the starry sky*
> *Face to face in all His glory,*
> *I shall see Him by and by!*
>
> Carrie E. Breck

And so while your family tends to your funeral, you are beholding the face of Christ. Though the family weeps at your departure, you would not return to earth even if the choice were given to you. Having seen heaven, you will find that earth has lost all of its attraction. As Tony Evans says, "Have a good time at my funeral, because I'm not going to be there!"

You only wish that those you left behind would know how important it was to be faithful to Christ. Looked at from the other side of the curtain, knowing what is now so clear to you,

you wish that you could shout to earth encouraging believers to serve Christ with all their hearts. You wish you had grasped this before the call came for you to come up higher.

Suddenly you realize that not everyone will have your experience. Some people—millions of them—will be lost forever because they did not take advantage of Christ's sacrifice on their behalf. You weep as you think of all the people still on earth who most probably will not be there.

You know that you would weep forever except that God comes to wipe the tears from your eyes.

It will all be true, just as Christ said.

CHAPTER 6

WHEN HADES IS THROWN INTO HELL

**Reasons to Disbelieve | Alternative Teachings |
The Justice of God | Greek Words for Hell |
Characteristics of Hell**

H ell disappeared. And no one noticed."
 With that terse observation, American church historian Martin Marty summarized our attitude toward a vanishing doctrine that received careful attention in previous generations. If you are a churchgoer, ask yourself when you last heard an entire sermon or Sunday school lesson on the topic.

An article in *Newsweek* said, "Today, hell is theology's H-word, a subject too trite for serious scholarship." Gordon Kaufman of Harvard Divinity School believes we have gone through a transformation of ideas, and he says, "I don't think there can be any future for heaven and hell."

Admittedly, hell is an unpleasant topic. Unbelievers disbelieve in it; most Christians ignore it. Even the staunchly biblical diehards are often silent out of embarrassment. Hell, more than any doctrine of the Bible, seems to be out of step with our times.

And yet we read that in the final judgment the unbelieving dead of all the ages stand before God to be judged, "Then Death and Hades were thrown into the lake of fire. . . . And if anyone's name was not found written in the book of life, he was thrown into the lake of fire" (Revelation 20:14–15). This is but one of many descriptions of hell found in the Bible. What shall we do with this teaching?

REASONS TO DISBELIEVE

This doctrine is often neglected because it is difficult to reconcile hell with the love of God. That millions of people will be in conscious torment forever is beyond the grasp of the human mind. Bishop John A. Robinson, who gained notoriety decades ago with his liberal views in *Honest to God*, writes,

> Christ . . . remains on the Cross as long as one sinner
> remains in hell. . . . In a universe of love there can be no
> heaven that tolerates a chamber of horrors; no hell for
> any which does not at the same time make it hell for
> God. He cannot endure that, for that would be a final
> mockery of his nature.[1]

The doctrine of hell has driven many people away from Christianity. James Mill expressed what many have felt. "I will call no being good, who is not what I mean by good when I use that word of my fellow creatures; and if there be a Being who can send me to hell for not so calling him, to hell I will go."[2]

One man said that he would not want to be in heaven with a God who sends people to hell. His preference was to be in hell so that he could live in defiance of such a God. "If such a God exists," he complained, "he is the devil."

To put it simply, to us the punishment of hell does not fit the crime. Yes, all men do some evil and a few do great evils, but nothing that anyone has ever done can justify eternal torment. And to think that millions of good people will be in hell simply because they have not heard of Christ (as Christianity affirms) strains credulity. It's like capital punishment for a traffic violation.

Thus millions of Westerners believe in some kind of afterlife, but it is one of bliss, not misery. Genuine fear of suffering in hell has vanished from the mainstream of Western thought. Few, if any, give prolonged thought to the prospect that some people will be in hell. Fewer yet believe they themselves will be among that unfortunate number.

ALTERNATIVE TEACHINGS

There are two alternative theories that vie for acceptance. One takes the hell out of forever; the other takes the forever out of hell.

Universalism

Universalism is the name given to the belief that eventually all men will arrive safely to heaven. Since Christ died for all people without exception, it follows, they say, that all will eventually be saved. God will overcome every remnant of evil, and all rational creatures (some would even include Satan) will eventually be redeemed.

Here is a verse universalists like to use. Paul taught that

in the fullness of time, there would be the "summing up of all things in Christ, things in the heavens and things on the earth" (Ephesians 1:10 NASB). And it is God's intention to "reconcile to himself all things, whether on earth or in heaven, making peace by the blood of his cross" (Colossians 1:20). The implication, we are told, is that everyone will eventually be brought into the family of God.

Unfortunately, this attractive interpretation has serious weaknesses. If the universalists' interpretation were correct, then Satan would also have to be redeemed, that is, reconciled to God. Yet it is clear that Christ did not die for him (Hebrews 2:16); therefore God would have no just grounds to pardon him, even if he repented.

What is more, the Scriptures explicitly teach that he along with the beast and the false prophet shall be "tormented day and night forever and ever" (Revelation 20:10). Here we have a clear statement that Satan shall never be redeemed but will exist in conscious eternal torment.

Yes, everything will be summed up in Christ. That means that all things will be brought under Christ's direct authority. Christ has completed everything necessary to fulfill God's plan of salvation. The order of nature shall be restored, and justice will prevail throughout the whole universe. As we shall see later, that restoration does not negate the doctrine of hell but instead necessitates it.

Universalists also quote other verses, such as, "Therefore, as one trespass led to condemnation for all men, so one act of righteousness leads to justification and life for all men" (Romans 5:18). A similar passage is 1 Corinthians 15:22: "For as in Adam all die, so also in Christ shall all be made alive." Universalists interpret these verses to mean that as all men are condemned for Adam's offense, so all men are justified by

Christ's act of righteousness.

Unfortunately, that interpretation fails for two reasons. First, the texts must be interpreted in light of others that clearly teach the eternal misery of unbelievers in hell. We simply do not have the luxury of isolating passages of Scripture.

Second, we must realize that the Bible frequently uses the word *all* in a restricted sense, as pertaining to all in a certain category rather than all without exception. Examples are numerous. Matthew tells us that "all Judea" went out to hear John the Baptist (Matthew 3:5–6). Luke records that a decree went out that "all the world should be registered" (Luke 2:1). And the disciples of John the Baptist complained that "all" were following Christ (John 3:26). In the passages written by Paul, it is clear that all who are in Adam die, whereas all who are in Christ shall be made alive. The "all" has limitations built into it by the context.

The final deathblow to universalism is in Matthew 12:32 NASB. Christ is speaking of the unpardonable sin: "It shall not be forgiven him, either in this age or in the age to come." In Mark 3:29 it is called an "eternal sin," indicating that it begins in this age and is carried on for all eternity without hope of reversal. How could those who have committed this sin be reconciled to God when Scripture clearly says they shall never be forgiven?

Universalism has never been widely accepted by those who take the Scriptures seriously. Obviously if this teaching were true, there would be no pressing reason to fulfill the Great Commission or to urge unbelievers to accept Christ in this life.

Conditional Immortality

Whereas universalism sought to take the "forever" out of hell, we now come to a theory that attempts to take the hell out of forever. Conditional immortality contends that all will not be saved, but neither will any be in conscious torment forever. God resurrects the wicked to judge them; then they are thrown into the fire and consumed. The righteous are granted eternal life, whereas the unbelievers are granted eternal death. Hell is annihilation.

Clark Pinnock asked how one can imagine for a moment that the God who gave His Son to die on the cross would "install a torture chamber somewhere in the new creation in order to subject those who reject him in everlasting pain?" He observes that it is difficult enough to defend Christianity in light of the problem of evil and suffering without having to explain hell too.

Pinnock believed that the fire of God consumes the lost. Thus God does not raise the wicked to torture them but rather to declare judgment on them and condemn them to extinction, which is the second death. Everlasting punishment, according to Pinnock, means that God sentences the lost to final, definitive death.

Pinnock's favorite text is: "And do not fear those who kill the body but cannot kill the soul. Rather fear him who can destroy both soul and body in hell" (Matthew 10:28). He assumes that if a soul is destroyed in hell it is annihilated.

Unfortunately, that interpretation will not survive careful analysis. Robert A. Morey points out in *Death and the Afterlife* that the word "destroyed" as used in the Bible does not mean "to annihilate." The Greek word *apollumi* is used in passages such as Matthew 9:17, Luke 15:4, and John 6:12, 27. In none of those instances does it mean "to pass out of existence." Morey writes: "There isn't a single instance in the New Testament where *apollumi* means annihilation in the strict sense of the word."[3] Thayer's Greek-English Lexicon defines destruction as "to be delivered up to eternal misery."

Unfortunately, annihilationism simply will not wash. Christ says that the lost will go into "eternal fire," which has been prepared for the devil and his angels. And then He adds, "These will go away into eternal punishment, but the righteous into eternal life" (Matthew 25:46). Since the same word *eternal* describes both the destiny of the righteous and the wicked, it seems clear that Christ taught that both groups will exist forever, albeit in different places. The same eternal fire that Satan and his hosts experience will be the lot of unbelievers.

In an earlier chapter we learned that the eternal conscious existence of unbelievers was already taught in the Old Testament. Daniel wrote, "Many of those who sleep in the dust of the earth shall awake, some to everlasting life, and some to shame and everlasting contempt" (Daniel 12:2). The wicked will experience shame and contempt for as long as the righteous experience bliss.

Finally, the occupants of hell are clearly said to experience eternal misery. Those who worship the beast and have received his mark "will drink the wine of God's wrath, poured full strength into the cup of his anger" (Revelation 14:10). Such will be

> tormented with fire and sulfur in the presence of the holy angels and in the presence of the Lamb. And the smoke of their torment goes up forever and ever, and they have no rest, day or night, these worshipers of the beast and its image, and whoever receives the mark of its name. (verses 10–11)

Notice that the fire does not annihilate the wicked but torments them. There, in the presence of the holy angels and the Lamb, there will be no periods of rest during which the wicked are unconscious of torment. They will never slip into peaceful nonexistence.

In Revelation 20 we have a similar scene. The beast and the false prophet have been thrown into the lake of fire. Satan is bound, but after a thousand years he is released to deceive the nations once more. At the end of that period, Satan is cast into the lake of fire. Notice carefully that the beast and the false prophet have not been annihilated during those one thousand years in hell. The fire has not consumed them: "And the devil who had deceived them was thrown into the lake of fire and sulfur where the beast and the false prophet were, and they will be tormented day and night forever and ever" (verse 10).

Hence, the teachings of universalism and annihilationism come to their deceptive end. Eternal, conscious torment is clearly taught—there is no other honest interpretation of these passages.

THE JUSTICE OF GOD

At the root of the debate is the question of whether hell is fair and just. Pinnock, you will recall, lamented that it was difficult enough to explain evil to the unbelieving world without having to explain hell too. Sensitive Christians, he says, cannot believe in eternal, conscious punishment.

To us as humans, everlasting punishment is disproportionate to the offense committed. God appears cruel, unjust, sadistic, and vindictive. The purpose of punishment, we are told, is always redemptive. Rehabilitation is the goal of all prison sentences. The concept of a place where there will be endless punishment without any possibility of parole or reform seems unjust.

How can hell be just? The following observations may not answer all of our questions, but I hope they will help us begin to see hell from God's perspective.

The Judgment Is Based on What They Did

In a previous chapter we learned that hades will eventually be thrown into hell. But before that happens every person will be resurrected and judged individually. "And I saw the dead, great and small, standing before the throne, and books were opened. Then another book was opened, which is the book of life. And the dead were judged by what was written in the books, according to what they had done" (Revelation 20:12).

No one is saved by works, to be sure. As we shall stress in the final chapter of this book, salvation is a gift of God, not of works. But for the unsaved the works are the basis of judgment. In other words, they will be rightly judged on the basis of what they did with what they knew.

Those who live without specific knowledge about Christ will be judged by the light of nature and their own conscience (Romans 1:20; 2:14–16). That does not mean that those who respond to general revelation will be automatically saved, for no one lives up to all that he knows. That is why a personal knowledge of Christ is needed for salvation. "And there is salvation in no one else, for there is no other name under heaven given among men by which we must be saved" (Acts 4:12).

But the light of God in nature and in the human conscience is still a sufficient basis for judgment. Whatever the degree of punishment, it will fit the offense exactly, for God is meticulously just. Those who believe in Christ experience mercy; those who do not (either because they have never heard of Him or because they reject what they know of Him) will receive justice. Either way, God is glorified.

Think of how accurately God will judge every unbeliever! Each day of every life will be analyzed in minute detail. The hidden thoughts and motives of each hour will be replayed, along with all the actions and attitudes. The words spoken in secret will be made public, the intentions of the heart displayed for all to see. They will have no attorney to whom they may appeal, no loopholes by which they can escape. Nothing but bare, indisputable facts.

I believe that the balance of justice will be so accurate that the pornographer will wish he had never published such material, the thief will wish he had earned an honest living, and the adulterer will regret that he lived an immoral life. Faithfulness to his marriage vows would not have earned him a place in heaven, to be sure, but it would have made his existence in hell slightly more bearable.

Before God, no motives will be misinterpreted, no extenuating circumstances thrown out of court. The woman who seduced the man will receive her fair share of punishment, and the man who allowed himself to be seduced will receive his. The parents who abused their child who turned to drugs to escape from the pain of rejection—all blame will be accurately proportioned.

We all agree that heaven is a comforting doctrine. What is often overlooked is that hell is comforting too. Our newspapers are filled with stories of rape, child abuse, and a myriad of injustices. Every court case ever tried on earth will be reopened; every action and motive will be meticulously inspected and just retribution meted out. In the presence of an all-knowing God there will be no unsolved murders, no unknown child abductor, and no hidden bribe.

Unbelievers Are Eternally Guilty

Hell exists because unbelievers are eternally guilty. The powerful lesson to be learned is that no human being's suffering can ever be a payment for sin. If our suffering could erase even the most insignificant sin, then those in hell would eventually be freed after their debt was paid. But all human goodness and suffering from the beginning of time, if added together, could not cancel so much as a single sin.

> *Could my zeal no respite know,*
> *Could my tears forever flow,*
> *All for sin could not atone;*
> *Thou must save, and Thou alone.*
> *"Rock of Ages"*

Sir Francis Newport, who ridiculed Christianity, is quoted as saying these terrifying words on his deathbed:

> Oh, that I was to lie a thousand years upon the fire that never is quenched, to purchase the favor of God, and be united to him again! But it is a fruitless wish. Millions and millions of years would bring me no nearer to the end of my torments than one poor hour. Oh, eternity, eternity! forever and forever! Oh, the insufferable pains of hell![4]

He was quite right in saying that a million years in hell could not purchase salvation. Tragically, he did not cast himself upon the mercy of God in Christ. Since no man's works or sufferings can save him, he must bear the full weight of his sin throughout eternity.

We Cannot Comprehend the Seriousness of Sin

We must confess that we do not know exactly how much punishment is enough for those who have sinned against God. We may think we know what God is like, but we see through a glass darkly. Jonathan Edwards said that the reason we find hell so offensive is because of our insensitivity to sin.

What if, from God's viewpoint, the greatness of sin is determined by the greatness of the One against whom it is committed? Then the guilt of sin is infinite because it is a violation of the character of an infinite Being. What if, in the nature of God, it is deemed that such infinite sins deserve an infinite penalty, a penalty that no one can ever repay?

We must realize that God did not choose the attributes He possesses. Because He has existed from all eternity, His attributes were already determined from eternity past. If God had not possessed love and mercy throughout all eternity, we might have been created by a malicious and cruel being who delighted in watching His creatures suffer perpetual torment. Fortunately, that is not the case. The Bible tells of the love and mercy of God; He does not delight in the death of the wicked. But it also has much to say about His justice and the fact that even the wicked in hell will glorify Him. To put it clearly, we must accept God as He is revealed in the Bible, whether He suits our preferences or not.

It is absurd in the extreme to say, "I don't want to be in heaven with a God who sends people to hell . . . I would rather go to hell and defy Him." I can't exaggerate the foolishness of those who think they can oppose God to their own satisfaction or to His detriment! In Psalm 2 we read that God sits in the heavens and laughs at those who think they can defy Him. Like the mouse who thinks it can stand against the farmer's plow or the rowboat poised to thwart the path of an aircraft carrier, it is insanity for man to think that he can oppose the living God, who is angry with sinners and is bent on taking vengeance on those who oppose Him.

Even as we look at the world today, we should not be surprised that God allows multitudes to live in eternal misery. Think of the vast amount of suffering (preventable suffering, if you please) that God has allowed on this earth. An earthquake in Iran kills thirty thousand, a tidal wave in Bangladesh kills fifty thousand, a tsunami takes over two hundred thousand lives, and famines in the world cause twenty thousand deaths every single day! Who can begin to calculate the amount of emotional pain experienced by babies, children, and adults? Yet we know that strengthening the earth's crust, sending rain, and withholding floods could all be accomplished by a word from the Almighty.

If God has allowed people to live in untold misery for thousands of years, why would it be inconsistent for Him to allow misery to continue forever? Charles Hodge asks, "If the highest glory of God and the good of the universe have been promoted by the past sinfulness and misery of men, why may not those objects be promoted by what is declared to be future?"[5]

If our concept of justice differs from God's, we can be quite sure that He will be unimpressed by our attempts to get Him to see things from our point of view. No one is God's counselor; no one instructs or corrects Him. He does not look to us for input on how to run His universe.

GREEK WORDS FOR HELL

The New Testament uses three different Greek words for hell. One is *tartarus*, used in 2 Peter 2:4 for the abode of evil angels who sinned during the time of Noah. "For . . . God did not spare angels when they sinned, but cast them into hell and committed them to chains of gloomy darkness to be kept until the judgment." In Jude 6 the word *tartarus* is used similarly.

The second and most often used word for hell in the New Testament is *gehenna*, a word for hell already used by the Jews before the time of Christ. The word is derived from the Hebrew "valley of Hinnom" found in the Old Testament (Joshua 15:8; 2 Kings 23:10; Nehemiah 11:30). In that valley outside Jerusalem the Jews gave human sacrifices to pagan deities. There too the garbage of the city was thrown, where it bred worms. That explains why Christ referred to hell as the place where "their worm does not die and the fire is not quenched" (Mark 9:48, 44, 46).

This picture of an unclean dump where fires and worms never die became to the Jewish mind an appropriate description of the ultimate fate of all idolaters. Thus the word became applied to the ultimate gehenna. The Jews taught, and Christ confirmed, that the wicked would suffer there forever. Body and soul would be in eternal torment.

For years, liberal scholars taught (and some sentimentalists still do) that Christ, who stressed the love of God, could never be party to the doctrine of hell. Yet significantly, of the twelve times the word gehenna is used in the New Testament, eleven times it came from the mouth of our Lord. Indeed, He spoke more about hell than about heaven.

The third word is *hades*, a word we have already studied in a previous chapter. I mention it here only because it is translated "hell" in the King James Version of the Bible. Most other translations simply leave it untranslated as "hades," so that it might be properly distinguished from hell.

What will the suffering of hell be like? We must guard

against undue speculation since the Scriptures do not describe the torments of hell in specifics. We must not fall into the error of the medievals, when guides taking tourists through the Vatican described hell in vivid detail. Yet, Jesus told a story that does give us a glimpse of hell, or more accurately, a glimpse of hades, which is a prelude to the final place of eternal punishment.

CHARACTERISTICS OF HELL

In a previous chapter we referred to Christ's story of the rich man who was in hades while his friend Lazarus was in Abraham's bosom. Christ's point was to show how the fortunes of these men were reversed in the life to come. The rich man was now in torment, the poor man in bliss.

But after the judgment, hades is thrown into the lake of fire. Yet, there is no doubt that some of the characteristics of hades continue, or more accurately, that the suffering of hades is intensified in hell.

A Place of Torment

Usually when we think of hell, we think of fire, since Christ spoke of the "fire of hell." In Revelation we read of "the lake of fire and brimstone."

There is no reason the torments of hell could not include physical fire, since the bodies of those present will have been re-created and made indestructible. Unlike our present bodies, those of the resurrected dead will not burn up or be extinguished. Literal fire is a possibility.

However, as we learned earlier, there is another kind of fire that will be in hell, a fire that may be worse than literal fire. That is the fire of unfulfilled passion, of desires that are never satisfied. Perpetually burning lusts never subside, and the tortured conscience burns but is never sated or appeased. There will be increased desire with decreased satisfaction.

Hell, then, is the raw soul joined to an indestructible body, exposed to its own sin for eternity. Hell is the place of unquenchable, raging guilt, without painkillers or sedation. Literal fire might be welcomed if only it would cleanse the tormented conscience.

Be assured of this: Neither the devil nor his angels will torment people in hell. Satan and his demons will be among the tormented; they will not be tormentors (Revelation 20:10).

A Place of Abandonment

In hades there was an unbridgeable chasm between the two men, but at least they could speak to one another. But it is unlikely that there will be the opportunity of such communication in hell. For one thing, "Abraham's bosom" was transferred directly into the presence of Christ at the ascension. For another, we have no suggestion in the New Testament that those who are in hell will be able to communicate with one another.

C. S. Lewis believed there would not be communication in hell, because it was a place of solitude. Jonathan Edwards believed that if unbelievers are next to one another they would only add to each other's agony through expressions of hatred, accusations, and curses. Of one thing we can be absolutely certain: No comfort will be derived from the presence of others. Consumed with the torment of raging, unforgiven sin, those in hell will never find comfort again.

However, the Scriptures teach that those who are in hell will be tormented in the presence of Christ and the holy angels (Revelation 14:10). Nothing is said about whether other people behold the sufferings of the damned, though God often invites righteous people or angels to behold the judgment He inflicts upon the wicked (Psalm 46:8–9; Isaiah 66:23–24; Revelation 19:17–21). The famous British preacher Charles Haddon Spurgeon wrote, "If there be one thing in hell worse than another, it will be seeing the saints in heaven. . . . Husband, there is your wife in heaven and you are among the damned. And do you see your father? Your child is before the throne, and you accursed of God and man are in hell!"

If believers do witness these events, we can be sure that they will agree completely with the justice displayed by God, for then they shall see all things from His point of view. Thus, the righteous can enjoy the bliss of heaven knowing full well the fate of the wicked in hell.

Though Dante added many of his own ideas to the superstitions of his day when he wrote *The Inferno*, the sign he read in the vestibule of hell does portray the biblical teaching of hopelessness and abandonment.

> *I am the way to the city of woe.*
> *I am the way to a forsaken people.*
> *I am the way into eternal sorrow.*
> *Sacred justice moved my architect.*
> *I was raised here by divine omnipotence,*
> *Primordial love and ultimate intellect.*
>
> *Only those elements time cannot wear*
> *Were made before me, and beyond time I stand.*
> *Abandon all hope ye who enter here.*
> *Canto 3.1–9*

Jonathan Edwards pointed out that those in hell will have no reason for entertaining any secret hope that after being in the flames many ages God will take pity on them and release them. God, says Edwards, will not be any more inclined to release them after a million ages than He was at the very first moment. Little wonder, Edwards said, that any description we give of hell can be but a faint representation of the reality!

A Place of Eternity

How long is eternity?

Visualize a bird coming to earth every million years and taking one grain of sand to a distant planet. At that rate it would take thousands of billions of years before the bird had carried away a single handful of sand. Now let's expand that illustration and think how long it would take the bird to move the Oak Street Beach in Chicago and then the other thousands of beaches around the world. After that, the bird could begin on the mountains and the earth's crust.

By the time the bird transported the entire earth to the far-off planet, eternity would not have officially begun. Strictly speaking, one cannot begin an infinite series, for a beginning implies an end. In other words, we might say that after the bird has done his work, those in eternity will not be one step closer to having their suffering alleviated. There is no such thing as half an eternity.

The most sobering thought that could ever cross our minds is the fact that the rich man in hades referred to above has not yet received the drop of water for which he so desperately longed. Today, as you read this book, he is still there awaiting the final judgment of the lake of fire. Eternity endures, and it endures forever.

A Place of Easy Access but No Exit

Entering hell is easy enough. All that one has to do is neglect Christ, the only one who can save us.

Jonathan Edwards, whom we have already quoted, gave more consideration to the doctrine of hell than any other theologian. His sermon "Sinners in the Hands of an Angry God" kept audiences spellbound, stripping from them any objections or excuses they might have had against the doctrine of hell. He made the point that there are some people now living for whom God has more anger than some who are now in hades (he called it hell) who have already died. Therefore, it was only the mercy of God that kept them from plunging into the abyss:

> There is nothing that keeps wicked men at any one moment out of hell, but the mere pleasure of God. . . . There is no want in God's power to cast wicked men into hell at any moment. . . . They deserve to be cast into hell, so divine justice never stands in the way. . . . They are now the objects of that very same anger and wrath that is expressed in the torments of hell . . . yea, God is a great deal more angry with great numbers that are now on the earth, yea doubtless with some who reread this book, who it may be are at ease, than he is with many of those who are now in the flames of hell.
> Unconverted men walk over the pit of hell on a rotten covering, and there are innumerable places in this covering so weak that they will not bear their weight, and those places are not seen. . . . There is the dreadful pit of the glowing flames of the wrath of God; there is hell's wide gaping mouth open; and you have nothing to stand upon, nor anything to take hold of, there is nothing between you and hell but air; it is only the power and mere

pleasure of God that holds you up. . . . His wrath burns against you like fire; he looks upon you as worthy of nothing else than to be thrown into the fire. . . . You hang by the slender thread, with the flames of divine wrath flashing about it and ready every moment to singe it, and burn it asunder.[6]

Powerful!

If reading this chapter has been frightening, the good news is that if God grants you the desire to trust Christ that you might escape hell, you are invited to do so. Indeed, we read, "Whoever believes in the Son has eternal life; whoever does not obey the Son shall not see life, but the wrath of God remains on him" (John 3:36). Thankfully, there is a way of escape; we can be forever shielded from the wrath to come!

WHEN THE CURTAIN OPENS FOR YOU

**Death by Suicide | Faith in God's Providence |
A Lesson in How to Die**

In the Middle East a fable is told of a merchant in Baghdad who sent his servant to the marketplace to run an errand. When the servant had completed his assignment and was about to leave the marketplace, he turned a corner and unexpectedly met Lady Death.

The look on her face so frightened him that he left the marketplace and hurried home. He told his master what had happened and requested his fastest horse so that he could get as far from Lady Death as possible—a horse that would take him all the way to Sumera before nightfall.

Later the same afternoon the merchant himself went to

the marketplace and met Lady Death. "Why did you startle my servant this morning?" he asked.

"I didn't intend to startle your servant—it was I who was startled," replied Lady Death. "I was surprised to see your servant in Baghdad this morning, because I have an appointment with him in Sumera tonight."

You and I have an appointment. Perhaps it will be in London, Taipei, or Chicago. Wherever, it is one appointment we will not miss. As C. S. Lewis observed, the statistics on death are impressive—so far it is one out of one!

Cancer, accidents, and a hundred different diseases lurk about waiting for an opportunity to devour us. Death awaits us as the concrete floor awaits the falling lightbulb. The first person who ever died was not Adam, the first sinful man; nor Cain, the man who would be a murderer, but Abel, the one who was righteous. We give a wry smile when we hear about the friendly undertaker who signed all of his correspondence, "Eventually yours."

DEATH BY SUICIDE

The suffering that often precedes death can be so excruciating that many people hope to leapfrog over the process of dying to get to death itself. Books explaining how to commit suicide are selling briskly; a growing number of people want to "control their own destiny" rather than be at the mercy of modern medicine. "Dying with dignity," we are told, is our right.

Strictly speaking, no one "dies with dignity." Ever since sin entered into the world and brought death with it, death has always been the final humiliation, the one unalterable fact that confirms our mortality and reduces our bodies to ashes.

Apparently, Jesus Himself hung on the cross naked, exposed to the gawkers outside the city of Jerusalem. We are thankful that none of us will likely have to endure such shameful public torture, but death is never pretty.

Another argument for assisting in death is that medical technology has artificially prolonged life. Rather than suffer, we now have doctors who take it upon themselves to help patients grant themselves "self-deliverance."

This is not the place to discuss the fallout of assisted suicide in society. We can only anticipate the pressure that will be placed on the elderly to end it all to save medical costs and to make it easier for their families. Very quickly the right to die can become the responsibility to die.

Those who do choose suicide (for whatever reason) should remember that death is not the end, but a doorway to an eternal existence. Sad to say, some who find the pain of dying intolerable will awaken in a realm that is even more terrible than earth could ever be. We should welcome death from the hand of God, but not force the hand that brings it.

A rather well-known pastor committed suicide. He had preached the gospel for many years; no doubt dozens, if not hundreds, were converted under his ministry, and yet there he lay on the grass with self-inflicted gunshot wounds.

Yes, Christians—genuine Christians—sometimes do commit suicide. I believe that such are in heaven by the only route by which any one of us shall make it—the grace of God. Of course those who end their own lives die as failures; their last act was murder (their own). And yet because they have come under the shelter of God's protection through Christ, they will be escorted into the heavenly gates.

As a pastor I have frequently had phone calls from distraught people wanting me to assure them that if they commit suicide they will go to heaven. I routinely tell them that they have other options—suicide is never an honorable way out of a difficulty. Whatever our need is, Christ has given us the resources to cope with the difficulties of life. That might mean making some tough choices, but there is "a way of escape."

Second—and this is important—it is presumptuous to commit suicide on the premise that all will be well on the other side. For one thing, many people who say they are Christians aren't. Thus for them suicide is a doorway to eternal misery. For another, we forget that we are accountable to Christ for the way we lived (and died) on earth. Though Christ will not parade our sins before us, our life will be carefully reviewed. It simply makes no sense to see Christ before He has called our name.

FAITH IN GOD'S PROVIDENCE

On November 8, 1994, Pastor Scott Willis and his wife, Janet, were traveling with six of their nine children on Highway I-94 near Milwaukee when a piece of metal fell off the truck ahead of them. Scott had no choice but to let the object pass under his vehicle; the result was that the rear gas tank exploded and five of the six Willis children died instantly in the flames. The sixth child, Benjamin, died a few hours later.

Scott and Janet were able to get out of the vehicle, sustaining burns from which they would later recover. Standing there watching their children die in the fire, Scott said to Janet, "This is the moment for which we are prepared." The courage of this couple was reported throughout the United States and the world. Christ walked with them through the deep sorrows of this tragedy.

"Every morning we awake we say, this is one more day

to prove the faithfulness of God. Every night we say, we are one day closer to seeing our children again." Such is the testimony of this couple who understood that children are a gift of God; and when God wants them back, He has the right to take them to Himself. Job, the Old Testament patriarch, would agree.

We say that the Willis family had an "accident," but was not this, from God's perspective, a providential happening? I believe so. What we call an accident might be a well-planned event to God.

Just think of the contingencies, the events that had to converge for the accident to happen. Here are a few: If only they had started their trip a minute earlier in the morning— or a minute later. Then again, if only the truck had been at a different location on the expressway, either a few seconds earlier or later. Or one can say, "If only that piece of metal had fallen earlier, or later, or if it had scuttled into the ditch rather than in the middle of the lane of traffic . . ."

With a little bit of ingenuity we could identify a dozen "if onlys." After all, this accident would not have happened unless a number of circumstances had converged at the right time and the right place.

Listen to the conversation at almost any funeral and you will hear some "if onlys."

"If only we had called the doctor sooner . . ."

"If only there would not have been ice on the highway . . ."

"If only we had noticed the lump sooner . . ."

"If only they had operated . . ."

"If only they had not operated . . ."

Let me encourage you to take those "if onlys" and draw a circle around them. Then label the circle, "The providence of God." The Christian believes that God is greater than our "if onlys." His providential hand encompasses the whole of our lives, not just the good days but the "bad" days too. We have the word *accident* in our vocabulary; He does not.

Accidents, ill health, or even dying at the hand of an enemy—God uses all of these means to bring His children home. As long as we entrust ourselves to His care, we can be confident that we are dying according to His timetable. We can't control events outside of us; we are, however, responsible for how we react to what happens in the seemingly random events of life. The fact is that God can send any chariot He wishes to fetch us for Himself.

Martha and Mary had their "if onlys" too (John 11:1–44). When Christ was told that His friend Lazarus was sick, He stayed away for two extra days so that Lazarus would already be dead and buried by the time He arrived in Bethany. The sisters individually voiced their complaint, "If only you had been here, my brother would not have died." Yet Christ wanted them to know that Lazarus had died within the will of God; he had died according to the divine schedule.

Nothing is gained by bemoaning the fact that "if we had only known then, things could have been different." We do not have to be like the woman who went to the grave of her husband every morning for fourteen years because she felt guilty. She had convinced her husband to go to a concert; en route they were in an accident and he was killed. Such false guilt is not from God, but is self-generated.

That woman—bless her!—could have spared herself much grief if she had but remembered that we are only humans and only God is God. She couldn't foreknow that the accident was going to happen that evening. We have all encouraged our mates to go somewhere they did not want to go; we all could have suffered a similar fate. We must see that

God is bigger than our mistakes; He is bigger than a piece of steel that falls randomly from a truck on the expressway. We must remember that those events that are completely out of our control are firmly within His grasp.

At the age of twenty-six, Lina Sandell Berg was accompanying her father aboard a ship across Lake Vattern in Sweden en route to the city of Gothenburg. The ship unexpectedly gave a sudden lurch and Lina's father, a devout Christian, fell overboard and drowned before the eyes of his devoted daughter. From her broken heart she wrote a song that many of us have often sung. As you read the words, find all the lines that affirm Lina's confidence that her father died within the protection and loving care of God.

Day by day and with each passing moment,
Strength I find to meet my trials here;
Trusting in my Father's wise bestowment,
I've no cause for worry or for fear.

He whose heart is kind beyond all measure
Gives unto each day what He deems best—
Lovingly, its part of pain and pleasure,
Mingling toil with peace and rest
Every day the Lord Himself is near me
With a special mercy for each hour;
All my cares He fain would bear, and cheer me,
He whose name is Counselor and Pow'r.

The protection of His child and treasure
Is a charge that on Himself He laid;
"As thy days, your strength shall be in measure,"
This the pledge to me He made.

Remarkably, Lina had confidence that the death of her father, which many would simply ascribe to the random fate of a windblown ship, died under God's loving care. She could write, "The protection of His child and treasure / Is a charge that on Himself He laid." Far from seeing this incident as a cruel oversight on God's part, she saw in her father's death an expression of loving protection! On the human side, he died because of the unexpected high wave; on the divine side, he died because God wanted him home.

As the time of our death approaches we can take comfort from the example of someone who parted the curtain and returned to tell us what to expect on the other side. Christ is our best example of how to face that final hour that most assuredly will come to us all. He died so that we could die triumphantly.

A LESSON IN HOW TO DIE

We never have to say of a believer, "He departed." Rather, we can say, "He has arrived." Heaven is the Christian's final destination. Thanks to Christ, we can be free from the fear of death. We can take comfort from Christ, who gave us an example of how to face that final hour.

He Died with the Right Attitude

Christ died with a mixture of grief and joy. Listen to His words in Gethsemane, "My soul is very sorrowful, even to death; remain here, and watch with me" (Matthew 26:38). The disciples failed him, so alone He pleaded with His Father, "My Father, if this cannot pass unless I drink it, your will be done" (verse 42).

He agonized as He contemplated becoming identified

with the sins of the world. He would soon become legally guilty of adultery, theft, and murder. As the sin-bearer, He knew that His personal holiness would come in contact with the defilement of sin. He was sorrowful unto death as He wrestled with the trauma that awaited Him.

But there was hope, too. His impending death was a doorway leading back to the Father; it was the path to victory. Before He went to Gethsemane, He spoke these words, "And now, Father, glorify me in your own presence with the glory that I had with you before the world existed" (John 17:5). We also read elsewhere that He endured the cross, "for the joy that was set before him . . . , despising the shame, and is seated at the right hand of the throne of God" (Hebrews 12:2). For the short term there was pain; but long term, there was glory and joy.

We should not feel guilty for facing death with apprehension, for Christ Himself experienced emotional agony the night before the horror of the cross. Yet, with the fear came comfort; joy and sorrow existed in the same heart. Death was, after all, the Father's will for Christ, and for us all.

A daughter said of her godly father, who died of cancer, "In his closing days, Dad spent more time in heaven than he did on earth." If we can look beyond the immediate heartache to the eventual glory, there is joy. The exit is grievous; the entrance is joyful.

He Died at the Right Time

The night of His betrayal Christ chose to eat the Passover with His disciples. "Now before the Feast of the Passover, when Jesus knew that his hour had come to depart out of this world to the Father, having loved his own who were in the world, he loved them to the end" (John 13:1). This was the hour into which was compacted the agony of Gethsemane, the betrayal of Judas, and the excruciating death of the cross. Interestingly, three times before this we read that "His hour had not yet come" (John 7:30; 8:20; see also 2:4). Until "the hour" arrived, His enemies were powerless against Him.

What sustained Christ? We read, "Jesus, knowing that the Father had given all things into his hands, and that he had come from God and was going back to God, rose from supper. He laid aside his outer garments, and taking a towel, tied it around his waist" (John 13:3–4). He had come to earth at an hour appointed by God, and now He was returning on schedule! There was not the slightest possibility that Christ would die sooner than God planned!

Christ died more quickly than most others who were crucified. The soldiers, you recall, did not break his legs because they "saw that he was already dead" (John 19:33). He died between three and six in the afternoon, just as the Passover lambs were being slaughtered. He died at the hour God planned, a striking reminder that He was indeed "the Lamb of God, which taketh away the sin of the world" (John 1:29 KJV).

He was only thirty-three years old, young by today's standards and those of ancient Middle Eastern culture. Why not fifty-three, so that He could have many more years of healing the sick, training the disciples, and preaching the love of God to the multitudes? No doubt people in those days wondered, even as they do today, as to why the righteous often die young whereas the wicked live to a ripe old age.

Yes, even the crime of the crucifixion was a part of God's good plan. "For truly in this city there were gathered together against your holy servant Jesus, whom you anointed, both Herod and Pontius Pilate, along with the Gentiles and the peoples of Israel, to do whatever your hand and your plan had predestined to take place" (Acts 4:27–28). They could not act until God's clock struck. The "hour" had to come!

Christ died young, but His work was finished. We don't have to live a long life to do all that God has planned for us to do. Some of God's best servants have died at an early age—early from our standpoint, at the right time from God's. They too have finished the work God gave them to do.

The death of a child seems like mockery since God is taking a life before he or she has the joy of accomplishment. As Jung says, "It is like putting a period before the end of the sentence." But a child's short life can fulfill the will of God. Though we do not understand it, that little one has "finished the work God has given him (or her) to do." Though now in heaven, the little one continues his or her ministry in the life of parents and relatives.

Jim Elliot, who himself was killed at a young age while doing missionary work among the Waodani Indians, said, "God is peopling Heaven; why should He limit Himself to old people?"

Why, indeed! If the Almighty wants to reach down and take one of His little lambs, or if He wishes to take a servant in the prime of life, He has that right. We think it cruel only because we cannot see behind the dark curtain.

Of course, looked at from our point of view, we can hasten our own death by bad eating habits and other forms of carelessness. And sometimes people deliberately cause the untimely death of another. Mothers who have abortions, thieves who kill their victims—in these instances God holds people responsible for their actions.

But let us boldly say that even when a believer is murdered by evil men (Jim Elliot serves as an example), such a one dies according to the providential plan of God. If Christ, who was brutally murdered by jealous religious leaders, died as planned by God, why should we think that a believer who is gunned down in a robbery is any less under the care of the Almighty? Car accidents, heart attacks, cancer—all of these are the means used to open the door of heaven to the children of God. The immediate cause of our death is neither haphazard nor arbitrary. The One who knows the number of hairs on our head and sees the sparrow fall has the destiny of every one of our days in His loving hands.

Our death is just as meticulously planned as the death of Christ. There is no combination of evil men, disease, or accident that can kill us as long as God still has work for us to do. To those who walk with faith in God's providence, they die according to God's timetable.

This fact should rid us of false guilt. The mother who thoughtlessly answered "Yes" to her little daughter who asked "May I cross the street?" only to see her hit by a truck—that blessed woman must understand that her little one also died under the providential hand of God. Could the Almighty not have arranged that the truck come to the intersection a moment later or earlier? Or could not the mother have been detained and arrived at a different time? Yes, even accidents occur within the circle of divine providence.

Sometimes ministers are reluctant to tell Christian families, "God took your child." Some think it is better to say, "Cancer took your child," or, "A drunken driver took your child." But the Christian can see beyond these immediate causes. He knows that God can control diseases and restrain the wicked. The immediate cause of death might be any number of things, but the ultimate cause is God. Yes, wicked men nailed Christ to the cross, yet we read, "But the Lord was pleased to crush Him, putting Him to grief" (Isaiah 53:10 NASB).

Let us clearly say that God took the six children of the Willis family. God took the woman whose cancer was discovered too late for treatment. God took the child who was gunned down in a drive-by shooting. And someday God will take you and me.

He Died in the Right Way

We've emphasized that there are many ways to die: disease, accidents, murder, to name a few. The circumstances differ for each individual. In God's plan, Christ was to die on a cross, for this was a symbol of humiliation and an unmistakable sign that He was cursed by God. It was death without dignity.

There was no sanitary hospital room, no blankets that would hide the shame of His bloodstained body. He died without dignity, crucified naked for all to see. Today most people die under heavy sedation so that their exit is made as peaceful as possible. When Christ was offered wine mingled with myrrh, He refused this ancient sedative so that He could be fully aware of His surroundings. He took all the horror that death could offer.

If the time of our death is under divine providential guidance, then so is the means. Christ predicted, for example, how Peter would come to the end of his earthly existence. "Truly, truly, I say to you, when you were young, you used to dress yourself and walk wherever you wanted, but when you are old, you will stretch out your hands, and another will dress you and carry you where you do not want to go." Then John adds, "This he said to show by what kind of death he was to glorify God" (John 21:18–19). In old age, Peter was tied to a cross and had his hands stretched out, apparently crucified upside down because he felt unworthy to be crucified in the same way Christ was. Can anyone deny that Christ chose the way in which Peter would die?

Most likely, our death will not be by crucifixion. But here again, we know that the ultimate choice will be made by God. The porter God chooses to summon us will come our way, knock on our door, and it will be time to leave. We are thankful that Christ could say, "Do not fear those who kill the body but cannot kill the soul. Rather fear him who can destroy both soul and body in hell" (Matthew 10:28). If we fear God, we need fear nothing else.

When the summons comes, it will be like sitting in a concert enjoying the music, only to have our name called before the performance is finished. It will be like building a house and being told that we are not able to live in it. This abrupt interruption of our plans will, however, lead us to our permanent home.

He Died for the Right Purpose

Christ's death was not simply the tragic end of a beautiful life. Within the will of God, His death accomplished redemption for the people whom God had chosen. Christ refers to these individuals as a gift given to Him from the Father: "Those whom thou hast given me" (John 17:11 KJV). When He cried, "It is finished!" the work was accomplished (John 19:30).

Obviously, our death does not accomplish redemption, but it is the means by which we experience the redemption Christ accomplished for us. Death is the doorway by which we can leave the limitations and pains of this existence and enter into the heavenly realm. Our death also serves a divine purpose.

Although we can be thankful for the wonders of modern medicine, there does come a time when believers must answer the call to "come up higher." So often when a Christian becomes ill, we immediately pray for his physical restoration. How can we be so sure that it is not God's time to have him enter into the inheritance that is reserved for him (1 Peter 1:4)?

When a person has lived a long life and has virtually no hope of recovery, we must simply commit him to God rather than use heroic measures to eke out one more day of pitiful existence. The day of our death is the day of our glorification. Death is the grand entrance, the door that swings into eternity. Eventually it will open in God's time and in God's way to let another child come home where he or she belongs.

He Died with the Right Commitment

Death can be a time of trust in God's deliverance. Christ's last comment was "Father, into your hands I commit my spirit!" (Luke 23:46). Thus He died entrusting Himself to the Father whom He so passionately loved. We too can die committing our eternity into the hands of our Father who is in heaven.

Many Christians believe that Christ descended into hell (or more accurately hades) before He went to the Father. This teaching has been reinforced by the Apostles' Creed, which says "He descended into hell."

On the day of Pentecost, Peter quoted Psalm 16:10 and applied it to Christ: "Because You will not abandon my soul to Hades, nor allow Your Holy One to undergo decay" (Acts 2:27 NASB). Apparently, Christ's soul did go to sheol or hades. However, we must remember that hades had two regions, one for the righteous and the other for the unrighteous. That Christ went to the righteous side can be shown by quoting His words to the repentant thief: "Today you will be with me in Paradise" (Luke 23:43).

Since Christ died before the thief did, our Lord was waiting for him; there in paradise they met again, this time to talk about the glories of eternity. The sins that the thief had committed had all been taken away in that moment when he exercised faith in the dying Christ.

Think of the faith that thief had! Humanly speaking, Christ seemed no better off than he himself was. Needless to say, Christ did not look like a Savior while writhing in pain on the cross. Yet there was something about Him that made the thief take notice. Perhaps the thief had heard about Christ long before they met at Golgotha. Or maybe it was the words Christ spoke and the attitude He displayed. Whatever the reason, the thief believed and was saved.

The other thief rejected Him, taunting, "Are you not the Christ? Save yourself and us!" (Luke 23:39). He thought only about the salvation of his body, not the salvation of his soul. If he died with such defiance as the Scriptures seem to teach, he did not join Christ in paradise.

Christ did not go to hades to suffer for us. All of the teaching of the New Testament emphasizes that His suffering took place on the cross where His blood was shed. There our debt was paid. As His soul left His body, He found Himself in the presence of God, along with the penitent thief. Three days later, Christ was raised from the dead with a glorified body and later ascended into heaven.

How shall we summarize our understanding of Christ's death? The immediate cause was the anger of the religious leaders and the cooperation of the Romans in carrying out this unjust execution. But the ultimate cause was God. "Yet it was the will of the Lord to crush him; he has put him to grief" (Isaiah 53:10).

Before his death, John Calvin had the same confidence

when he said, "Thou, Lord, bruisest me. But I am abundantly satisfied since it is from Thy hand."

Death can steal nothing from a Christian. Health, wealth, and joy—all of these come in greater abundance when the spirit goes to God.

William Cowper combined both the story of redemption and the story of the penitent thief in his song when he wrote:

There is a fountain filled with blood
Drawn from Immanuel's veins;
And sinners, plunged beneath that flood,
Lose all their guilty stains.

The dying thief rejoiced to see
That fountain in his day;
And there may I, though vile as he,
Wash all my sins away.

When this poor lisping, stamm'ring tongue
Lies silent in the grave,
Then in a nobler, sweeter song,
I will sing Thy pow'r to save.

Our future existence is not in the hands of doctors, nor in the hands of disease, nor in the hands of the drunk who runs into our car along the highway. Our life is in the hands of the Almighty, who can use any means He wishes, including the above, to have us brought into the heavenly gates.

Perhaps today our name will be called.

CHAPTER 8

KNOWING TODAY WHERE YOU WILL BE TOMORROW

What God Requires | Making Sure

Those of us who have traveled in foreign countries know the importance of a passport. Regardless of your status or charisma, that document is what qualifies you for entry and acceptance among the people in a different land.

We need a passport to get into heaven, if that is the country where we wish to go. Those who have such a visa can rejoice in their citizenship long before their arrival. Paul wrote, "But our citizenship is in heaven, and from it we await a Savior, the Lord Jesus Christ" (Philippians 3:20).

Indeed, the redeemed are spoken of as having been raised with Christ and already seated in heaven (Ephesians

2:6). Because we are legally there we should not expect that crossing the border will be a hassle. What matters is that we have qualifications that are recognized by the "Keeper of the Keys."

Don't imagine for a moment that you will get to heaven without the right credentials. You will not be there because your wife has a right to enter; you will not be there because you have a child who is already there. No, this is an individual matter, and only those with the right document will be allowed entry.

This is just another way of saying that no one can enter into heaven without God's specific approval. Our problem, of course, is that God will not accept us just as we are. We cannot come to heaven's gates hoping for leniency. We cannot come pleading for special favors once we have slipped through the parted curtain. Visas are not available on the other side of the border.

WHAT GOD REQUIRES

How perfect do you have to be to enter into heaven? The answer, quite simply: as perfect as God. In fact, if you are not as perfect as He is, don't even think that you will enter into the kingdom of heaven! Christianity, whether Catholic or Protestant, has always taught that we must be as perfect as God to enter through those pearly gates.

The question, of course, is: How can we as sinners be as perfect as God? The answer: God is able to give us all of His perfections; His righteousness can be credited to our account so that we can enter into heaven immediately at death without so much as an intermediate stop.

When Christ died on the cross, He made a sacrifice for

sinners, which God accepted. Though Christ was perfect, God made Him legally guilty of all of our sins. In turn, we receive His righteousness. "For our sake he made him to be sin who knew no sin [Christ], so that in him we might become the righteousness of God" (2 Corinthians 5:21).

What grace!

What this means is that Christ was regarded as a sinner when He bore our sin; we are regarded as saints when we receive His righteousness. Though very imperfect, we are regarded as "the righteousness of God." God has exceedingly high standards, but thanks be, He meets them for us!

Perhaps you think that you have sinned too much to receive such a gift. Well, I want you to know that God is able to save great sinners—criminals, in fact. The amount of our sin is not a barrier; it is our unbelief that cuts us off from God's mercy and pardon.

When we receive Christ's righteousness, another miracle happens to us at the same time. God gives us a new nature; He changes us from the inside out. Christ said to Nicodemus, a Jewish religious leader, "Truly, truly, I say to you, unless one is born again he cannot see the kingdom of God" (John 3:3). Obviously, we cannot cause ourselves to be born again. That is something that God must do for us.

What must we do to receive the gift of righteousness and a new nature within? The answer is to admit our helplessness, to acknowledge that we are dependent on God's mercy. Then we must transfer all of our trust to Christ as our sin-bearer; we must believe in Him as the One who did all that we will ever need to stand in God's holy presence. To believe in Christ means that as best we know, we trust Him for all that we need in this life and in the life to come.

How sure can we be that we will spend eternity with

God? We can be so sure that death need not terrify us. Yes, there is mystery; yes, we all are apprehensive of taking leave of this body to wake up in the world to come. But when we have trusted Christ, we know that He walks with us through the parted curtain.

In the New Testament, Paul taught that those who belong to Christ can be very sure that they will enter heaven. Though these verses contain some theological words, you will understand what Paul is getting at. "For those whom he foreknew he also predestined to be conformed to the image of his Son, in order that he might be the firstborn among many brothers. And those whom he predestined he also called, and those whom he called he also justified, and those whom he justified he also glorified" (Romans 8:29–30).

We are already glorified! In effect, our arrival in heaven has already taken place. Those whom God chooses to be His—that is, those whom He foreknows and predestines—these are the ones who are justified, and all of these are guaranteed a safe passage into their heavenly home. None is lost en route; in God's mind they already have their glorified bodies! For God "calls into existence the things that do not exist" (Romans 4:17).

Here is another promise for those who face death. Paul said that nothing can separate God's children from His love. Then he adds, "For I am sure that neither death nor life, nor angels nor rulers, nor things present nor things to come, nor powers, nor height nor depth, nor anything else in all creation, will be able to separate us from the love of God in Christ Jesus our Lord" (Romans 8:38–39). Death is not any more successful than life in separating us from Christ's love.

What is Christ's attitude toward our homecoming? Repeatedly in the New Testament Christ is spoken of as sitting "at the right hand of God." But there is one reference to His leaving His seat and standing; He is welcoming one of His servants home. As Stephen was being stoned, we read that "being full of the Holy Spirit, he gazed intently into heaven and saw the glory of God, and Jesus standing at the right hand of God" (Acts 7:55 NASB).

Thus the seated Son of God stood to welcome one of His own into the heavenly realm. A believer's death may be unnoticed on earth, but it is front-page news in heaven. The Son of God takes note. He will be there to welcome us.

D. L. Moody at death caught a glimpse of heaven. Awakening from sleep he said, "Earth recedes, Heaven opens before me. If this is death, it is sweet! There is no valley here. God is calling me and I must go!"

Just before John Bunyan died, he said, "Weep not for me, but for yourselves. I go to the Father of our Lord Jesus Christ, who will through the mediation of His blessed Son receive me though a sinner; there we shall meet to sing the new song and remain everlastingly happy, world without end."

Remember the words of Hamlet in Shakespeare's play? In a moment of deep contemplation he mused, "To be, or not to be: that is the question" (III.i.56). He was contemplating suicide because life had become unbearable. Yet when he thought of where that might lead him, he continued,

> *Whether 'tis nobler in the mind to suffer*
> *The slings and arrows of outrageous fortune,*
> *Or to take arms against a sea of troubles,*
> *And by opposing end them? To die: to sleep;*
> *No more; and by a sleep we say we end*
> *The heart-ache and the thousand natural shocks*
> *That flesh is heir to, 'tis a consummation*

Devoutly to be wish'd. To die, to sleep;
To sleep: perchance to dream: ay, there's the rub;
For in that sleep of death what dreams may come
When we have shuffled off this mortal coil.
(III.i.58–67)

Hamlet finds suicide both attractive and repulsive. If he could be sure that it would rid him of his sea of troubles, he would do it; but he fears that "undiscover'd country from whose bourn / No traveller returns" (III.i.79–80). His present ills might be pleasant in comparison to the fate that would await him.

Compare Hamlet's dilemma with that of Paul:

> For to me to live is Christ, and to die is gain. If I am to live in the flesh, that means fruitful labor for me. Yet which I shall choose I cannot tell. I am hard pressed between the two. My desire is to depart and be with Christ, for that is far better. But to remain in the flesh is more necessary on your account. (PHILIPPIANS 1:21–24)

Hamlet says, "Live or die, I lose!" Paul says, "Live or die, I win!"

What a difference Christ makes!

MAKING SURE

Here is a prayer you can pray, a prayer that expresses your desire to transfer your trust to Christ alone for your eternal salvation. This prayer can be the link that will connect you to God. And if you pray it in faith, God will receive you.

Dear God,

I know that I am a sinner and there is nothing that I can do to save myself. I confess my complete helplessness to forgive my own sin or to work my way to heaven. At this moment I trust Christ alone as the One who bore my sin when He died on the cross. I believe that He did all that ever will be necessary for me to stand in Your holy presence.

I thank You that Christ was raised from the dead as a guarantee of my own resurrection. As best as I can, I now transfer my trust to Him. I am grateful that He has promised to receive me despite my many sins and failures.

Father, I take You at Your word. I thank You that I can face death now that You are my Savior. Thank You for the assurance that You will walk with me through the deep valley.

Thank You for hearing this prayer.

In Jesus' name. Amen.

Here are some promises that are given to all who trust Christ alone for their entrance into the kingdom.

- Christ said, "I am the resurrection and the life. Whoever believes in me, though he die, yet shall he live, and everyone who lives and believes in me shall never die" (John 11:25–26).
- The author of Hebrews wrote, "Since therefore the children share in flesh and blood, he himself likewise partook of the same things, that through death he might destroy the one who has the power of death, that is, the devil, and deliver all those who through fear of death were subject to lifelong slavery" (Hebrews 2:14–15).
- Paul asked, "O death, where is your sting?" (1 Corinthians 15:55).

• John assures us, "And I heard a voice from heaven saying, 'Write this: Blessed are the dead who die in the Lord from now on.' 'Blessed indeed,' says the Spirit, 'that they may rest from their labors, for their deeds follow them!'" (Revelation 14:13).

We do not know who will be next to hear the divine call. Let us be ready when it comes.

NOTES

Introduction

1. C. S. Lewis, "The Weight of Glory," in *The Weight of Glory and Other Addresses*, rev. and exp. ed. (New York: Macmillan, 1980), 18–19.

Chapter 1: Attempting to Peek behind the Curtain

1. Tom Howard, *Christianity Today*, March 29, 1974, 31.
2. Martha Smilgis, "Hollywood Goes to Heaven," *Time*, June 3, 1991, 70.
3. James A. Pike, *The Other Side* (New York: Doubleday, 1968), 115.
4. Raymond Moody, *Life After Life* (Covington, Ga.: Mockingbird, 1975).
5. Melvin Morse, *Closer to the Light* (New York: Ivy, 1990), 33.
6. Betty J. Eadie and Curtis Taylor, *Embraced by the Light* (Placerville, Calif.: Gold Leaf, 1992).
7. Ibid.

8. Philip J. Swihart, *The Edge of Death* (Downers Grove, Ill.: InterVarsity, 1978).
9. Maurice S. Rawlings, *Beyond Death's Door* (Nashville: Nelson, 1978).

Chapter 2: The Descent into Gloom

1. For a more complete discussion of sheol and hades, see *Death and the Afterlife*, by Robert A. Morey (Minneapolis: Bethany, 1984), 72–87.

Chapter 3: The Ascent into Glory

1. For a more complete critique of soul sleep, see Robert A. Morey, *Death and the Afterlife* (Minneapolis: Bethany House, 1984), 199–222.
2. Joseph Bayly, *The View from a Hearse* (Elgin, Ill.: David C. Cook, 1969), 36.

Chapter 4: Welcome! You Have Arrived!

1. Steve Saint, "Did They Have to Die?" *Christianity Today*, September 16, 1996, 26.

Chapter 5: Living in the New Jerusalem

1. David Gregg, *The Heaven-Life* (New York: Revell, 1895), 62.
2. Richard Whately, *A View of the Scripture Revelations Concerning a Future State*, 3d ed. (Philadelphia: Lindsay & Blakiston, 1857), 214–15.
3. Wilbur M. Smith, *Biblical Doctrine of Heaven* (Chicago: Moody, 1968), 253.
4. Joseph Seiss, *Lectures on the Apocalypse* (New York: Charles C. Cook, 1901), 3:412–13; quoted in Wilbur Smith, *Biblical Doctrine,* 249.

Chapter 6: When Hades Is Thrown into Hell

1. John A. Robinson, "Universalism: Is It Heretical?" *Scottish Journal of Theology,* June 1949, 155.
2. Percy Dearmer, *The Legend of Hell* (London: Cassell, 1929), 74–75.
3. Robert A. Morey, *Death and the Afterlife* (Minneapolis: Bethany, 1984), 90.
4. Walter B. Knight, *Knight's Master Book of New Illustrations* (Grand Rapids: Eerdmans, 1956), 159.
5. Charles Hodge, *Systematic Theology*, vol. 3, pt. 4 (Grand Rapids: Eerdmans, 1956), 159.
6. Warren Wiersbe, *Treasury of the World's Great Sermons* (Grand Rapids: Kregel, 1977), 198–205.

Your Eternal Reward

Interior design: Erik M. Peterson
Cover design: Smartt Guys design
Cover image of gates copyright © albund / Shutterstock / 158678495. All rights reserved.

ISBN-10: 0-8024-1317-8

CONTENTS

CHAPTER 1

TEARS IN HEAVEN

Tears in heaven! In the minds of many Christians, *tears* and *heaven* simply do not belong together. Like war and peace, light and darkness, health and sickness, these simply cannot coexist.

But I believe there are good reasons why there will be tears in heaven. When we reflect on how we lived for Christ, who purchased us at such high cost, well might we weep on the other side of the celestial gates. Our tears will be those of regret and shame, tears of remorse for lives lived for ourselves rather than for Him who "loves us and released us from our sins by His blood" (Revelation 1:5 NASB). Perhaps we would never cease crying in heaven if God Himself did not come and wipe the tears from our eyes (Revelation 21:4).

The judgment seat of Christ is, to our shame, almost universally ignored among Christians. Most whom I have talked with think it will not be a very significant event. When I ask why, I usually get one of several reasons, often based on some misconceptions that have found their way into the minds of so many.

False assumptions die hard. I discovered that I could not teach the subject of the judgment seat of Christ until I had dislodged some impressions that had largely emptied this doctrine of its significance. Until we are willing to set aside these opinions, we will not be able to appreciate the rich teaching of the Bible on this topic. Nor will we be transformed by a doctrine that should impact our daily lives.

Here are some common assumptions that must be challenged if we are to recapture the biblical teaching on the judgment seat of Christ.

THREE MISCONCEPTIONS

Leading the list of mistaken ideas is the belief that there cannot be a serious review of our lives at the judgment seat of Christ because as believers our sins are forgiven and "cast . . . into the depths of the sea" (Micah 7:19). After all, the argument goes, as far as God is concerned, our past failures and sins do not exist. "Doesn't Calvary cover it all?" a friend of mine asked when I suggested that some people might experience deep regret along with lost privileges at the judgment seat of Christ. For him, the judgment seat of Christ is really no judgment at all. All believers will pass the judgment seat with flying colors.

Not so.

Let us hear the words of Paul. "For we must all appear before the judgment seat of Christ, so that each one may be recompensed for his deeds [done] in the body, according to what he has done, whether good or bad" (2 Corinthians 5:10 NASB). That phrase, "whether good or bad," rids us of the cherished hope that our failures can never return to haunt us. It reminds us that our Father in heaven judges us even though we are secure in the knowledge that we are His children forever.

Recall the story of Ananias and Sapphira, who lied about the price of some property they had sold so that they might withhold a percentage of the proceeds while pretending to give all the money to the church (Acts 5:1–11). Though they were Christians, they were smitten by God and instantly died for their dishonesty. Perhaps when they arrived in heaven they might have said to themselves, "How could this have happened? Peter told us that Calvary covered it all!"

This experience of Ananias and Sapphira, along with others like it in the New Testament, is a powerful reminder that *God judges justified sinners*. And if He judges us on earth, sometimes even to the point of physical death, it is certainly not difficult to believe that He will judge us in heaven for the way we lived here. As Jim Elliff says, "Such warnings virtually bleed from the pores to Scripture." So it is.

King David, who committed the twin sins of adultery and murder, was judged for his sin even after he had confessed it and was assured of God's forgiveness. Nathan said: "The LORD also has taken away your sin; you shall not die. However, because by this deed you have given occasion to the enemies of the LORD to blaspheme, the child also that is born to you shall surely die" (2 Samuel 12:13–14 NASB).

If Ananias and Sapphira remind us that God judges us for unconfessed sin, David reminds us that *God judges us for sins that have been confessed and forgiven.* Judicial forgiveness is one thing, but the discipline the Father inflicts on His wayward children is quite another.

Yes, those who trust Christ alone for their salvation are redeemed, eternally forgiven, and legally perfect before God. We are not under condemnation but have "passed out of death into life" (1 John 3:14). We enter heaven with the righteousness of Christ credited to our account; we are accepted on the basis of His worthy merit. To this all Christians must say "Amen."

But—and this is important—we should not conclude that every Christian will do well at the judgment seat of Christ. We can suffer serious loss; many of us might stand in shame before Christ as we see our lives pass before us. It is not true, as some teach, that ten minutes after our personal confrontation with Christ our meeting will have little significance because all of us will essentially receive the same reward. What happens at the judgment seat can have permanent consequences.

There are degrees of punishment in hell and degrees of reward in heaven. This does not mean that heaven will be divided into the haves and the have-nots. Eventually, everyone will be happy in heaven because God will comfort us by wiping the tears from our eyes. Everyone will be a servant and enjoy the fellowship afforded to all who enter the presence of God through Christ. But we shall not all have the same privileges, for the way we live will have a ripple effect that will go on for an eternity. Paul did not see a contradiction between teaching justification by faith and the related fact that we shall be judged for all our "deeds [done] in the body" since our conversion. The hows and whys will be explained in later chapters.

A second misconception is the belief that even after we have been converted our works have no merit before God. When the Reformers preached (and rightly so) that we are saved by grace alone and not by works, some theologians went on to say that our works after salvation are also nonmeritorious. They concluded that in heaven all Christians will either receive the same reward, or else any differences will be due to God's sovereign will. Many Bible students since that time have accepted the same basic premise.

Almost all Christians agree that some believers will receive the approval of Christ, whereas others will receive censure and disapproval; nevertheless, it is argued, any negative consequences will soon be forgotten. If some would have a different status in heaven, the argument goes, that would imply that works had some merit, which God accepted, and this, it is said, would be contrary to the grace of God.

Let us test this premise.

Of course, I passionately agree that when we put our faith in Christ we are declared righteous by God because of Christ and not because of our works. Our deeds before our conversion are of no merit in the sight of God. "For by grace you have been saved through faith; and that not of yourselves, it is the gift of God; not as a result of works, so that no one may boast" (Ephesians 2:8–9 NASB). If anyone reading this book thinks that he will be saved because of human effort, he will be tragically disappointed for all of eternity.

But works done *after* we have received the free gift of eternal life are special to God. Indeed, the same passage (quoted above) that affirms we are saved by faith alone because of grace continues: "For we are his workmanship, created in

Christ Jesus for good works, which God prepared before-hand, that we should walk in them" (v. 10). These works are sought by God and honor Him. We should strive to please Him, and for such works we shall be rewarded. Although we shy away from thinking that something we do has merit, Christ did not hesitate to promise that those who performed sacrificial acts would be "repaid" (Luke 14:14).

Melanchthon, Luther's confidant and a theologian in his own right, made an important distinction between works prior to salvation, which lack merit, and those after conversion, which he calls meritorious. He wrote:

> We teach that good works are meritorious—not for the forgiveness of sins, grace, nor justification (for we obtain these only by faith) but for other physical and spiritual rewards in this life and in that which is to come, as Paul says (1 Corinthians 3:8), "Each shall receive his wages according to his labor." Therefore there will be different rewards for different labours. . . . There will be distinctions in the glory of the saints.[1]

Of course, the works we do after our conversion do not have merit in and of themselves; they have merit only because we are joined to Christ. He takes our imperfect works and makes them acceptable to the Father. Also, we should not think that God must pay us like an employer who has a legal obligation to pay his employee. As we shall learn later, our good deeds are done only because God gives us the desire and ability to do them. They are a gift of His grace to us. Furthermore, no child is expected to work for his inheritance; indeed, it is not possible that he could "earn" all that the Father is pleased to give him.

But—and this must be stressed—the father *tests* his son

to prove him worthy; the father uses that which is least to see if his child can be trusted with a greater share of the inheritance. *Dependability on earth translates into greater responsibility in heaven.* Just so, Christ will judge us on the basis of our worthiness, and thus our present faithfulness or lack thereof will have eternal, heavenly repercussions!

This does not mean that rewards are based on a day's pay for a day's work. God will reward us out of proportion to the work we have done. Though it appears that He would have no reason to reward us, He has placed Himself under a loving obligation to do so. If He didn't reward us, the author of Hebrews says, He would be "unjust." "For God is not unjust so as to forget your work and the love which you have shown toward His name, in having ministered and in still ministering to the saints" (Hebrews 6:10 NASB).

When we consider that the ultimate reward is to rule with Christ as a joint-heir, charged with the responsibility of authority over all God's possessions, it is clear that rewards are never earned in the usual sense of the word. God has obligated Himself to give us rewards, but this is strictly because of His grace. We can demand nothing; indeed, after we have done our best we are still unworthy servants, having "done only that which we ought to have done" (Luke 17:10 NASB). God has chosen to give us what we have no right to either demand or expect. *We are rewarded because of His generosity, not His obligation.*

A third and final misconception is that it is selfish to think of rewards as a proper motivation to serve Christ. After all, the argument goes, we should serve God out of love, and love alone. Shouldn't a basketball player give his best just for the sheer love of the game?

Furthermore, I have heard it said, "Will we not cast our

crowns before Him anyway?" implying that we will give up our rewards and they will not mean anything beyond our initial meeting with Christ. This is based on the assumption (false, in my opinion) that the rewards are nothing more than the crowns themselves. Certainly rewards are sometimes spoken of symbolically as crowns, but the rewards themselves have to do with levels of responsibility that will be given to us. Regardless of what we do with our crowns, our rewards will reach into eternity.

Of course, it is quite right that we should serve God simply because He is God and worthy of our devotion. Yes, we should serve Him because we love Him rather than wanting a better position in the kingdom. Servants should simply serve, expecting nothing in return. But, as we shall see, there is more than one motivation for serving Christ. Love is one; fear, another.

Another motivation for serving is a strong desire that we would please Christ, who is eager to share His inheritance with us. It is not selfish to want Christ's approval. He wants us to win the right to rule with Him in the kingdom, and that should be our passionate yearning. A basketball player who loves the game will give his best, but he would be especially motivated if he knew the coach whom he loves had chosen to openly reward the faithful.

Let's not overlook the connection Paul makes between pleasing Christ and doing well at the judgment seat of Christ. "Therefore we also have as our ambition, whether at home or absent, to be pleasing to Him. *For* we must all appear before the judgment seat of Christ" (2 Corinthians 5:9–10 NASB, italics added). I would like to hear Christ say, "Well done, thou good and faithful servant" (Matthew 25:21 KJV), and I believe you would too. I would like to live in such a way that Christ would count me worthy to rule with Him. You feel the same way. Obviously no credit goes to us; in heaven, ruling with Christ will have no overtones of pride and self-seeking. But being found worthy to rule because we love Christ was Paul's desire and should be ours.

Christ often and unapologetically motivated the disciples with the prospect of rewards. He told them that they should put their treasures in heaven where their money would have more security and a better rate of return. "But lay up for yourselves treasures in heaven, where neither moth nor rust destroys and where thieves do not break in and steal" (Matthew 6:20). In a future chapter we shall see that He often promised them that if they were sacrificially obedient their "reward will be great" (Luke 6:35; see also 6:23; Hebrews 10:35).

Think of the biblical saints who were driven to serve Christ because of the prospect of a reward. Abraham was willing to leave Ur and live in tents, "for he was looking for the city which has foundations, whose architect and builder is God" (Hebrews 11:10 NASB). He died without having received the promise, but it was this promise that motivated him to obey God. He was rewarded in the life to come.

Moses was willing to leave the treasures of Egypt, "choosing rather to endure ill-treatment with the people of God than to enjoy the passing pleasures of sin, considering the reproach of Christ greater riches than the treasures of Egypt; for he was looking to the reward" (Hebrews 11:25–26 NASB). A careful calculation made him realize that it made sense to give up the visible earthly reward for the invisible future reward. Anyone who exchanges a lesser reward for a greater one is wise.

Paul feared that he might fail and thus be disqualified in

the race of life (1 Corinthians 9:27). He urged believers in Philippi to prove themselves to be blameless in this perverse generation, "holding fast the word of life, so that in the day of Christ I will have reason to glory because I did not run in vain nor toil in vain" (Philippians 2:16 NASB). He was motivating them to do well "in the day of Christ." In fact, he wanted "reason to glory" in the life to come.

Christians who piously avoid any suggestion that the prospect of rewards should motivate us would be wise to admit their mistake and take up the challenge of Jonathan Edwards:

> Resolved: To endeavor to obtain for myself as much happiness in the other world as I possibly can, with all the power, might, vigor and vehemence, yea violence, I am capable of, or can bring myself to exert, in any way that can be thought of.[2]

I agree with Iosif Ton, who points out that rewards are not decorative medallions in which we can take pride. "The deepest reward is in the very fact that we will become what our Creator intends us to become. It is the reward of being made into the likeness of Christ. When we will be like Him, we will be qualified to share with Him in the inheritance, and to work with Him in important positions of high responsibility over the whole universe."[3] Our rewards are a continuation of our responsibilities begun on earth.

I am convinced that those who have been unfaithful will suffer serious loss. I agree with A. J. Gordon, who wrote, "I cannot think of a final divine reckoning which shall assign the same rank in glory, the same degree of joy to a lazy, indolent and unfruitful Christian as to an ardent, devoted, self-denying Christian."[4] If this life is a training ground for greater responsibilities, believers will be thoroughly judged; then once eternity begins they will differ in glory as lightbulbs differ in brightness.

Hell will not be the same for everyone, and heaven will not be the same for everyone. The way we live here will have eternal, unchangeable, and profound consequences. The cup of cold water given in the name of Christ will not be forgotten; nor will the impure, self-indulgent Christian inherit the full blessings of the kingdom.

Earl Radmacher says that "the person I am becoming today, is preparing me for the person I shall be for all of eternity." Much will change about us in eternity, but much shall also remain the same. We will be the same people we were here on earth, though with a new nature and eventually a new body. And because our position in eternity will be momentous, the life I live today is momentous—*eternally* momentous! *Only in this life can we impact our eternity.*

We must pause long enough to let the reality of standing before Christ sink into our consciousness. Just Christ and you. Just Christ and me.

TWO JUDGMENTS

To be clear, we must distinguish between two different judgments. Each involves a different group of people, each occurs at a different time, and those who are judged have a radically different destination.

The judgment seat of Christ, to which I have already referred, will take place when Christ returns to take all believers to be in heaven with Him. The purpose of this judgment will be to evaluate us so that we can be properly rewarded for the way we have faithfully (or unfaithfully) served here on earth.

All who appear at this judgment will be in heaven, but the question that needs to be settled is the extent of our rule (if any) with Christ. This judgment is the subject of this book.

In contrast, the Great White Throne Judgment convenes many years later, just before the final phase of eternity begins. All who appear here will be thrown into the lake of fire, or what is called hell. The purpose of this judgment is to assess the degree of punishment that will be experienced for all of eternity. (I discuss this judgment briefly in chapter 10 of this book.)

There is a popular notion that we will appear before God to determine whether we will go to heaven or hell. But there is no such judgment mentioned in the Bible. Whether we go to heaven or hell is determined already in this life. At death, those who know Christ as Savior go directly to heaven where the judgment seat of Christ will take place; those who do not know Him go to a place called hades and will eventually be brought before God at the Great White Throne Judgment. Either way, everyone will encounter God.

That you will appear before God is more certain than the sunrise. And the judgment at which you will be summoned is determined in this life, based on your relationship with Christ. There is no opportunity to reroute your travel plans after you have died. One minute after you die, your eternal destination is unalterably fixed.

Standing at the Great White Throne Judgment will be hordes from every country of the world, from every religion in the world, with the best intentions in the world. They will learn too late that God is serious about justice, and if Christ does not bear their punishment, they must bear their own. And since it is not possible for them to now accept Christ on the other side of death, they will be "thrown into the lake of fire" (Revelation 20:15).

If you are not sure at which judgment your name will be called, you still have the opportunity to settle the matter. You must admit your sinfulness and transfer all of your trust to Christ alone, for only He can fit you for heaven. "Whoever believes in the Son has eternal life; whoever does not obey the Son shall not see life, but the wrath of God remains on him" (John 3:36).

In fact, if you want more information on how to be sure of heaven, I suggest you skip to chapter 10. I've included the terrifying biblical description of the Great White Throne Judgment, along with an explanation of how you can avoid this frightful event. Take time to make your peace with God *now*.

THE PURPOSE OF THIS BOOK

For several years I pondered the possibility of studying the judgment seat of Christ, or what is called the *doctrine of rewards*. It is with sobriety and not a little trepidation that I have finally had the courage to preach and write about this subject. The fact that you and I will be one-on-one with Christ, and He shall review our lives, is enough to give us pause.

The thesis of this book is that *the person you are today will determine the rewards you will receive tomorrow.* Those who are pleasing to Christ will be generously rewarded; those who are not pleasing to Him will receive negative consequences and a lesser reward. In other words, your life *here* will impact your life *there* forever.

If the knowledge that we will give an account to Christ "for [the] deeds [done] in the body, . . . whether good or bad" (2 Corinthians 5:10 NASB) does not motivate us to faithful living, it is quite possible that nothing else will. Here at last we must own up to the question of how much we really do love Christ. In that day there will be no place to hide.

Resist the temptation to think about how others might fare while standing in Christ's presence. Indeed, no doctrine should make us more hesitant to judge our brothers and sisters, for we shall stand before the same Christ as they. Let us not think we can do God's work of judgment for Him. There is a place for church discipline, but there is no place for a critical, unforgiving, judgmental spirit.

Also resist the temptation to hide behind a preconceived theological bias that would render the judgment seat of Christ of little consequence. Read with an open mind, willing to grapple with the full impact of what God has revealed. Along the way we will continue to expose those misinterpretations that have weakened the biblical teaching on the subject.

Join me on a journey that will challenge your thinking and, I pray, change your life. Let's prepare for that day when you and I will be alone with Christ; just reality and no pretense. Matthew Henry wrote, "It ought to be the business of every day to prepare for our last day."

Let's begin the journey.

CHAPTER 2

YOU'LL BE THERE

Imagine staring into the face of Christ! Just the two of you, one-on-one! Your entire life is present before you. In a flash you see what He sees.

- No hiding.
- No opportunity to put a better spin on what you did.
- No attorney to represent you.
- The look in His eyes says it all.

Like it or not, that is precisely where you and I shall someday be. "*For* we must all appear before the judgment seat of Christ, so that each one may be recompensed for his deeds in the body, . . . *whether good or bad*" (2 Corinthians 5:10 NASB, italics added).

The judgment seat of Christ is often called the *Bema* (the Greek word for judgment seat used by Paul in 2 Corinthians 5:10, quoted above). Literally, the *Bema* refers to a raised platform that was used for the assembly where speeches were given and crowns were awarded to the winners. In ancient Rome the Caesars sat on a tribunal to award those who had made heroic contributions in winning the battle.[1] The *Bema* of Christ dwarfs all other tribunals, for here we shall be called into account before the all-knowing Judge.

Think this through: God gives us the faith by which we believe in Christ, and yet for this faith He gives us the gift of eternal life. God then works within us so that we might serve Him, and for our service He honors us with eternal rewards or *privileges*. Of course we don't deserve those rewards! But we are the sons and daughters of a loving Father who is more benevolent than we could possibly expect Him to be. He delights in giving to those who do not deserve His love.

"I'll be content to sit in the back row!" a friend of mine quipped when I brought up the subject of rewards in heaven. Looked at in one way, he echoed the sentiment of all of us. I interpreted his remark as a genuine expression of humility, the deep conviction that we deserve absolutely nothing. To have a seat in heaven, even if in the farthest corridor, is to enjoy an undeserved honor indeed. Anyone who feels differently has not yet seen his sinfulness before God!

But considered in a different light, his remark might betray a serious misunderstanding of the nature of rewards. What if those who "sit in the back row" are there because they have displeased Christ in their earthly sojourn? What if it was the Father's good pleasure to have us "sit in the front row," but we forfeited this privilege because of carnal living? Let us keep in mind that the idea of rewards is not ours; it is the Father's desire to bless us beyond all human reason. *We should be all that we can be on earth so that we can be all that we could be in heaven!*

I agree with Jim Elliff, who has observed that the people who piously care so little about eternal rewards are often killing themselves trying to accumulate a great "reward" now. They profess to be content with a "little shack in heaven," but want a much bigger one on earth! The Bible teaches that there is nothing wrong with ambition, just as long as we focus it on heaven rather than earth.[2]

We do not desire rewards for the reward itself, but because rewards are a reflection of Christ's approval of us. It is not wrong to want to be in the front row if such an honor is reserved for those who hear Christ say, "Well done, thou good and faithful servant" (Matthew 25:21 KJV).

CHARACTERISTICS OF JUDGMENT

Paul begins in 2 Corinthians 5:10, "For we *must* all appear before the judgment seat of Christ" (italics added). There is this similarity between the *Bema* and the Great White Throne Judgment: attendance at one or the other is required. There can be no exception, no special deferment. When God calls our name, we will be there. We cannot hide, for God will *find* us; we cannot scheme to make ourselves look good, for God shall *see* us. We cannot excuse ourselves, for God *knows* us.

We Will Be Judged Fairly

Who will judge us? This is the "judgment seat of Christ." Christ, who knows us completely, loves us in spite of ourselves.

We are judged by our Savior. He who died to save us, now stands to judge us. Because we are judged by One who loves us, we know that our judgment will be tempered with mercy. We'll be judged by One who wishes us well rather than by one who is anxious to condemn us. The Christ of the throne is the Christ of the cross.

Our Savior is also our Brother. He has invited us to join His family; we share the same Father; thus, our names have been called for fellowship at the family table. To Mary Magdalene, a woman who had been possessed by evil spirits, Christ said, "I am ascending to my Father and your Father, to my God and your God" (John 20:17). This judge will be merciful and fair because His Father is our Father. This is family business.

Even so, if we are unfaithful here on earth, the judgment could be severe. Immediately after Paul says that we shall be recompensed for the deeds done in the body, whether good or bad, he adds, "Therefore, knowing the fear of the Lord, we persuade others" (2 Corinthians 5:11). Interestingly, he connects the fear (or terror) of the Lord with the judgment seat of Christ. Some scholars who think that our judgment will be a positive experience for everyone teach that Paul must now be giving a warning to unbelievers. But obviously such an interpretation makes an unnatural break in Paul's thought. He knew that the judgment seat of Christ for some believers would be fearful indeed.

Christ often gives severe warnings to His redeemed church. To the congregation in Ephesus, whom He loved, He said, "Remember therefore from where you have fallen; repent, and do the works you did at first. If not, I will come to you and remove your lampstand from its place, unless you repent" (Revelation 2:5). Our Savior and Brother will administer only that which is right and just. But He will not wink at our disobedience. He does not play favorites nor step aside when meticulous adjudication is called for.

We can be quite sure that we will be judged only for what we have done since our conversion to Christ. The apostle Paul expected to do well at the judgment seat of Christ even though he had persecuted the church, jailing Christians in his preconversion days. Yet this man who claimed he was the chief of sinners said just before he died:

> For I am already being poured out as a drink offering, and the time of my departure has come. I have fought the good fight, I have finished the race, I have kept the faith. Henceforth there is laid up for me the crown of righteousness, which the Lord, the righteous judge, will award to me on that Day, and not only to me but also to all who have loved his appearing. (2 Timothy 4:6–8)

These are encouraging words for those who have a sinful or criminal record extending back to their preconversion days. The question to be answered at the judgment is how we have behaved as one of God's sons. We'll not be judged on what we did from the time of our *first* birth, but on what we did since our *second* birth.

Also, we will discover that every believer had the same potential to receive Christ's approval of "well done." Rewards are based on our faithfulness to opportunities presented to us since our conversion.

We Will Be Judged Thoroughly

When Paul says we shall "appear" at the judgment seat of Christ, he uses the Greek word *phaneroō*, which means "to be made manifest." The imagery is that we shall be "turned inside out." One Bible scholar, Philip Hughes, says the word *manifest* means "to be laid bare, stripped of every outward facade of respectability, and openly revealed in the full reality of one's character. All of our hypocrisies and concealments, all our secret, intimate sins of thought and deed, will be open to the scrutiny of Christ."[3]

We will be judged "for [the] deeds [done] in the body . . . whether good or bad" (2 Corinthians 5:10 NASB). The good deeds will be lovingly remembered. That cup of cold water given in the name of the Lord will not be forgotten. Those whom we helped who cannot repay us—such deeds will attract the attention of the Judge. (Later we will be discussing in more detail exactly what Christ will be looking for when He investigates our lives.)

That which is "bad," or worthless, will most assuredly be a negative counterbalance for that which is classified as "good." Because Christ is omniscient, every single detail can be brought into the final verdict, with every motive and action accounted for in context. Everything hidden today will be relevant in that day.

We've all known churches that have split over one or more issues, sometimes doctrinal, sometimes personal. Some people want the pastor to stay; others are convinced he should leave. Rumors circulate from one member to another; telephone lines buzz with charges and counterclaims. Usually people are hurt on both sides and hidden animosities simmer for years to come.

The Corinthian church had the tendency to fight and bicker among themselves, just as we often do. In 1 Corinthians Paul admonishes them, "Therefore do not pronounce judgment before the time, before the Lord comes, who will bring to light the things now hidden in darkness and will disclose the purposes of the heart. Then each one will receive his commendation from God" (1 Corinthians 4:5).

Some disputes must wait until the judgment seat of Christ for resolution. Of course, we should do all we can to see that these matters are settled in this life. But we all know that our best efforts often fail. We can judge a person's behavior, but we cannot judge his motives. To know who is right and who is wrong we shall have to wait for God. I shall return to this theme in a later chapter.

I'm told that there is a central location on the Internet that records all the "visits" of millions of subscribers. Somewhere, there is a person who could tally every website you and I have ever contacted. On the Web there is much that is good and helpful as well as that which is destructive and evil. Whether good or bad, our actions are recorded.

Just so, God has His vast information network. Everything we have done or said is known to Him. He can, if necessary, "download" the information at a moment's notice. And whatever He chooses to reveal to us, whether it be little or much, we will not dispute the facts. We won't need to ask for dates, times, and places, for all such details are known to Him.

Later I shall discuss the question of whether we will actually see our sins. For now, let me simply say that we can be sure that our sins will provide input into the evaluation. "For if we would judge ourselves, we should not be judged" (1 Corinthians 11:31 KJV). Unconfessed sin, sin that we have rationalized and idolized, will play a special part in the revelation and judgment.

If this seems fearful, remember that this judgment is also comforting. We've all had the experience of being criticized unfairly, even by our friends. When our motives are misinterpreted, when lies are spread by those who would delight in our downfall, such experiences are difficult indeed.

At the *Bema* the false accusations leveled against you will be brought to light. Cruelty, gossip, and misunderstandings will be cleared up. The judgment will be as detailed as it has to be to satisfy justice. All the "he said" and "she said" arguments will cease. Here the specifics are finally revealed; nothing but facts, nothing but the truth—the whole truth and nothing but the truth. If you need vindication, you will have it; if you need to be shown that you were in error, you will have that too.

Woodrow Kroll says, "Just as day brings light from the sun to reveal the hidden things of darkness, so that day will bring light from the Son to reveal the hidden things of darkness done in our bodies. However, many hidden things which are good will be revealed as well. . . . It will be both a day of vindication and a day of disappointment."[4] No time will be needed to gather evidence; no jurors will be selected to hear the arguments. Every detail has been known by Christ from the foundation of the world.

We will not dispute the outcome. We will not disagree with Christ, not because we are afraid to, but because we will have no reason to! If we have a question, it will be answered, but it is more likely that we will be speechless. We will see what He sees and know that His verdict is eminently just.

We Will Be Judged Impartially

When Paul outlined the principles by which God will judge us, he assured his readers that "God shows no partiality" (Romans 2:11). Indeed, the judgment of God is according to truth, that is, according to reality. No special advantages are given to the wealthy; those who counted on perks and power in this life find themselves stripped of every crutch, all forms of manipulation. Every trapping of man will fade into insignificance in the presence of the One who discerns the "thoughts and intents of the heart" (Hebrews 4:12 KJV).

Nor will pastors and missionaries be given preferential treatment. Those who have given their lives to serve Christ, often at great personal sacrifice, might receive a greater reward, but they are judged by the same standard of faithfulness. In fact, those who teach the Word of God will be judged by "a stricter judgment" (James 3:1 NASB) because they were given greater responsibility. Every detail will be evaluated within its larger context.

Most of us live in houses or apartments that are beautifully kept on the outside. But inside there is a mixture of cleanliness and dirt; perhaps a neat den but a closet filled with junk. During the tornado season the walls of houses are often blown off and everything within the closets and drawers lies visible to those who walk by. Just so, Christ will walk through our lives that now will be without walls. He will inspect the *rubies* as well as the *rubble*. He will show us whatever might be relevant to the judgment at hand.

In the presence of Christ, our outer image will give way to the reality of our inner character. The color of our skin, the size of our income, and our fame or lack of it will suddenly be irrelevant. This is one courtroom in which no one has an advantage. The Judge will determine what we did with what He gave us.

George Whitefield was a famous English preacher who had a profound ministry here in the United States during the first Great Awakening. His preaching on the new birth, coupled with an emphasis on predestination, caused both conversions and controversy. He said that the only epitaph he desired for his tombstone was:

Here lies George Whitefield;
What sort of man he was
The great day will discover

Although I'm told that Whitefield did not get his wish to have these words on his grave, they are true just the same. Only the judgment seat of Christ will reveal the sort of man he really was. The newspapers that criticized him will be silent. His biographers, whether friend or foe, will not be recruited for the final assessment. In the presence of Christ the opinions of men will be woefully irrelevant, whether critic or admirer. The divine verdict is the only one that matters.

We Will Be Judged Individually

If you are familiar with church life, you know that we have a strong tendency to judge one another regarding dos and don'ts. We like to judge others in questionable matters according to our own standard. In the first century, the Roman church was practically split over the question of whether it was proper to eat meat offered to idols, or whether it was right to eat meat at all. Paul stressed that we should not judge each other in these matters; petty arguments must be put aside. Listen to his words:

> But you, why do you judge your brother? Or you again, why do you regard your brother with contempt? For we will all stand before the judgment seat of God. . . . *So then each one of us will give an account of himself to God.*"
> (ROMANS 14:10–12 NASB, italics added)

Here again, Paul uses the word *Bema*, a reference to our one-on-one encounter with Christ. Underline that word *himself:* "Each one of us will give an account of *himself* to God." You will give an account of yourself; I shall give an account of myself. We will not have to speak in behalf of someone else. So let us stop carping about others; before our own Master we will each stand or fall.

Whenever I have been asked to sing in a choir, I try to sing softly, embarrassed that I might be off pitch. I can get by without being noticed, especially if there is a strong bass section. What I would never do is sing a solo! But when we stand before Christ, we will, figuratively speaking, have to sing our own song. There will be no comparisons with others; no one to cover for us, no opportunity to point out that we have more to show than someone else.

Will the judgment be private or public? I think it probably will occur in the presence of others, including angels before whom Christ promised to confess that we are His (Luke 12:8). Recall that in the parable of the talents, the slave who hid his talent (*mina*) was reprimanded and the king gave some important orders. "Then he said to the bystanders, 'Take the mina away from him and give it to the one who has the ten minas'" (Luke 19:24 NASB). Those who were present saw what happened and actually played a role in taking the mina away from one slave and giving it to another. The judgment was public indeed.

If you find this terrifying, take comfort in the fact that it will not matter whether our friends are present or not. For one thing, we will all be together; no one will be in a position to gloat, nor will there be much opportunity to be surprised. There will be some good and bad in all of us.

More important, I'm convinced that when we look into the eyes of Christ, what others think will not matter. A student giving a recital on the piano cares only what his teacher thinks. To a football player, the censure or affirmation of the coach means much more than the boos or cheers of the fans.

In the presence of Christ, we will be oblivious to those who are around us. The expression on His face will tell it all. The judgment will be very "up close and personal," but also public.

Since there are millions of Christians, some people have questioned whether it is possible for Christ to judge us individually. The point is that there would not be enough time for millions of encounters, especially if it is done in the seven-year period beginning at the Rapture and ending with the glorious return of Christ. But let us not limit Christ's ability. We do not know how long each judgment will take; also, research will not be needed to get all the facts. Christ can cause our entire lives to be present to us in a moment of time. There will be no files to shuffle, no witnesses that must be called to confirm the data.

We Will Be Judged Graciously

If it is a mistake to think that our failures can never return to haunt us, it is equally an error to think that the purpose of the *Bema* is that God might vent His pent-up anger at our carnality and selfishness. No, that anger has been absorbed for us by Christ, who died on the cross. He bore our eternal punishment and was the target of God's righteous indignation on our behalf. Nor is the purpose of the *Bema* that we might do better next time. There is no "next time," since we will now serve Christ perfectly. At issue is neither payment for our sins nor God's desire to "even the score."

The purpose of the judgment seat of Christ is to properly evaluate us, to grade us so that our position in the coming kingdom is made clear. This life is like a college-entrance exam that helps us know where we shall be slotted in the kingdom of the coming King. To quote Hughes again, this judgment "is not a declaration of gloom, but an assessment of worth, with the assignment of rewards to those who because of their faithfulness deserve them and a *loss* or withholding of rewards in the case of those who do not deserve them."[5]

Imagine a father who promises his son a ride in his personal airplane if only the lad will mow the lawn six weeks in a row. Six weeks later the boy's record is one of failure: he mowed the lawn only three times, skipped two weeks, and the last time only partially completed the job. The test period is over, and the father tells the boy what he should already know: his dream of taking a flight above his town will not come to pass.

The father is not angry, but saddened by the boy's lack of faithfulness. He does not formally "punish" his son for his negligence. He does, however, reprimand the son, and the boy must live with consequences of his unfaithfulness. He must stand by while another boy in the neighborhood responds to the same challenge and is rewarded with a Saturday morning flight. What hurts most, however, is the look on his father's face. All that is punishment enough.

Christ will not be angry, but disappointed. We will be "recompensed for [the] deeds [done] in the body, . . . whether [they be] good or bad." After the judgment is over and eternity begins, we will be denied privileges; perhaps some of us will not get to reign with Christ because of unfaithfulness.

If you feel distraught because of your sins and failures, take heart. All of us have experienced the depths of our own evil hearts and actions. As we shall discover, those sins that we judge through personal repentance will not be brought to light, except insofar as they will result in a loss of rewards.

But those sins that we tolerate, the matters that are unresolved between us and God and His people—these will be the specific subject of review and judgment.

In the midst of failure there will be grace. I'm convinced that Christ will find some things for which we will receive reward. Paul says, "Then each man's praise will come to him from God" (1 Corinthians 4:5b NASB). Perhaps there will not be much for which we are praised, but Christ will search the Cosmic Internet and find something for which He can commend us.

Despite our propensity to sin, every one of us can live a life that will receive the Lord's approval rather than His rebuke. Indeed, our struggle against sin, if successful, is worthy of reward. Today, in dependence upon Christ, we can live in light of that Great Day.

LIVING IN LIGHT OF
THE JUDGMENT

We've already learned some lessons that should affect the way we live. First, keep in mind that *this life is training for the next*. We are to be learning the rules of the kingdom; we are apprentices for something better. God's purpose is to mature us in faithfulness and service so that we will be a credit to Him on earth and a companion for Christ in heaven.

Second, *every day we live is either a loss or a gain so far as our future judgment is concerned*. How we live today will help determine the words we hear from Christ tomorrow. Remember, the person we are today will determine the rewards we receive in the future.

When Billy Graham was once asked by Diane Sawyer in a television interview how he would like to be remembered, sadness came across his face. "I would like to hear the Lord say to me, 'Well done, thou good and faithful servant,' but I don't think He will."

Two thoughts came immediately to mind. First, I surmised that Billy Graham was being more humble than he had to be! Here is a man who has preached the gospel to more millions than any other man in history. I think of his grueling schedule, the pressures and the heavy responsibilities he has borne. "Of course, he will do well at the *Bema*," I speculated.

My second thought: If Billy Graham does not think he will receive Christ's approval, what hope is there for the rest of us? Surely, if rewards are based on results, Billy Graham will be somewhere at the head of the line.

But in this respect Billy Graham was quite right. When he stands before Christ, his fame will not influence the outcome. Nor will the adulation of millions affect Christ's personal evaluation. Nor the fact that hundreds of thousands have come to Christ through his ministry. Like Whitefield, the manner of man Billy Graham was *"that day shall declare."*

This leads us to a third lesson. *Rewards are not based on results or size of ministry.* Some of us have had more widespread influence than others. Many who have served in mission fields can claim but few converts after lives of hardship and intense personal cost. Others are called to vocations in factories, farms, and within the home; some serve for many years, others for few. We will not be rewarded by a scale that asks for the number of souls saved, the number of sermons preached, or the number of books written. Comparisons with someone else will be off-limits.

Nor will we be rewarded for the length of time we serve. New converts can also receive Christ's approval. We will be judged on the *basis of our loyalty to Christ with the time, talents, and treasures that were at our disposal.* In other words, we are judged for the opportunities that were given to us, be they few or many, great or small. All believers have the potential to be generously rewarded.

To some who perhaps did not expect to be rewarded but were diligent about their calling, Peter wrote, "As long as you practice these things, you will never stumble; for in this way the entrance into the eternal kingdom of our Lord and Savior Jesus Christ will be abundantly supplied to you" (2 Peter 1:10b–11 NASB). Others who did not live diligently, those who cared little about whether they were pleasing the Lord or not, will experience "shame at his coming" (1 John 2:28).

What is God's purpose for us in eternity? What rewards can we win or lose? What will Christ be looking for?

Keep reading.

CHAPTER 3

WHAT WE CAN GAIN

G lance over my shoulder and read this letter that arrived in my mailbox:

> I know someone who has appeared in several X-rated films. Since then she has become a Christian. But she worries that since these films are irretrievable and have been distributed all over the world, the harm they are doing will continue even after she dies.
>
> Will this interfere with her salvation? In other words, how will she be able to share in the joy of heaven, while as a direct result of what she did on earth, others continue to

sin? She feels that she is leaving a legacy of evil. Can you offer any consolation?

Yes, thanks to the promises of Scripture, I believe I can offer some consolation. First, her past life will not interfere with her salvation. Christ died for sinners, even terrible sinners—yes, even pornographers and criminals. Our great-grandfather Adam left a worse "legacy of evil" than this woman, but God covered him with the skin of animals to cover his shame. These skins were symbolic of the coming of Christ, who would be killed so that we could be clothed in His righteousness. Many people have ongoing consequences of sins committed in their preconversion days. Yet, we can be secure in God's forgiveness even when the consequences of our sin continue. This forgiveness is a free gift given to those who acknowledge their sinfulness and trust Christ alone for their salvation.

Second, yes, this lady can look forward to joy in heaven, for at the judgment seat of Christ she will only be judged for what she did since she was saved, not what was done in her preconversion days. Having been forgiven much, she can indeed love much, and therefore be rewarded much. In fact, quite possibly, this woman will get to sit alongside of Christ and rule with Him forever.

The gift of salvation is not a reward for *works,* but a reward for *faith,* a faith that God has actually given to us! But when we are rewarded at the *Bema,* it will be based on our works; it will be according to our loyalty. I don't mean to say that we will receive what we deserve; as we will repeatedly emphasize, we will receive *far more* than we deserve, for God abounds in loving-kindness. We will not be paid in the sense that we will receive a day's pay for a day's work, but we will be paid in the sense that God will give us a hundred times more than we deserve. As Woodrow Kroll says, "Rewards are a gracious wage."

If your employer handed you a check late Friday afternoon and said, "This is a gift," you might not be amused. The implication would be that you don't deserve it; the check is simply an expression of compassion. But if you received a certificate for a two-week vacation in Hawaii because you were top salesman for the month, you would have "earned" the trip even though the reward would be far out of proportion to your effort. Christ, as we have already learned, did not hesitate to say that the faithful would be "repaid" by the Father.

The prospect of being found worthy to rule with Christ is the subject of this chapter. What Christ enjoys by divine right, He is willing to share with us by divine mercy! Today we are invited to catch a glimpse of the high honor to sit on Christ's throne and participate with Him in ruling the universe. "And there will no longer be any night; and they will not have need of the light of a lamp nor the light of the sun, because the Lord God will illumine them; and they will reign forever and ever" (Revelation 22:5 NASB). The journey from here to there is a love story that begins in the past and will end in this most glorious future.

Many Bible teachers simply take it for granted that everyone who enters heaven will get to rule with Christ. But many other passages suggest that this reward will be given to those who proved to be trustworthy on earth; if everyone in heaven does rule, some will be given greater positions of responsibility. I believe that there is much to gain at the judgment seat of Christ; thus there is also much we can lose.

THE LOVE STORY

To explain the whys and hows, I must describe this drama in three scenes. The plot begins in the Garden of Eden and ends in heaven. Stay with me as I summarize God's purpose for the human race in general and His own people in particular. Step-by-step we shall better understand God's ultimate intentions for us all.

And now the story.

The Past: Adam and Eve

The story begins in the Garden of Eden, where God chose to create mankind in His own image. "Let Us make man in Our image, according to Our likeness; and let them rule" (Genesis 1:26 NASB).

Neither angels nor animals were created in the image of God; this was the privilege only of mankind. This means that we share God's communicable attributes: personality, wisdom, love, truth, justice. Also, it means that we have an amazing capacity for God-likeness. We can be more like God than any other creature.

Let us ponder the details.

God fashioned man from the dust of the ground and "breathed into his nostrils the breath of life, and the man became a living creature" (Genesis 2:7). Soon after, Adam began to name the animals and take charge of the earth, just as God commanded. Yet in this idyllic paradise, something—or rather someone—was missing. God said, "It is not good that the man should be alone" (v. 18). No matter how beautiful the creation, no matter how close the fellowship between the man and God, Adam was incomplete. "There was not found a helper fit for him" (v. 20). So God set out to find a companion for him; more accurately, He set out to create the companion Adam needed.

Now when God created Eve, He did not create her from the dust of the ground. Right from the beginning He wanted to show the organic unity of the human race, the solidarity that exists between the members of the human family. He especially wanted to demonstrate the oneness of a man and his wife. So God formed Eve from Adam's rib so that he could say, "This at last is bone of my bones and flesh of my flesh" (v. 23).

The helper—the bride—was "found." She would meet her husband's needs but also get to rule with him over the creation. Notice the plural pronouns. The Lord said, "Let *them* have dominion over the fish of the sea and over the birds of the heavens and over the livestock and over all the earth and over every creeping thing that creeps on the earth" (Genesis 1:26, italics added). The woman was to be a co-ruler with Adam, exercising with him the dominion over all creation. She was to enjoy full partnership in the divinely ordered plan. Whatever Adam and Eve did, they were to do together.

Only humans have the concept of family. Angels were created individually; they were never babies who eventually grew up and became adults. Angels don't have cousins, grandparents, aunts, and uncles; they have no brothers or sisters. They have only a functional unity; that is, they exist for the common purpose of serving God. But there is no *organic* unity between them.

In contrast, Adam and Eve would beget children in their likeness. Cain would marry one of his sisters and have brothers and cousins. This solidarity is exactly what God needed to fulfill His eternal purpose. Stay with me on this.

To recap: Adam was the first man, and from him a bride

was created who would be able to exercise dominion with him. God was intent on finding a helpmate suitable for him.

Sin ruined all of this. Adam and Eve fell into the devil's trap, and their right to rule was forfeited. Satan picked up the scepter and asserted himself as ruler of the world. But Adam did not lose his place as the head of the human family. Although we, as his descendants, would, I'm sorry to say, be dysfunctional in varying degrees, Adam would still be the representative of the human race. The image of God would be *effaced* but not *erased*.

The love story between Adam, Eve, and God was in difficulty. Instead of ruling the world, we as humans would now be ruled by the world. Disease, destruction, and death would be the legacy bequeathed to this planet. We would sow, but not be sure that we would reap; we would establish friendships, but would be overcome by jealously, mistrust, and hatred.

Thankfully, this is only the first chapter in the story. God will intervene to dispel the darkness and keep the romance alive.

The Present: Christ and the Church

The Almighty was not content with the fellowship of the Trinity in eternity past. The Father, Son, and Holy Spirit were in eternal harmony in purpose and action; their relationship was beautiful and perfect. Yet apparently there was something missing—the fellowship of creatures would better display God's attributes. Mankind's plunge into sin would give God a gracious opportunity to showcase His love and intentions.

So the Almighty chose to clean up the mess Adam and Eve had created. Specifically, He had a Son named Christ, who would stand at the head of a whole new race of humanity. This Son is known as the "second Adam," for He will succeed where the first Adam failed. Adam was only a replica of God, but Christ is the perfect "image of the invisible God" (Colossians 1:15). Such a perfect image that He is, in fact, God.

Long before the Fall, God the Father promised a gift of redeemed humanity to His Son. The Son would purchase these people and they would be united as one body to share in His love and honor. And because this bride would be purchased at high cost by the Bridegroom, the intensity of the love would be evident for all to see.

Think this through. *Just as God sought a bride for Adam, so God sought a bride for His Son, Jesus Christ.* He chose to prepare a companion who would be able to share His Son's rule over the universe, someone who would enjoy His dominion. This bride would be loved, honored, and invited to join Christ on the throne of the universe.

Thanks to God, millions of people will belong to the number of the redeemed, united in one consciousness, one purpose, and one love. Just as the body is one and has many members, so also is the body of Christ: many members all unified in one body; one bride for God's most beloved Son.

So Christ stands at the head of new humanity, a new family. When we are born into this world, we are born of the seed of Adam, which is called "corruptible seed" (1 Peter 1:23 KJV; "perishable," NASB). We share the nature of our fallen parents and grandparents. When we are "born again" (John 3:3, 7), we receive God's seed that we might be replicas of His Son. We are begotten of "incorruptible" seed, God's seed (1 Peter 1:23 KJV; "imperishable," NASB), so that we can be "partakers of the divine nature," members of God's own family (2 Peter 1:4). *We are to be like Christ to the extent that the finite can be like the infinite; we are as much like Him as the creature can be like the Creator.*[1]

What is God's purpose for us here and now? We, as God's chosen bride, are being prepared for future responsibilities. In the words of one writer, God's intention "is the production and preparation of an Eternal Companion for the Son, called the Bride, the Lamb's Wife."[2] We are being tested to see whether we are worthy of such responsibilities.

Intimacy between a husband and wife should mirror this divine agenda. As husbands, we are to showcase the beauty of our wives, just as God is going to put the church on display in "all her glory" (Ephesians 5:27 NASB). We are to recognize our wives as co-heirs, fulfilling the role Eve was to have over the earth. Read these familiar words with new appreciation:

> Husbands, love your wives, just as Christ also loved the church and gave Himself up for her, so that He might sanctify her, having cleansed her by the washing of water with the word, that He might present to Himself the church in all her glory, having no spot or wrinkle or any such thing; but that she would be holy and blameless. (EPHESIANS 5:25–27 NASB)

We are not yet married to Christ, but we are engaged. During these days God is preparing us for the wedding. This is a time of purification, a time of testing and training. We are being primed for the coming marriage along with the rights and privileges that accompany it. Just as the bride is to enjoy the same honors as her husband, even so, the church inherits the honors of God's eternal Son.

And a greater chapter has yet to be written.

The Future: The Bride Is Enthroned

We cannot have the honor of being a joint-heir with Christ unless we are His relatives. To participate in His title deed to the universe, we must be members of His family.

We qualify because Christ is our brother. He came to Bethlehem not as an angel, but in the form of mankind. "For surely it is not angels that he helps, but he helps the offspring of Abraham" (Hebrews 2:16). Christ had to become one of our relatives in order for God to shower us with the honors reserved for members of His family. Unless we were God's sons and daughters, we could not legally receive the family inheritance.

God had one "only begotten Son" (John 3:16 NASB), but He longed for more sons, specifically sons who would be, at least in some respects, like His own.

> For it was fitting for Him, for whom are all things, and through whom are all things, in bringing many sons to glory, to perfect the author of their salvation through sufferings. For both He who sanctifies [Christ] and those who are sanctified [those whom Christ redeemed] are all from one Father; for which reason He is not ashamed to call them brethren. (HEBREWS 2:10–11 NASB)

Let me stress one more time that we are brothers with Christ because we share the same Father. We all know how embarrassing a wayward brother can be to the rest of the family. One woman I know disowned her brother because he was such a reprobate! We might think that Christ would be chagrined to be called our brother, but He is not. No matter how badly we reflect on the family, He does not disown us. We share family privileges, and He loans us the family name. He loves His brothers and sisters. He delighted in bringing "many sons into glory."

In our earthly existence when a father dies, the brothers and sisters share the family fortune. Of course, our Father in heaven does not die, but we do. And when we get to heaven, we are "heirs." When the title deed is read, we are partners; we share the Son's estate. "The Spirit himself bears witness with our spirit that we are children of God, and if children, then heirs—heirs of God and fellow heirs with Christ, provided we suffer with him in order that we may also be glorified with him" (Romans 8:16–17).

If you are a believer, expect to hear your name when God's last will and testament is opened. Since we are joint-heirs, the will cannot be dispensed unless we receive our inheritance. As it turns out, Christ is "heir of all things" (Hebrews 1:2), and as His brothers and sisters we are fellow heirs in an eternal, heavenly existence. We do not know all that this inheritance includes.

Certainly every believer will have an eternal, indestructible body, just as Christ has; we will not be limited by distance or endurance. Also, every believer will have proximity to the Father, the ability to behold Him in all of His beauty, to spend an eternity studying the wonders of His attributes and purposes.

If we want to know more about our future existence, we must only look at Christ after the Resurrection. He had a beautiful and powerful body that masked radiant glory. All of His brothers and sisters will be like Him.

> See how great a love the Father has bestowed on us, that we would be called children of God. . . . Beloved, now we are children of God, and it has not appeared as yet what we will be. We know that when He appears, we will be like Him, because we will see Him just as He is.
> (1 JOHN 3:1–2 NASB)

We should not be surprised that John motivates us to pure lives in light of such a prospect. He continues, "And everyone who thus hopes in him purifies himself as he is pure" (v. 3). Far from giving us license to sin, the grace of Christ should drive us to holiness. We should want to be like our Savior and brother.

Our famous brother does not keep us at a distance. He invites us to share His throne in the coming kingdom and beyond. We will be His bona fide partner, His judicial equal. We who are a gift from the Father to the Son, we who are the bride and eternal companion for the Son might well be startled by this promise, "To him that overcometh will I grant to sit with me in my throne, even as I also overcame, and am set down with my Father in his throne" (Revelation 3:21 KJV).

Let's take this slowly. As a reward for the Son's faithfulness, He was invited to sit on the throne of the Father. If we are overcomers, we are invited to sit with Christ on the Father's throne He rightfully inherited. So if the Son sits on the Father's throne and we sit on the Son's throne, are we not sitting on the throne of God?

At this point we have reached the limits of our comprehension; we cannot grasp what the text means. We understand the words, but the implications elude us. We can only listen with John, who heard these words from the throne: "The one who conquers will have this heritage, and I will be his God and he will be my son" (Revelation 21:7). Surely we are in awe of the generosity of God.

Of course, we should never think that we shall either become God or take His place. There is no room in the Bible for the "potential divinity of man." No, God has picked us up from the pit of sin and lifted us to dizzy heights. We shall forever be the creature and He the Creator. This is not proof of man's greatness and potential, but rather an example of God's love and undeserved grace! *It has nothing to do with what we have been able to make of ourselves, but everything to do with what God has chosen to make of us!*

Angels, bless them, are not qualified to reign with Christ. For one thing they are not brothers to Christ, and therefore do not share in the family inheritance. For another, they were not chosen to be Christ's eternal companion. They do the will of God with joy and holy obedience, but they are not participants in God's plan for the Son to purchase a bride for Himself.

Let me say again: We shall be as much like Christ as it is possible for the creature to be like the Creator; as much as the finite to be like the infinite. We shall be co-rulers with Christ, sitting on His throne, bought by Him, loved by Him, and honored by Him. (What this might mean is discussed in more detail in chapter 9.)

A PROMISE TO THE FAITHFUL

Does the Bible teach that all believers will get to reign with Christ? Does it matter whether we train for heavenly rule? Will everyone inherit the kingdom equally? Will all the saints share an equal honor at the marriage supper of the Lamb?

God has always reserved special rewards for those who are most faithful. When Israel left Egypt, the nation had been redeemed by God. At least a remnant of those who died in the desert, as far as we know, will be in heaven. They were redeemed by the blood of the Lamb; they experienced redemption from Egypt. And yet they died without entering into the fullness of God's promise; they missed Canaan.

The land was a promise of additional blessing for those who were faithful. Of the older generation, only Joshua and Caleb qualified.

Even Moses was excluded from the land of Canaan because of his disobedience. He will be in heaven, but he forfeited his earthly inheritance. In the Old Testament it was possible to be regenerate, belong to God, and still miss out on the extra blessing of inheritance. Salvation was a gift through faith, but the added blessing was dependent on obedience.

Today, we are not concerned about entering into the land of Canaan, but the same principle applies. Just as some did not enter into the land and yet made it to heaven, even so some will be in heaven but without experiencing the fullness of reward. Rewards are always dependent on faithfulness.

Paul made it clear that slaves were to serve their masters as they would serve Christ. If they were devoted, the Lord would give them *the reward of the inheritance*. Some would accept his challenge; possibly others did not.

> Whatever you do, work heartily, as for the Lord and not
> for men, knowing that from the Lord you will receive
> the inheritance as your reward. You are serving the Lord
> Christ. For the wrongdoer will be paid back for the
> wrong he has done, and there is no partiality.
> (COLOSSIANS 3:23–25)

Slaves could accept unjust wages with the assurance that Christ would personally reward them for their faithfulness. Of course, if they could better their position, that would be acceptable, but they lived in a culture where there was no opportunity to redress the wrongs. But if slaves served their masters as if they were Christ, Christ would reward them. Their reward was dependent on their works.

All believers have God as their inheritance, but there is another inheritance, an additional one given to those who are faithful. All believers will get to be heirs, but they will not inherit the same things.

Christ made the same point to His disciples.

> Truly I say to you, that you who have followed Me, in the regeneration when the Son of Man will sit on His glorious throne, you also shall sit upon twelve thrones, judging the twelve tribes of Israel. And everyone who has left houses or brothers or sisters or father or mother or children or farms for My name's sake, will receive many times as much, and will inherit eternal life.
> (MATTHEW 19:28–29 NASB)

Imagine the payback! To leave father and mother for the sake of Christ is to receive "many times as much" and "inherit eternal life." Obviously eternal life is a gift given to those who believe on Christ, but the expression "inherit eternal life" apparently refers to an additional acquisition, something more than simply arriving in heaven. It refers to a richer experience of being appointed by Christ to be in charge of the affairs of the cosmos as a ruler or judge. Salvation is guaranteed to those who accept Christ by faith; rewards are not. Entering heaven is one thing; having a possession there is quite another. One is the result of faith; the other, the reward for faith plus obedience.

The Bible is a realistic book. It does not assume that all believers will be faithful. Indeed, there are many examples of unfaithfulness of believers. History itself proves that many true Christians have buckled under persecution and have even denied Christ to save their lives or the lives of their families. In fact, many deny Christ just to save their jobs or their reputations. Others are seduced by the temptations of this world.

The Bible nowhere expressly says that some believers will not reign with Christ. However, the promises of reigning with Him are almost always explicitly tied to obedience, faithfulness, or being an overcomer. As Paul wrote in 2 Timothy 2:12, "If we endure, we will also reign with him; if we deny him, he also will deny us." In the Revelation it says, "The one who conquers and who keeps my works until the end, to him I will give authority over the nations" (2:26).

Either some Christians will not get to rule with Christ or they will rule over a lesser territory. If we remember the parable of the talents, we will keep in mind that one unfaithful servant had his talent taken from him and given to another. While others reigned over cities, he did not. All that he could hope for was to be admitted into the kingdom; he could not inherit its most prized positions.

WEDDING PREPARATIONS

Earlier I mentioned that we are engaged to Christ, but someday we will be married to Him. We have in the Bible a rather detailed description of the "marriage supper of the Lamb" (Revelation 19:9), for which we must be properly dressed. At every wedding in which I have participated, the attenders are always interested in what the bride is wearing. The style of the dress and the choice of flowers and veil are all the focus of attention. We read:

> "Let us rejoice and be glad and give the glory to Him, for the marriage of the Lamb has come and His bride has made herself ready." It was given to her to clothe herself in fine linen, bright and clean; for the fine linen is the righteous acts of the saints. (REVELATION 19:7–8 NASB)

The righteous acts of the saints! What are these righteous acts? Certainly not the acts that declared us justified before God; we cannot stress too often that we did not work for the garments of righteousness that Christ gives us. These are different garments.

In order to attend the marriage supper of the Lamb, we need two different suits of clothes. The first is the righteousness of Christ, the gift that admits us into heaven. This is a free set of clothes, the garments by which we are ushered into heaven's courts. "For our sake he made him to be sin who knew no sin, so that in him we might become the righteousness of God" (2 Corinthians 5:21).

But the second suit of clothes is a wedding garment for the marriage supper. This suit is not the righteousness of Christ, but rather the deeds we have done for Christ on earth. Christ has made us ready for heaven; we must make ourselves ready for the wedding feast. We must distinguish between what only God can do and that which we can have a part in doing.

What are we doing today? We are sewing the garments that we shall wear at the marriage supper of the Lamb. We are making sure that we will not be so scantily clad that we shall be ashamed. John warns, "And now, little children, abide in him, so that when he appears we may have confidence and not shrink from him in shame at his coming" (1 John 2:28).

If you ask how these garments became so "white and clean," I reply that many of our imperfect works are made perfect in the sight of God through Christ. God takes what we do, and if it is done for Him, these deeds are made white and clean. Just recently, a woman died who was faithful to Christ throughout her long life. Many years ago I stopped by her house to run an errand, and as she came to the door, her face was flush with tears. She apologized for crying, explaining, "You caught me in the middle of my prayer time for my family." I think she was sewing a garment for the wedding; my suspicion is that she will be well clothed at the marriage supper.

The purpose of our trials and temptations is to train us for ruling with Christ. We are learning the laws of the kingdom, responding in faithful obedience. We are given the opportunity of becoming overcomers so that we might inherit the promises. "For this light momentary affliction is preparing for us an eternal weight of glory beyond all comparison" (2 Corinthians 4:17). Place all of your trials on one end of a scale and the eternal weight of glory on the other, and it will go "plunk"! It is the weight of a feather versus a cubic foot of gold!

A family I know lost both of their children to prolonged and severe battles with cancer. And now, as I write, the father himself is down to 125 pounds, expected to die at any time of the same disease. What is God's purpose in all of this? It is to increase the eternal joy of the saints. Not the present joy, to be sure, for the moment seems to be utterly devastating, but *we can only become overcomers when there is something that must be overcome!*

We want life to be smooth, secure, uninterrupted. God has a different agenda. He is purifying us, testing us, training us so that we might be presented to Him as a pure church, ready to take our place sitting next to Christ on His throne. The English preacher Spurgeon wrote: "O Blessed axe of sorrow that cuts a pathway to my God by chopping down the tall trees of human comfort."

Our desire to pass our test and receive Christ's approval is not prideful; rather, it motivates us to worship a God who would be so generous with His undeserving children. We can only wonder at Christ's gracious words: "Fear not, little flock, for it is your Father's good pleasure to give you the kingdom" (Luke 12:32). Let me repeat that the idea that we should reign with God's Son is not ours, but His. God's desire is to display His wonder and grace throughout all of eternity, "so that in the coming ages he might show the immeasurable riches of his grace in kindness toward us in Christ Jesus" (Ephesians 2:7).

In the next chapter we shall discuss in more detail what it means to "suffer loss." We will attempt to answer the question of what it might be like to enter into heaven minus the rewards reserved for the faithful.

We shall learn that if we are unwilling to suffer loss for Christ in this life, we shall surely suffer loss in the life to come. Let us examine our hearts lest we be among those who do not hear Christ's "Well done."

CHAPTER 4

WHAT WE CAN LOSE

There is a story about a man who was trudging through a blistering desert. He was faint with thirst, and to his delight he came across a well with a pump. Next to the pump sat a small jug of water with a sign, "Please use this water to prime the pump. The well is deep so you will have enough water for yourself and your containers. Please fill the jug for the next traveler."

Should the man play it safe and drink the jug of water, assured that his parched lips would at least get some relief? Or should he take the risk of pouring the water down the pump in hopes of getting all he would need?

Do we believe God's promises that He will repay us if we take the risk of serving Him with a whole heart? Or do we live as if this is the only life that matters? Christ warns, "Whoever finds his life will lose it, and whoever loses his life for my sake will find it" (Matthew 10:39). If I give up the control of my life to God, I shall find it; if I maintain control, I shall lose it.

If we think of heaven as a theme park, we must emphasize that the entrance ticket is free. Christ must be received by faith; we are saved "not of works, lest any man should boast" (Ephesians 2:9 KJV). But if we want to go on some of the rides, if we want to be rewarded and not be embarrassed at the sadness we cause Christ, we must be faithful on earth. The entrance is free, but some additional benefits are based on merit.

THE JUDGMENT OF FIRE

Perhaps the most vivid picture of the judgment seat of Christ is Paul's metaphor given to the church at Corinth. He pictures a building with a strong foundation, capable of holding the weight of the walls and roof, but these materials must be tested. What kinds of substances were used in the building? Can this structure withstand the test of time? Only when the building is set aflame is the answer made clear. And yes, some builders will suffer loss.

Unfortunately, this passage has often been interpreted as a reference to carnal Christians who supposedly believed on Christ but lived lives of open fleshly rebellion. And yet, when they die, we are told, they will be in heaven, "saved as by fire." But Paul did not write this to give carnal Christians at least a bit of comfort. His point, I believe, lies in another direction.

He begins by saying that he cannot speak to the believers at Corinth as to spiritual men, but as to "people of the flesh, as infants in Christ" (1 Corinthians 3:1). But keep in mind that these believers were learning how to exercise their gifts; they were supporting the church and interested in spiritual growth. They were not modern carnal Christians who made a commitment to Christ in their youth, then wasted their lives in wanton sin. Their carnality revealed itself in the immaturity of putting their favorite man on a pedestal; some followed one leader, others another (vv. 3–4).

To address these petty jealousies, Paul uses two metaphors. The first is *agricultural:* "I planted, Apollos watered, but God gave the growth" (v. 6). The praise is given to God's part in the work, namely, the miracle of life, the marvel of growth. Rewards are never far from Paul's mind, so he adds, "He who plants and he who waters are one, and each will receive his wages according to his labor" (v. 8).

Then, second, he presents an *architectural* metaphor. "According to the grace of God given to me, like a skilled master builder I laid a foundation, and someone else is building upon it. Let each one take care how he builds upon it" (v. 10). He is speaking about the leaders who build churches; he is giving both warning and encouragement to those who have responsibility within the congregation.

Now we come to the crucial verses:

> Now if any man builds on the foundation with gold, silver, precious stones, wood, hay, straw, each man's work will become evident; for the day will show it because it is to be revealed with fire, and the fire itself will test the quality of each man's work. If any man's work which he has built on it remains, he will receive a reward. If any

man's work is burned up, he will suffer loss; but he himself will be saved, yet so as through fire.
(1 CORINTHIANS 3:12–15 NASB)

Paul's point is that some leaders are trying to build the church with poor materials; they gather a congregation quickly, but there is nothing transforming about their ministry. They might work hard, but because their energy is misdirected, they will have nothing that lasts in glory.

Others are trying to build with precious stones; they have a ministry based on the Word of God, prayer, and the Spirit. They value character, which D. L. Moody defined as "what a man is in the dark." They know that they will be judged, not just for what they *did* but for who they *are*. As veteran missionary to India Amy Carmichael used to say, "The work will never go deeper than we have gone ourselves." These shall receive a reward.

The person who is "saved so as by fire" is indeed a Christian, but his leadership has been flawed. He has relied too heavily upon himself, his techniques, and his training. He did not approach the work with a spirit of dependence and faith; he did not do the work with Spirit-directed faithfulness. He will be "saved so as by fire."

Though Paul's point is intended for the leaders of the church, it can be applied to all of us. We are all building our lives, day by day; each of us will be tested, and each life will reveal a mixture of precious stones and stubble.

Imagine for a moment that all of our deeds were turned into either precious metals or trash, and then torched. The kind of life we lived would become evident by the size of the fire. The question would be: What was left when the flames died out? The more carnality and selfishness, the more "wood, hay, straw" and the less "gold, silver, precious stones." This metaphor helps all of us come to terms with the thoroughness of God's judgment.

The Final Judgment of Sin

Will we actually see our sins at the judgment seat? Perhaps Hoekema is right when he suggests that the sins and shortcomings of believers will be "revealed as forgiven sins, whose guilt has been totally covered by the blood of Christ."[1] If so, we could see our sins, which would be represented to us as forgiven by God's grace.

What we do know is that Paul taught clearly that we will receive the consequences of our wrongs at the judgment. He reminded slaves to serve their masters as they would Christ, "knowing that from the Lord you will receive the reward of the inheritance" (Colossians 3:24 NASB). Then he adds, "For he who does wrong will receive the consequences of the wrong which he has done, and that without partiality" (v. 25 NASB). Even if our sins are represented as forgiven, we cannot escape the conclusion that our lifestyle is under judicial review, with appropriate rewards and penalties. We will suffer for our "wrongdoing." And even what is hidden will be brought to light.

The respected theologian John Murray, when speaking of the judgment seat of Christ, says that God will leave nothing at loose ends; in fact, since believers will be fully sanctified, they will desire such a judgment: "Besides, it is against the gravity of their sins that their salvation in Christ will be magnified, and not only the grace but the righteousness of God will be extolled in the consummation of their redemption."[2]

We should not think that the loss of rewards means that Christ takes from us something we once had. As Woodrow

Kroll says, "We are not stripped of rewards as an erring soldier is stripped of his stripes."[3] We receive no heavenly rewards on earth, so there is nothing that can be taken away from us; only when we stand before our Master are rewards given out. But the absence of rewards is serious indeed.

If we do have rewards coming to us, no one can take them from us. Christ warned the church at Philadelphia, "I am coming quickly; hold fast what you have, so that no one will take your crown" (Revelation 3:11 NASB); He did not mean that someone can steal our reward. Indeed, Christ said that those who have treasures in heaven will *not* have them stolen. Christ warns, however, that we *can* forfeit our reward by default and by failing to use the opportunities God gives us. Someone else can take our crown only if we let him get in the way of our relationship with God.

Three descriptive phrases help us visualize just how thorough this judgment will be. Paul wrote that our works will "become evident," for the day will "show it" because it is to be "revealed with fire" (1 Corinthians 3:13 NASB). The imagery is that of a person who has his pockets turned inside out to reveal every particle of lint. We will watch as Christ does the revealing, the analyzing, the judging.

The Kinds of Materials

Two kinds of materials are contrasted. We can find a pile of wood, hay, and stubble almost anywhere, especially in rural areas. Precious gems are quite another matter. Hold them in your hand, and they are of more value than mounds of wood and straw. So it is not how *much* we do for Christ, but rather *what* we do and *how* we do it. Of course, this does not mean that we should do as little as possible for Christ, insisting that we have made up for our slothfulness through "quality."

Paul's point is simply that much of what we do, if done in the wrong way and for the wrong reasons, is worthless.

Why do our works have to be subjected to the flames? The natural eye cannot easily tell the difference between these building materials. Not even Paul was confident that he could always separate junk from gems. From our perspective, a believer might have nothing but an impressive pile of combustible material; but when torched, nuggets of gold might be found embedded in the straw. Conversely, what we thought was a gold brick of some notable saint might just be the end of a wooden beam. Only the fire can separate the real from the fake.

- Our thoughts and intentions will be judged. "For the word of God is living and active . . . and able to judge the thoughts and intentions of the heart. And there is no creature hidden from His sight, but all things are open and laid bare to the eyes of Him with whom we have to do" (Hebrews 4:12–13 NASB). We who are adept at hiding our true selves from others, and even fooling ourselves, will suddenly have no place to hide. The piercing, probing, omniscient eyes of Christ will see through us.

- Our words will be judged. "I tell you, on the day of judgment people will give account for every careless word they speak" (Matthew 12:36). And that which is spoken in a bedroom will be shouted from the housetop, for "nothing is covered up that will not be revealed, or hidden that will not be known" (Luke 12:2). Obviously, not everything said in our bedrooms will be shouted from the housetops. Christ is speaking of those sins we have covered and refused to bring to Him in confession and repentance.

• Our motives will be judged. "But to me it is a very small thing that I may be examined by you, or by any human court; in fact, I do not even examine myself. For I am conscious of nothing against myself, yet I am not by this acquitted; but the one who examines me is the Lord. Therefore do not go on passing judgment before the time, but wait until the Lord comes who will both bring to light the things hidden in the darkness and disclose the motives of men's hearts; and then each man's praise will come to him from God" (1 CORINTHIANS 4:3–5 NASB).

If we should not pass judgment before the time, it can only be because the unresolved disputes among believers will be adjudicated at the *Bema*. There the injustices among God's children will be brought to light, truth will triumph, and the righteous will be vindicated.

Consider:

• An American missionary organization raised money for property, including buildings, in a country of Europe. When the chairman of the European board resigned, a local board member was able to usurp authority, rewrite the constitution of the organization, and declare himself owner. This Christian leader, in effect, stole the property from the Christian organization, expelled its leadership, and put the church and newly built apartments in his name.

• A Christian couple had a bitter divorce. There were so many lies, deceptions, and deep hurts that counselors couldn't establish agreement on so much as a single point. The husband eventually abandoned his wife and children and yet used their names as dependents on his income tax forms.

It might be tempting to think that these Christians will walk through heaven's gates hand in hand, with old animosities forgotten. Yes, of course, at that time all believers will have new natures and will not be subject to grudges and bitterness. But this does not mean that what happened on earth will be hidden. Paul taught that the believers in Corinth should not think they have to settle every issue, but wait for Christ to do it. What is the purpose of exposing the secrets of the hearts if it is not to bring final reconciliation to unresolved disputes? (See 1 Corinthians 4:3–5, quoted on the previous page.)

If you have had your reputation ruined by a vindictive believer, take comfort in the fact that the truth shall someday be revealed. Is not the *Bema* the place where injustices on earth shall finally be addressed? Is not this why Paul said we should not take revenge but leave the matter with God? "Never take your own revenge, beloved, but leave room for the wrath of God, for it is written, 'Vengeance is Mine, I will repay,' says the Lord" (Romans 12:19 NASB).

Christ will untangle the disputes that baffled us on earth. He will bring to light "the things hidden in the darkness and disclose the motives of men's hearts" (1 Corinthians 4:5 NASB). Justice can only triumph if the participants see injustices addressed and resolved. The judgment seat of Christ will be the place where God will satisfy our craving to have masks torn away, lies exposed, and reality prevail. The wrongdoers will finally admit the truth, and the victims will be vindicated; forgiveness among believers will be both given and accepted. Only then will justice prevail.

Recently I was told that a known Christian leader is actually a fake, a man who is using gullible Christians to garner funds for himself and his family. Yet he preaches messages that have biblical content; he is generally believed to have been converted out of an atheistic family. Perhaps people have been converted from hearing him preach. Whether he will be judged at the *Bema* or the Great White Throne, we can take comfort in the fact that someday the facade will fall and all that will be left is reality.

What would it be like to "suffer loss"? What would the consequences be if we did see our deeds disintegrate behind a cloud of smoke? What memories might we take with us into eternity? Notice the contrast between the two men. "If any man's work which he has built on it remains, he will receive a reward. If any man's work is burned up, he will suffer loss; but he himself will be saved, yet so as through fire" (1 Corinthians 3:14–15 NASB). The man who suffers loss is pictured as running out of a building that is engulfed in flames and collapsing behind him. He is saved; indeed, he arrives in heaven just as surely as his faithful brothers and sisters. But he has lost the opportunity for a full reward.

LOSING OUR REWARD

What kind of lifestyle might cause us to *lose* our inheritance? We can lose our reward both by the sins we commit and the opportunities we squander. Certainly all believers inherit heaven with its opportunity to serve Christ and worship at the throne. But there is another inheritance, a special reward given to the faithful. This second kind of reward is sometimes spoken of as "inheriting eternal life."

Earlier I pointed out that some scholars teach that to

enter the kingdom is one thing; to *inherit* the kingdom, quite another. We say that King Hussein inherited the kingdom of Jordan, which he has ruled for many years. But there are many other people who live within the country but are not participating in his rule.

To *possess* eternal life you simply need faith in Christ; to truly *inherit* it, you need faith and obedience.[4] If we keep in mind that to "inherit eternal life," or to "inherit" the kingdom, is an extra reward for faithful service, we will read many passages of Scripture differently.

Paul wrote, "For this you know with certainty, that no immoral or impure person or covetous man, who is an idolater, has an inheritance in the kingdom of Christ and God" (Ephesians 5:5 NASB). Who are these people who will not have an "inheritance in the kingdom of Christ and God"? In context, Paul is warning Christians about their behavior. He assumes that Christians can be deceived and live like the "sons of disobedience." We have all known Christians who struggle with sexual addictions, or Christians who are greedy and idolatrous. We've all known Christians who live with these sins even when coming under God's heavy hand of discipline. The Bible assumes what we know by experience, namely, that Christians can do evil deeds and be caught in terrible sins. Some die in such a spiritual condition.

Covetousness, which is also listed as one of these transgressions, lies deeply buried within every one of us. We all can identify with the war for ownership that rages within the soul. If with Christ's help we do not master such sins, they will assuredly master us. If Paul meant that those who practice such vices will not *enter* the kingdom, our own assurance of final salvation would be in constant jeopardy. Any one of us could be overtaken by such a sin and die in disgrace.

Perhaps what Paul meant is this: those who practice such sins will not be barred from entering the kingdom, but will be barred from inheriting it. If one or more of these sins characterizes their Christian lives, and they refuse to judge the evil, they will forfeit the honor of kingdom rule.

Similar teaching occurs in Paul's instructions to the church in Galatia. In fact, here the list of sins that will prevent people from "inheriting the kingdom of God" is even longer.

> Now the deeds of the flesh are evident, which are: immorality, impurity, sensuality, idolatry, sorcery, enmities, strife, jealousy, outbursts of anger, disputes, dissensions, factions, envying, drunkenness, carousing, and things like these, *of which I forewarn you, just as I have forewarned you, that those who practice such things shall not inherit the kingdom of God.* (GALATIANS 5:19–21 NASB, italics added)

Again Paul speaks of those who will forfeit certain kingdom privileges because of their sinful lifestyle. Although we must admit that many so-called carnal Christians are not Christians at all, we also must recognize that serious failure is possible for genuine Christians. And this will be revealed at the *Bema.*[5]

I freely admit that most scholars disagree with the above interpretation. They teach that Paul's description refers to the unconverted, who will miss the *Bema* entirely and be judged at the Great White Throne Judgment. To live a lifestyle characterized by these sins, it is said, is proof that one is not a Christian. They would argue that Christians might *lapse* into these sins, but their lives will not be *characterized* by them.

It is not my intention to settle this interpretive question. Either way, Paul's words are a sober warning to all of us. First, we must examine whether we are living lives that are free of these sins that God so strictly judges. Surely many who claim to be believers and yet practice these sins are self-deceived. We must remind ourselves that it is possible to *profess* to have eternal life, and not *possess* it. In other words, many whose lives are characterized by these sins will find themselves on the wrong side of the celestial gates.

But second, I'm sure we would agree that when genuine Christians allow such sins to become a part of their lives, their reward will be diminished. Faithfulness not only means that we are committed to good deeds, but also that we are free of evil ones. One result of the new birth is a love for God and a dislike for sin. If as a child of God we tolerate what our Father hates, we will incur His discipline in this life and the next.

If we ask the question how God evaluates lives that are so mixed with failures and successes, if we wonder how God balances twenty years of faithful ministry with a year of moral failure, we cannot answer. If God spelled out specifically what we must do to "inherit" the kingdom and the number of failures that we must have on our record before we "forfeit" it, you can be sure that some of us would want to do the bare minimum to balance the ledger!

Certainly, those whose lives were characterized by these sins shall suffer greater loss than those who struggled with such sins but continually judged them through confession and repentance. Indeed, even if the sins we have forsaken and confessed will only be represented as lost rewards, they shall still greatly affect the outcome of our judgment. If we have wasted our lives, we will still suffer loss even if we should repent just before our death.

When the church at Corinth was experiencing God's

heavy hand of discipline for disrespect at the Lord's Table (indeed, some were smitten with sickness and others had actually died), Paul had this admonition: "But if we judged ourselves rightly, we would not be judged. But when we are judged, we are disciplined by the Lord so that we will not be condemned along with the world" (1 Corinthians 11:31–32 NASB).

The more consistently we judge our sins through repentance and yieldedness, the less severe will be our future judgment. Even if we should lapse into known sin, we must never make our peace with it. Unjudged sin, that is, sin that we presumptively commit, can, I believe, bar us from enjoying the full potential of our rule with Christ.

Don Carson, professor at Trinity International University, says that when he was in Europe he spoke to a student who was cheating on his wife while far away from home at a university in Germany. When Carson pointed out that this would incur the discipline of God, the adulterer responded, "Well, of course, I expect God to forgive me—that's His job!" Carson did not believe that this man was a Christian, but if a believer were to adopt such an attitude, he most assuredly would be reprimanded and denied a reward.

In the Scriptures there are many warnings to those who would misuse the grace of God. There are also many encouragements to those who strive against sin but at times lose the battle. The desires of our hearts and the direction of our lives will all be taken into account when we stand before Christ.

Keep in mind that our entire life will be evaluated. The times of spiritual victory will be assessed along with our failures. Because God is generous, He will find more good in our lives than we know is there. Remember, Paul assured us that in that day "each man's praise will come to him from God" (1 Corinthians 4:5 NASB).

A second way we can forfeit our inheritance is by refusing to accept the joys of sacrifice and single-minded devotion to Christ. Rewards are based on our consistent faithfulness to follow Christ, even at great cost. God gives each of us time, talents, and treasure. To squander these, living as though these gifts are ours and not His, is to risk forfeiting our right to rewards.

In the next chapter we will consider more specifically what Christ will be looking for when He judges us. We will list ways in which we can please or displease Him. Not everyone need leave father and mother; not everyone need suffer persecution to have an abundant entrance into the kingdom. But if we neglect our duties, we will answer for our negligence.

A MAN WHO SUFFERED LOSS

We all struggle with the concept of negative consequences at the judgment seat of Christ. Many Christians think that Christ would never reprimand us at the *Bema*. Our sins have been washed away, and God cannot judge us for our carnality, selfishness, and wasted lives, we think. Because we are not under condemnation, we feel secure that any loss we suffer cannot be too serious.

But, as we have learned, God does judge His people on earth even though they are forgiven and justified. Ananias and Sapphira were judged by death for their dishonesty; carnal believers in Corinth died because of their disrespect for the Lord's Table (1 Corinthians 11:30). The simple principle is that God does not let His children get by with disobedience even though their place in heaven is secured and their transgressions legally forgiven. He judges them even though they will not have the opportunity to do better next time.

I agree with Kendall, who says, "We must deduce that there is no contradiction between Paul's doctrine of justification and his conception of the judgment of God; and that being declared righteous so as to escape the wrath of God... does not exempt us from rewards and punishment in the Last Day."[6] Thanks to Christ's sacrifice for us, we are spared the eternal penalty for our sin; we will, however, be judged for our response to opportunities that were laid before us. I can't lose my salvation, but there is something I *can* lose!

Let us try to imagine what the judgment seat of Christ will actually be like. If only we could meet someone who experienced it! The closest we can come to a firsthand account is to recall a parable Christ told about a man who suffered loss—significant loss—though he apparently was "saved . . . so as through fire" (1 Corinthians 3:15 NASB).

A nobleman called his servants and gave each of them some money and then left on his journey. One was given five talents; another, two; and a third, just one. Two of the servants seized the opportunity. "Immediately the one who had received the five talents went and traded with them, and gained five more talents. In the same manner the one who had received the two talents gained two more" (Matthew 25:16–17 NASB).

When the master returned, he called his servants to give an account of his money. When the five-talent servant presented him with ten talents, the master commended him. "Well done, good and faithful slave. You were faithful with a few things, I will put you in charge of many things; enter into the joy of your master" (v. 21 NASB). The servant whose two talents were now four talents heard the same kind words.

This corresponds to life as we know it. We are not given the same number of talents in life; some are given one, others are given two, while a few are given five or ten. God does not expect five-talent ability from a two-talent man. But since rewards are based on faithfulness to opportunity, both the two-talent man and the five-talent man received the same reward.

The third servant had hidden his money in the ground where no thief could find it. Perhaps he expected to be awarded for prudence, but he surely was not prepared for the response that awaited him. "You wicked, lazy slave, you knew that I reap where I did not sow and gather where I scattered no seed. Then you ought to have put my money in the bank, and on my arrival I would have received my money back with interest" (vv. 26–27 NASB).

Then he added, "'Therefore take away the talent from him, and give it to the one who has the ten talents.' For to everyone who has, more shall be given, and he will have an abundance; but from the one who does not have, even what he does have shall be taken away" (vv. 28–29 NASB).

Wicked! Lazy!

The master's words stung. What had this servant done to receive such harsh condemnation? Apparently feeling inferior because he had compared himself to those who had more talents than he, he said, in effect, "If I can't have five talents, I won't use the one I do have!" If he couldn't be a five-talent man, he didn't want to be a one-talent man. The sin of comparison crippled him.

This servant also feared failure and lacked the motivation to overcome his fears. This was not just pessimism about the economy; he had made a willful decision to choose the easy path. He didn't want to take the risk of investment. He thought that a box in the dirt would be safer than an investment at the bank.

He was discontented with his talent, and so he was discontented with his God. God was cruel and powerful, reaping where He had not sown and gathering where He had not scattered. He was making unreasonable demands. I believe the servant was a bitter man because he felt cheated. He thought he was digging a hole for his talent, but actually he was digging a hole for himself. But God wasn't buying his excuses!

What did he lose?

First, *he lost the approval of his master.* "You wicked, lazy slave" (v. 26 NASB). Perhaps Christ will speak similar words to some of us in the day of judgment. These words are, after all, an expression of disappointment and grief. If we have been unfaithful, we shall be rebuked.

Second, the servant faced *temporary rejection.* "Take away the talent from him, and give it to the one who has the ten talents" (v. 28 NASB). Perhaps this helps us understand Paul's words:

> The saying is trustworthy, for:
> If we have died with him, we will also live with him;
> if we endure, we will also reign with him;
> if we deny him, he also will deny us;
> if we are faithless, he remains faithful—for he cannot deny himself.
> (2 TIMOTHY 2:11–13)

Paul seems to be saying that it is possible that we will not endure, in which case we might not reign with Him; it is also possible that we can deny Him, in which case He will deny us. If so, we can rejoice that even if we are faithless He will remain faithful. He will not reject us as one of His children, but as one of His servants.

Or consider the words of Christ: "For whoever is ashamed of Me and My words in this adulterous and sinful generation, the Son of Man will also be ashamed of him when He comes in the glory of His Father with the holy angels" (Mark 8:38 NASB). Imagine Christ temporarily being ashamed of us because we were ashamed of Him!

Again, I must point out that many interpreters would refer these passages of Scripture to the unconverted. No believer, it is argued, would ever permanently deny Christ; nor would any believer be consistently ashamed of Christ. Yet, in context, these warnings are addressed to believers. Paul said that if "we" deny Him, He will also deny "us." Apparently he thought that such failure was a possibility for him.

Third, the servant was *denied rule in the kingdom.* "'Therefore take away the talent from him, and give it to the one who has the ten talents.' For to everyone who has, more shall be given, and he will have an abundance; but from the one who does not have, even what he does have shall be taken away" (Matt. 25:28–29 NASB). In a similar parable in Luke, the unfaithful servant explicitly forfeited rule over the cities (Luke 19:11–27). In the passage in Matthew, the text records that he was cast into "outer darkness; in that place there will be weeping and gnashing of teeth" (Matt. 25:30 NASB).

It is difficult to know how the judgment of this servant should be interpreted. Some scholars think that his strict judgment proves he was an unbeliever and perhaps Christ intended that we understand the parable as a warning to those who pretend to believe but their lifestyle belies their profession.

However, Warren Wiersbe represents those interpreters who point out that we need not see this treatment as punishment in hell, but rather the deep remorse of a man who was an unfaithful servant. He grieves deeply in the darkness outside of the King's palace, but he is still a servant and thus will be welcomed back into the King's estate. Wiersbe writes, "The man was dealt with by the Lord, he lost his opportunity for service, and he gained no praise or reward. To me that is outer darkness."[7]

We must caution that we should not build our theology on parables but remember that they were told to illustrate a central point. Christ used this story to alert His disciples to the danger of squandered opportunities. There is warning for all of us who are tempted to hide our talent in the dirt, either because of fear or self-centeredness. And when we stand before Christ in a state of purity with our glorified bodies, the sins we committed on earth will look more hideous than we could ever have thought them to be. Grief, *deep* grief, is understandable.

Can we say that some believers will be *punished* at the judgment seat of Christ? Certainly our eternal punishment was borne by Christ; thus, we are not under condemnation by God. But is not God's severe discipline of His children on earth a form of punishment? Would not the rebuke of Christ and the loss of rewards be a form of punishment for lives carelessly lived in the face of marvelous opportunities? Is not the purpose of any judge to hand out rewards or punishment?

Let us at least boldly affirm that the negative consequences of the judgment are far-reaching. This is a judgment, an accounting of how our lives were lived, with appropriate rewards either given or withheld. In fact, we do not know whether it is even possible to recover from our showing at the *Bema*. Perhaps those who suffer loss shall miss some opportunities for all of eternity. Hoyt wisely keeps us balanced when he writes, "To overdo the sorrow aspect of the judgment seat of Christ is to make heaven into hell. To underdo the sorrow aspect is to make faithfulness inconsequential."[8]

We should not think that the unfaithful Christian will spend eternity in the outskirts of God's kingdom, cowering in a dark corner. Heaven will not be comprised of two great companies, the faithful and the unfaithful. Most of us will fall somewhere in between; and, of course, everyone will be happy, everyone fulfilled, everyone serving. But the unfaithful Christian missed a splendid experience of receiving Christ's approval. Everyone in the kingdom will be a child of God, everyone a servant, but it appears that not everyone will get to rule with Christ.

People think that as long as their ledger shows neither gain nor loss that is sufficient. No, the talent given to this servant had to earn a profit. He had to be willing to take a risk for the sake of the king and his kingdom. He had to be willing to take his jar of water and prime the pump, believing that his small investment would result in all the water he would ever need.

There is a story, a legend that comes to us from India. A beggar saw a wealthy rajah come toward him, riding in his beautiful chariot. The beggar took the opportunity and stood by the side of the road holding out his bowl of rice, hoping for a handout. To his surprise, the rajah stopped, looked at the beggar, and said, "Give me some of your rice!"

The beggar was angry. To think that this wealthy prince would expect his rice! Gingerly, he gave him one grain of rice.

"Beggar, give me more of your rice!"

In anger, the beggar gave him another grain of rice.

"More please!"

By now the beggar was seething with resentment. Once again he stingily gave the rajah another grain of rice and then walked away. As the chariot went on its way, the beggar, in his fury, looked into his bowl of rice. He noticed something glitter. It was a grain of gold, the size of a grain of rice. He looked more carefully and found just two more.

For every grain of rice, a grain of gold.

If we clutch our bowl of rice, we shall lose our reward. If we are faithful and give God each grain, He gives us gold in return.

And the gold God gives will survive the fire.

CHAPTER 5

WHAT CHRIST WILL BE LOOKING FOR

The more honest we are, the more tempted we will be to conclude that we will not receive any rewards. Most of us see ourselves, at least to some degree, as represented in the attitude of the unfaithful servant who buried his talent and was reprimanded by his master. As we ask God to search our hearts, we see little that is good and much that is tainted. Is there any hope that we will hear, "Well done, thou good and faithful servant"?

The thought of a thorough judgment that even exposes our hidden motives and private thoughts is more frightening than comforting. We had hoped that we could slip into heaven, sit in a back row, and not have to face our dismal performance on earth. Now that we know that everything we have thought, done, or said since our conversion will have input into the outcome, we are not sure whether we want to die to be with Christ. We hope that there will be nuggets of gold amid the wood, hay, and stubble, but they probably will be few and far between. At least that is how all honest Christians feel.

How can any one of us expect to receive anything at all? Let us honestly affirm that not a one of us has all of the works that the Bible presents as being worthy of a reward. Our opportunities are limited, our lives too short, and our hearts too sinful. Some Christians are confined to a wheelchair; or they might be in prison, where the opportunities to serve are few.

Our motives are seldom as pure as we would like them to be; if our inner lives were exposed for all to see, we would want to live alone on a deserted island.

It is time for some encouragement.

First, let us keep in mind that the value of a deed depends upon the attitude of the heart. If we wanted to do more for Christ but could not because of human limitations, God will take our desires into account. We will be judged on the basis of faithfulness to the opportunities presented to us.

For example, when it comes to giving, Paul stresses the attitude of the heart. "For if the readiness is there, it is acceptable according to what a person has, not according to what he does not have" (2 Corinthians 8:12). If you give ten dollars but would give more if you had it, you will be rewarded for more than the amount you gave. If you intended to give a dollar you, will be rewarded for a dollar even if you inadvertently placed a twenty-dollar bill on the plate! The widow's two mites were almost worthless when we consider the huge budget needed to finance the temple worship. Yet Christ said, "This poor widow hath cast more in, than all they which have cast into the treasury," for she "cast in all that she had, even all her living" (Mark 12:43–44 KJV). Her gift was especially precious because she gave from her heart, unaware that Christ was watching. Her generous character counted.

We should notice in passing that a good motive does not mean that we enjoy doing a particular deed. Surely the slaves in Paul's time did not delight in treating their masters (often cruel) as they would treat Christ. God often asks us to do hard things, to suffer unjustly, and to endure suffering of every sort. The test of a motive is whether it is done for Christ, quite apart from whether the experience was pleasant or not.

Second, keep in mind that Christ takes our deeds, if done in His name, and makes them acceptable to the Father. Truth is, even when we serve with a motive that is as selfless as humanly possible, our deeds are still tainted with sin. We help a woman across a street, but often it is to make ourselves feel good because we all want to be needed. And perhaps that evening we can tell our family that we did our good deed for the day. We give money to the work of the church and secretly hope that the word will get out that we are among the generous.

One day a young woman abandoned her car and was walking along the street in obvious distress. I stopped and learned that her car had run out of gas. So I drove to a gas station, purchased a can filled with gas, and drove back to her car. As I was pouring gas into her car while standing in the ditch dressed in my business suit, the thought came to me, *I wish that all the people of Moody Church could see me now!*

Mixed motives.

How can these works become acceptable to God? Can we be rewarded for deeds done with motives that are not entirely loving, free of all self-interest? Yes, here again our Savior prepares us for the day when He will be our Judge. We are not to work for Christ as an employee for an employer; we are to work for Him as sons and daughters within a loving family. *Christ works in us and for us to please the Father!*

Christ takes our acts done with our good intentions and cleanses them so that they might be acceptable to God. Peter wrote, "You yourselves like living stones are being built up as a spiritual house, to be a holy priesthood, to offer spiritual sacrifices acceptable to God through Jesus Christ" (1 Peter 2:5). *Sacrifices acceptable through Christ!*

We've learned that good deeds done before our conversion are of no merit whatsoever; but the reason that good deeds after our conversion have merit is because they are presented to the Father through Christ! Because we are joined to Christ, we might say that He sees Christ as having done them!

Paul said that we should approve the things that are excellent "so that you may approve what is excellent, and so be pure and blameless for the day of Christ, filled with the fruit of righteousness that comes through Jesus Christ, to the glory and praise of God" (Philippians 1:10b–11). Through Jesus Christ our deeds of righteousness are "to the glory and praise of God." The Reformers were right: before our salvation our deeds have no merit whatever in God's sight. But they should also have stressed that after our conversion we can present ourselves to God, and this offering becomes "a living sacrifice, holy and acceptable to God, which is your spiritual worship" (Romans 12:1b).

God is especially pleased when He sees His Son in us. Thus after our conversion, our deeds should no longer originate in the flesh but in the work of the Spirit. Christ taught, "Abide in me, and I in you. As the branch cannot bear fruit by itself, unless it abides in the vine, neither can you, unless you abide in me. . . . for apart from me you can do nothing" (John 15:4–5). Obviously, apart from Christ we can do many things; but we can do nothing that will last.

Christ calls us to bear fruit that endures. Although fruit perishes quickly, there is a kind of fruit that will last forever. This is the fruit of the Spirit, the supernatural work of the Holy Spirit in our lives. *The works that are most acceptable are those done with the conviction that there is no merit in us but in Christ.*

The good deeds Christ will be looking for have common characteristics: a willingness to sacrifice, a joyous faith, and a commitment to persevere as did Moses. "And without faith it is impossible to please him, for whoever would draw near to God must believe that he exists and that he rewards those who seek him" (Hebrews 11:6). And, of course, at the root is a love for God, a willingness to serve, knowing that whatever the Father gives us is good for us. Yes, it is true that *God looks for the works that He Himself has wrought in us!*

Here are the deeds that are especially highlighted, the deeds that bring the promise of "great reward" (Hebrews 10:35).

WHAT CHRIST IS LOOKING FOR

The Joyful Acceptance of Injustice

Christ was straightforward about the reward connected with bearing insults for His sake. "Blessed are you when others revile you and persecute you and utter all kinds of evil against you falsely on my account. Rejoice and be glad, for your reward is great in heaven, for so they persecuted the prophets who were before you" (Matthew 5:11–12). If you are fired from a job because of your faith in Christ, if you are ostracized from the company perks, if you are bypassed in the pay scale because your convictions will not allow you to be dishonest—rejoice, for your reward is great in heaven!

A doctor friend of mine says that he is considered a troublemaker because he keeps calling on his hospital administration to embrace integrity. Even fellow Christians think he should not rock the boat because everyone is affected. But he is a Christian with clear convictions, and he cannot be satisfied until he has done what he can to get the hospital to own up to its procedures and practices.

The author of Hebrews warned his readers that if they did not suffer for Christ successfully, they would be losers. "Therefore do not throw away your confidence, which has a great reward" (10:35). The deep conviction that God was testing them in their distress would give them the courage to remain loyal even though their property was being seized and they were being ostracized for their faith. The knowledge of a "great reward" would give them the motivation they needed.

Peter wrote, "For this is a gracious thing, when, mindful of God, one endures sorrows while suffering unjustly" (1 Peter 2:19). Our cross is simply the trouble we wouldn't have if we were not Christians. Let us accept such trouble in the name of Christ and rejoice! God is watching.

Financial Generosity

Christ repeatedly spoke about money as being a test of our loyalties. He said, in fact, that if we cannot be entrusted with the mammon of unrighteousness, we should not think that we will be given more important spiritual responsibilities. He chided the Pharisees for their love of money and then said, "For that which is highly esteemed among men is detestable in the sight of God" (Luke 16:15 NASB).

Here is His familiar promise:

> Do not lay up for yourselves treasures on earth, where moth and rust destroy and where thieves break in and steal, but lay up for yourselves treasures in heaven, where neither moth nor rust destroys and where thieves do not break in and steal. For where your treasure is, there your heart will be also. (MATTHEW 6:19–21)

In our churches we are very careful not to reveal how much people give; gifts are strictly confidential. There are two reasons for this. One is that we might give in secret so as to be rewarded openly. The other is that we might not be tempted to treat the large donors with greater respect. But the real reason might be because we give so little we would be embarrassed if everyone knew how much we gave. But if that which is secret will be revealed, the day is coming when our checkbook will be carefully examined.

However, it would be a mistake to think that we will be judged solely on the basis of what we gave to the church, the poor, and missions. Let us never forget that all of our money belongs to God. This means that whatever we spend to live on, whatever we invest or inherit—we shall be accountable for all of it. Blessed is the child who looks into the face of his heavenly Father and asks for wisdom to use all his resources for the glory of God. (Since the subject of money was so frequently discussed by Christ, we shall consider investment strategies in the next chapter.)

Hospitality

Suppose Christ was scheduled to pay a visit to your church, and the pastor was looking for a home in which He could stay. Imagine the lineup of anxious Christians, all insisting that He come home with them!

Indeed someday Christ will invite people into His kingdom and say, "For I was hungry and you gave me food, I was thirsty and you gave me drink, I was a stranger and you welcomed me, I was naked and you clothed me, I was sick and you visited me, I was in prison and you came to me" (Matthew 25:35–36).

And when His people are startled because they do not remember having personally done this, Christ responds, "Truly I say to you, to the extent that you did it to one of these brothers of Mine, even the least of them, you did it to Me" (v. 40 NASB). We can sign up to have Christ visit us! We can take Him home with us any night of the week.

And what do we get in return? That depends, of course, on the attitude with which we exercised our hospitality. Christ describes the kindness that will not escape His notice.

> When you give a dinner or a banquet, do not invite your friends or your brothers or your relatives or rich neighbors, lest they also invite you in return and you be repaid. But when you give a feast, invite the poor, the crippled, the lame, the blind, and you will be blessed, because they cannot repay you. For you will be repaid at the resurrection of the just. (LUKE 14:12–14)

Christ did not shy away from calling rewards "repayments." If you want to please Christ, find the poor, the physically challenged, and the lonely and throw a feast for them. You will be "repaid" in the day of resurrection.

If you are tempted to envy a prophet because your own gifts are so small in comparison, you can receive a "prophet's reward."

> Whoever receives you receives me, and whoever receives me receives him who sent me. The one who receives a prophet because he is a prophet will receive a prophet's reward, and the one who receives a righteous person because he is a righteous person will receive a righteous person's reward. (MATTHEW 10:40–41)

Edwin Markham wrote a poem about waiting for an appointment to meet with Christ.

> *How the Great Guest Came*
> *Why is it, Lord, that your feet delay?*
> *Did you forget this was the day?*
> *Then soft in the silence a voice he heard,*
> *Lift up your heart for I kept my word.*
> *I was the beggar with bruised feet,*
> *I was the woman you gave to eat,*
> *I was the child on the homeless street.*

With a child standing beside Him, Christ said, "Whoever receives one such child in my name receives me" (Matthew 18:5).

The Spiritual Disciplines

The Jews had three spiritual disciplines they habitually practiced: the giving of alms, prayer, and fasting. Christ warned that these should not be exercised publicly to be seen of men. Indeed, those who do these things to look good "have their reward in full" (Matthew 6:5 NASB).

- "But when you give to the needy, do not let your left hand know what your right hand is doing, so that your giving may be in secret. And your Father who sees in secret will reward you" (vv. 3–4).
- "But when you pray, go into your room and shut the door and pray to your Father who is in secret. And your Father who sees in secret will reward you" (v. 6).
- "But when you fast, anoint your head and wash your face, that your fasting may not be seen by others but by your Father who is in secret. And your Father who sees in secret will reward you" (vv. 17–18).

Christ taught that it is possible to succeed in the eyes of men and fail in the eyes of God. If we serve to be seen of men, we will be rewarded by them. To quote Christ, we will "have [our] reward in full." We will not be rewarded twice. If we get all of our strokes in this life, we should expect no repayment in the life to come. *We are rewarded by the person whose praise we seek.*

In fact, when we are overlooked or taken for granted, and when the credit for what we do goes to someone else, we can rejoice, for God will give us a greater reward. Secret deeds often have purer motives than public ones. Blessed are those who have many secrets with God.

Of course, we will be judged not only by whether we practiced the disciplines of the Christian life. We will also be held accountable for the way in which we lived the whole of life. All of our time, talent, and treasure belongs to God.

Faithfulness in Our Vocation

The painful fact is that many people simply never find the right job/gift mix. Multitudes—perhaps the majority of the workforce—dislike what they are doing. But the need for money forces them into jobs that ignite boredom, frustration, and conflict. Many are underpaid.

Put yourself in a time machine and go back two thousand years and imagine that you are one of the 60 million slaves in the Roman Empire. You have no rights, no chance for a promotion, no court of appeals. To such, Paul wrote that they should serve their masters as they would serve Christ.

> Slaves, in all things obey those who are your masters on earth, not with external service, as those who merely please men, but with sincerity of heart, fearing the Lord. Whatever you do, do your work heartily, as for the Lord rather than for men, knowing that from the Lord you will receive the reward of the inheritance. It is the Lord Christ whom you serve. (COLOSSIANS 3:22–24 NASB)

Paul is not insensitive to their plight. He urges their masters to be fair, and he knew that the only way he could fight slavery in those days was by preaching the gospel. This would transform both slave and master so that there might be mutual respect and fairness. But even in the absence of such circumstances, Paul could exhort slaves to serve their masters as if serving Christ because they would be recompensed by Him. The Lord will make up for the wages they didn't receive and the mistreatment they endured—and then some!

In the world, greatness is determined by the number of people you rule; power is the name of the game. In the kingdom, greatness is determined by the number of people you serve. Humility is the badge of highest honor. Indeed, Christ Himself was exalted because He came not to be served, but to serve and give His life for us. "He humbled himself by becoming obedient to the point of death, even death on a cross.

Therefore God has highly exalted him" (Philippians 2:8–9, italics added).

Ironically, if you want to have the possibility of ruling at Christ's right hand, don't seek it by trying to find a lofty position and use it as a stepping-stone to something greater. Find the most lowly position, and perhaps God will grant you an exalted position. "Humble yourselves, therefore, under the mighty hand of God so that at the proper time he may exalt you" (1 Peter 5:6).

Blessed are those who change masters without changing jobs! If we visualize receiving our paychecks from Christ and not our employer, we will view our work very differently. And someday we will be generously compensated. God will not only judge you for how you taught your Sunday school class but for how you did your job on Monday morning.

Servanthood, as we shall learn in a future chapter, is the stepping-stone to greatness. Even better, servanthood *is* greatness.

Loving the Unlovable

Christ taught that there was a difference between divine love and human love. Human love depends upon the one who is loved. If you meet my needs, if I find you attractive, and if our personalities are compatible, I will love you. Understandably, human love changes. "You're not the woman I married!" a man shouts, giving his rationale for a divorce.

In contrast, divine love depends upon the lover; divine love says I can go on loving you even if you have stopped loving me. Divine love is based on a decision that continues even if the one who is loved changes. Divine love says, "You cannot make me stop loving you."

In this context, read Christ's words: "But I say to you

who hear, Love your enemies, do good to those who hate you, bless those who curse you, pray for those who abuse you" (Luke 6:27–28). This kind of love even loves enemies. And if we want to know whether such tough love will really be worth the cost, Christ continues, "But love your enemies, and do good, and lend, expecting nothing in return, and your reward will be great, and you will be sons of the Most High, for he is kind to the ungrateful and the evil" (v. 35). *Your reward will be great!*

So often we pray, "O God, make me godly." We want to be like God. Then God sends a difficult person into our life—perhaps a quarrelsome coworker—and we complain, insisting that He remove the "thorn" from us. But these trials are given to us that we might become "godly."

You have it from Christ Himself. "Your reward shall be great!"

Doctrinal Integrity

In a letter written by the apostle John to a church that evidently was known as "the chosen lady" (2 John 1 NASB), he warned the believers that there were many false teachers who could do a great deal of damage within the assembly. There were, he said, many deceivers, who denied that Jesus Christ has come in the flesh. They were, in effect, antichrists.

The believers were to watch out for the disastrous spiritual effects that might result from any compromise with their ideas. If they did not do so, they might lose some of their reward. "Watch yourselves, so that you may not lose what we have worked for, but may win a full reward" (v. 8). Notice that if they did fail, they might not lose their entire reward, but would lose their "full reward."

Certainly those who refuse to guard the doctrine of the

faith are liable to discipline and loss of reward. Sound doctrine, on the other hand, will merit a more complete reward in the day of judgment.

Investment in People

Only people span the gap between time and eternity. Paul writes: "For who is our hope or joy or crown of exultation? Is it not even you, in the presence of our Lord Jesus at His coming?" (1 Thessalonians 2:19 NASB). God's people are His most highly prized possession. To love those who are His, to invest in their spiritual well-being, is to attract special consideration. Exercising our gifts for the benefit of the body merits eternal reward.

Our investment in the lives of others varies in accordance with our gifts and opportunities. Some will sow, others water, still others reap; yet each shall be properly rewarded. These words, quoted before, deserve to be repeated:

> I planted, Apollos watered, but God gave the increase. So then neither he who plants is anything, nor he who waters, but God who gives the increase. Now he who plants and he who waters are one, and each one will receive his own reward according to his own labor.
> (1 CORINTHIANS 3:6–8 NKJV)

Please do not overlook the last line: "Each one will receive his own reward according to his own labor." There is a specific connection between the opportunities I accept and the rewards I receive.

Watching for Christ's Return

Christ has always insisted that wise servants look out for their master's arrival. He says:

> Stay dressed for action and keep your lamps burning, and be like men who are waiting for their master to come home from the wedding feast, so that they may open the door to him at once when he comes and knocks. Blessed are those servants whom the master finds awake when he comes. Truly, I say to you, he will dress himself for service and have them recline at table, and he will come and serve them. If he comes in the second watch, or in the third, and finds them awake, blessed are those servants! (LUKE 12:35–38)

We admire the apostle Paul for his endurance in preaching the gospel. We wish we had his revelations and opportunities. Yet we have the opportunity to be rewarded just as he was. When he was about to die, he looked back and could say: "I have fought the good fight, I have finished the race, I have kept the faith" (2 Timothy 4:7). He expected to receive "the crown of righteousness, which the Lord, the righteous judge, will award to me on that Day, and not only to me but also to all who have loved his appearing" (v. 8).

Whatever interpretation we give to the "crown of righteousness," we can have it too! To love the appearing of Christ is to receive a special welcome into heaven.

When soloist George Beverley Shea was asked what he would like to be when Christ returned, he said, "On pitch!" Let us all be ready to praise the Lamb when He returns.

Acceptance of Suffering

While speaking on the West Coast, I met a man whose wife had a rare, debilitating disease. He had to give her constant care, for she was confined to a wheelchair. Worse than the physical limitations, however, were her mental and emotional states of anger and continual discontent. If they went to church, she might appear pleasant, but on the way home she would berate him for everything from his own conversations with people to his driving. "I receive no thanks, no kind words, no sense of teamwork," he told me.

I was so moved by his story that I told him, "I don't expect to see you in heaven!" He was shocked, of course, but then I continued. "You will be so close to the throne, and I will be so far back, I will not see you!" And I meant every word. There are some people whom God calls to a special kind of suffering. Their faithfulness is of great reward.

When Christ returns, all of us would like to have something to present to Him. Peter wrote, "That the tested genuineness of your faith—more precious than gold that perishes though it is tested by fire—may be found to result in praise and glory and honor at the revelation of Jesus Christ" (1 Peter 1:7). Trials are given to us that we might be able to develop the faith that is precious to Christ. This faith, although a gift of God to us, nevertheless will be found to the praise and honor of Christ.

Of course, if I am faithful, I will have the same opportunity to be "close to the throne," as I put it. Furthermore, there are many ways to receive rewards. We've already listed more deeds than any one of us could consistently do. We will not be chided for the deeds we could not perform, though we undoubtedly will be shown what our lives could have been like had we lived them faithfully for Christ. We can rejoice: "For God is not unjust so as to overlook your work and the love that you have shown for his name in serving the saints, as you still do" (Hebrews 6:10).

We do not know everything we would like to know about rewards. We simply do not understand how Christ will balance our good deeds with those that are worthless. We must be content to know that Christ will be fair and generous. Whatever He does will be acceptable; no one will question His judgment. He will meticulously separate the perishable from the imperishable.

Upon hearing of the assassination of John and Betty Stamm in China in 1934, Will Houghton, former president of Moody Bible Institute, wrote these words:

> So this is life. This world with its pleasures, struggles and tears, a smile, a frown, a sigh, friendship so true and love of kin and neighbor? Sometimes it is hard to live—always to die!
>
> The world moves on so rapidly for the living; the forms of those who disappear are replaced, and each one dreams that he will be enduring. How soon that one becomes the missing face!
>
> Help me to know the value of these hours. Help me the folly of all waste to see. Help me to trust the Christ who bore my sorrows and thus to yield for life or death to Thee.

If we could catch a glimpse of heaven, we would strain to make the best use of the opportunities presented to us. Our lives, said James, are "a mist that appears for a little time and then vanishes" (4:14). There is much that awaits us on the other side.

And now we turn to the one matter Christ referred to repeatedly, a sensitive subject that gives us the potential of great failure or great reward.

Don't stop now.

CHAPTER 6

TAKING IT WITH YOU

You can "beat the system"!

Perhaps you heard of the employer who fired his branch manager for squandering money. The manager was humiliated and at a loss as to how he might earn a living. Physically, he was not strong enough to do hard labor and he was too filled with pride to beg for food. He did not know anyone who would give him a job that would be in keeping with his aptitudes and desires.

An idea struck him. If he got busy and made some friends, they might give him a job or at least a place to stay for the next few weeks. If he talked money, they would listen.

Before he cleaned out his desk he called some of his master's clients and made a proposal. He would renegotiate their contracts so that they did not have to pay the boss all they owed. For example, if they owed a hundred bushels of wheat, he cut the amount to fifty; the man who owed a barrel of oil now owed only a half-barrel. Needless to say, the patrons were grateful.

When his boss discovered this bit of wheeling and dealing he was angry, but he did have to commend his steward for shrewdness. If he had stolen the money, he could have been sent to prison; but he didn't steal, he just "gave it away." He was smart to use money to make friends so that after he was fired he would know some people who would do him a good turn.

Perhaps you recognize this story as the one Christ told to illustrate the wise use of money. He does not commend the morals of the man (He calls him an "unrighteous steward"), but He does commend him for his cleverness. Then He adds, "For the sons of this age are more shrewd in relation to their own kind than the sons of light. And I say to you, make friends for yourselves by means of the wealth of unrighteousness, so that when it fails, they will receive you into the eternal dwellings" (Luke 16:8–9 NASB).

This is not a chapter about giving, but *investing*. If we use money wisely, we can "beat the system." We can "take it with us" with handsome dividends. This chapter, perhaps more than any other, will give specific instruction on how to make sure that there will be a reward waiting for us in heaven. If you are a wise investor, listen carefully.

PRINCIPLES OF SOUND FINANCIAL MANAGEMENT

What we need is a philosophy of money, an opportunity to step back and look at it from God's point of view. When we are finished, we will never see wealth in the same way again. And we will discover that money can bridge the gap from this life to the next.

Here are five principles of sound financial management. The sooner we memorize them, the more productive we will be in this life and the greater our reward in the next.

Money Is Loaned, Not Owned

Thousands of Christians mismanage their money because they see it through a skewed lens. They think that the money put in the offering plate is God's, but the rest is theirs to spend as they please. And because of this misunderstanding, God is not free to bless them. The steward in Christ's parable owned nothing, but he was put in charge of everything. He knew that not a dime of what he managed belonged to him. He also knew that he was being watched and would have to give an account for what he did with all that was given.

Christ states flatly that money is not ours. "And if you have not been faithful in the use of that which is another's, who will give you that which is your own?" (Luke 16:12 NASB). Our money belongs to "another." Some of our wages are already garnished for federal and state taxes before we bring our check home. Bills have to be paid; creditors remind us that some of our money is theirs. Our money is "another's."

And even if we should save some of it, we might lose it in a stock market crash, and then it will surely become another's. And if money is not taken away from us, we will be taken away from it. It never was ours to keep. God loaned it to us, and He will receive it back.

The first step to receive God's blessing is to consciously recognize His ownership over all we possess. We must make Him Lord of our bank accounts, stocks, bonds, and mutual funds. Yes, our retirement accounts too. Then we have to pray for wisdom to manage all of this according to His principles and long-range intentions.

Yes, we might keep some of these savings, but we will always look at money differently once we realize that none of it is *owned;* it is only *loaned.* Accountability is now never far from our minds.

If you have never done so before, consciously transfer your money, real estate, and other assets into the hands of God. Trust Him to give you the wisdom to use these wisely and productively. A farmer whose crop was knocked down by hail said he felt bad until he remembered whose crop it really was. God, he realized, has a right to do what He wishes with that which belongs to Him.

Better it be in His hands than ours.

Money Should Be Transmuted into More Lasting Investments

During the Middle Ages alchemists experimented to find a chemical that would turn lead into gold. The intention was to transform common metals into something more valuable. In a different way, we do this all the time; we are always changing money into something else. This process is called *transmutation.*

For example, just yesterday one of our daughters needed a prescription filled. So I went to the bank, but I did not return home to give her money to eat; if so, she would have needed more than a prescription! I did take the money to the drug store and transmuted it into medicine; I also transmuted it into groceries and a newspaper. Transmutation means the changing across to something else.

If you are a smart investor, you will always be thinking of ways to transmute your money into more secure investments. When stocks are down, look for money market funds; when inflation is out of control, you might want some of your investments in precious metals. The wiser you are, the more carefully you will watch for secure returns. Christ taught that there were even better investments. We can transmute our funds to bridge the gap between earth and heaven. We can use our money to make friends who will welcome us into "eternal dwellings."

This can be done indirectly. The Christians at Philippi supported Paul in his missionary ventures, and now that he was imprisoned in Rome they sent a gift to help him. Paul wrote to thank them, but he does not say anything about what the gift meant to him, but rather what it meant to *them*. He writes, "Not that I desire your gifts; what I desire is that more be credited to your account" (Philippians 4:17 NIV). Giving does not help the recipient as much as it helps the giver himself, who is upping his tally in the accounts of heaven.

When we support missionaries who make converts, when we help in the lives of those who spread the gospel, we are hearing about something of ultimate value. But these values are obtained by starting on the lower level. Who pledged $1,000 for missions last year? Who decided to support that missionary couple that went to Haiti? Whoever did it learned the secret of taking something of lower value and transmuting it upward to something of higher value. That's wisdom.

There is a story told of a European princess, a fervent

Christian, who was burdened to start an orphanage for street children. She did not have any money of her own, so she told her husband she wanted to sell the jewels he had given her so that she could help the orphans.

Of course he was reluctant. "Don't you appreciate the jewels?" he would ask. "Of course," she would reply. "But there are homeless children we could help."

Eventually he gave in. She sold the jewels for many thousands of dollars and was able to build the orphanage. The children came and were fed and shown love. They memorized verses of Scripture and sang songs. One day the princess returned to her husband. "I found my jewels today!" she said through tears of joy. "I found my jewels, the bright happy eyes of the children who were rescued from the streets. I found my jewels!"

Smart woman! She beat the system!

All of our lives we are told that we "cannot take it with us." We are told we have to leave it all behind. Of course, we cannot take dollars and jewels with us, but if we transmute these into heavenly values, we can meet our money in another life. The princess found a way to get her jewels on the other side of eternity; she took them all the way to heaven. Forever.

Luther would commend this woman. He said, "I have held many things in my hands, and I have lost them all. But whatever I have placed in God's hands, that I still possess." If the value of an investment is determined by its security and rate of return, investing in the lives of those who will live forever brings the best dividends. God does not want us to give so that we become poorer; rather, we are to give so that we might become richer.

Giving to God's work is like investing in a mutual fund. You are contributing to a variety of ministries, each of which will have a high rate of return in new investments that jump the gap between time and eternity, between earth and heaven. "Lay up for yourselves treasures in heaven, where neither moth nor rust destroys and where thieves do not break in and steal" (Matthew 6:20).

Of course, we can also make such investments more directly. We can spend money to take our friends out to dinner and share the good news of the gospel with them. We can buy Bibles and books and distribute them in our community. We can welcome our neighbors into our homes.

We can also help the poor, befriend the unemployed, and take a cake to the widow across the street. If done for Christ, we will not lose our reward; it will be waiting for us in the heavenly kingdom.

Money Is a Test for Greater Privileges

Christ turns our view of money upside down.

He says, "He who is faithful in a very little thing is faithful also in much; and he who is unrighteous in a very little thing is unrighteous also in much. Therefore if you have not been faithful in the use of unrighteous wealth, who will entrust the true riches to you?" (Luke 16:10–11 NASB).

First of all He calls it "a very little thing." Now, if you know anything about the world, you know that money is a "very big thing"! Money is the lifeblood of business; it lies at the heart of "the deal." People lie for it, steal for it, scheme for it, and die for it.

A recent newspaper article titled "Not for Love but for Money" begins, "The romantic ideal of 'live now, pay later' is becoming increasingly dated in England." The report goes on to say that more people than ever now take financial security into account when sizing up a potential marriage partner.

"Romance is no longer enough," the report says. "People want to marry someone with some money."

For us, money is not "a little thing."

Second, Christ calls it "unrighteous mammon." We might paraphrase it "filthy lucre." Not very complimentary, but woefully true. Just look at what people have done for money!

Haddon Robinson, whose message on this parable has impacted my own thinking, points out that Christ does not play word games like we do. We often hear it said, "There is nothing wrong with money. It's just the *love* of it that's wrong!" But, notes Robinson, we use this cliché as an excuse, a convenient cover for our covetousness. We tell ourselves we really don't *love* money. Mind you, we date it, snuggle up to it, fantasize about it, scheme about it, hoard it—but we don't *love* it!

Christ does not let us by with neat rationalizations. He calls money what it is because He knows what people have done to get it. He knows the businessman who has cheated, the prostitute who has sold her body, the family that has feuded over settling an estate. He knows how covetous we are and that "covetousness . . . is idolatry" (Colossians 3:5).

Let's not miss Christ's three contrasts.

- If we are unfaithful in a "very little thing," how can God entrust us with something greater in the world to come?
- If we fail in the responsible use of the "the mammon of unrighteousness," how can we be counted worthy of the greater riches in the kingdom?
- If we misuse "that which is another's," how can the Lord entrust us with the inheritance He desires to give us?

Money is a test to see whether we are worthy to rule with Christ, able to assume full responsibilities in His reign and glory. Those who have the wisdom to transmute their funds into more permanent treasures are wise indeed. Consider: many of us have money deducted from our paychecks to help fatten our retirement accounts. This might be prudent, considering the fact that we will probably live well beyond the days of our earning power. But think how irresponsible we are if we do not similarly have money set aside regularly to specifically advance the kingdom so that we might have many friends who welcome us into "eternal dwellings"!

I've known Christians who put a twenty-dollar bill in the offering plate if they just happen to have that much in their wallet. They do not have a giving plan that resembles their saving plan. They do not give as much as they can and then wish they could give more. They are unfaithful, and their status in heaven will reflect it.

If we cannot be trusted to wisely administer God's money on earth, what makes us think we will be capable stewards in heaven? Greed here on earth means we forfeit the right to enter into all that could be ours in heaven. And what we don't use, we will lose, just as the unfaithful servant discovered when the king returned.

Money is our trust. God is testing us to see whether we are prepared for the larger responsibilities that await the faithful.

Money Must Be Our Servant
or It Will Be Our Master

Christ ended this parable by saying, "No servant can serve two masters, for either he will hate the one and love the other, or he will be devoted to the one and despise the other. You cannot serve God and money" (Luke 16:13).

We cannot be a full-time slave to two masters. If we serve God with our whole heart, the seductive love of money will be squeezed out. We must fight to make money our servant, asking God to root its power out of our lives. Even then, it will seek to grow again, for money is seductive and deceitful. We must agree with John Wesley, who said, "I value all things only by the price they shall gain in eternity."

Our hearts cannot have two ultimate loyalties.

Money Must Be Transmuted
for Heaven or Lost Forever

The Pharisees to whom Christ told this parable were livid. They did not buy into this "use your money for people who will be in heaven" message. We read, "The Pharisees, who were lovers of money, heard all these things, and they ridiculed him" (Luke 16:14). No lover of money likes what Christ had to say.

In order to convince them that money would not help them once they died, Christ told a story about a rich man who was "clothed in purple and fine linen and who feasted sumptuously every day. And at his gate was laid a poor man named Lazarus, covered with sores" (vv. 19–20). Incredibly, in the life to come their fortunes were reversed! Lazarus was carried by angels into Abraham's bosom; the rich man was delivered to hades, where he languished in darkness, isolation, and torment. Lazarus, who endured so much ill treatment when he was living, was now comforted; the rich man was in agony.

Christ's point is not that we are saved by being poor. He means to teach us that riches will not help us when we die. We cannot use them to hire an attorney to plead our case; we cannot use them to build ourselves a home or purchase some creature comforts. To the Pharisees who loved money, Christ was saying, "Riches are deceptive! They cannot provide what you really need!" Only those who consciously transfer their funds to heaven understand true values.

THE DAY YOUR DOLLARS DIE

Germany lay in ruins.

Millions of refugees wandered the streets in German cities amid the rubble of bombed-out buildings and disheveled streets. Years would be necessary to rebuild. The memory of Adolf Hitler would never be forgotten.

Willard Cantelon, in his book *The Day the Dollar Dies*, recounts the story of a little German mother who wanted to assist in the building of a Bible school on the outskirts of the destroyed city of Frankfurt. She held her money with pride and tenderness, as though it was a part of her very life. She had earned this money with hard work and had constantly guarded it in the war's destructive years. Now "she was investing it in a worthy cause and beamed with pride as she offered her contribution."

Cantelon continues, "How could I tell her she had held this money too long? Why did it fall to my lot to shock this sensitive soul with the news that her money was virtually worthless? Why had she not read the morning paper, or heard the announcement that the new government in Bonn had canceled this currency?"[1]

That Sunday in June of 1948, a staggering number of Germans committed suicide. Millions lost their savings because the mark had been canceled by their government. If only they had exchanged their money for something that would survive the economic collapse!

If this dear lady—bless her—had brought her money sooner, those marks could have helped pay for the renovation of the facilities or the tuition of students. Too bad that she had to hear those disappointing words, "Madam, I'm awfully sorry, but I cannot accept your money."

Someday, every dollar, every piece of gold, and every jewel will be devalued, wiped out forever. Peter wrote: "But the day of the Lord will come like a thief, in which the heavens will pass away with a roar and the elements will be destroyed with intense heat, and the earth and its works will be burned up" (2 Peter 3:10 NASB).

So much for Wall Street. Goodbye to stocks, bonds, property, and gold. Goodbye to houses, condos, and cars. The wise investor will put his money in a place that will bring the greatest dividends for the longest time. We cannot take dollars and Krugerrands with us unless we transmute them into something that will bridge the gap between earth and heaven.

On a wall in a New York rescue mission there are these lines:

> *Angels from their realms on High*
> *Look down on us with wondrous eye*
> *That where we are but passing guests*
> *We build such strong and solid nests*
> *But where we hope to dwell for aye*
> *We scarce take heed one stone to lay.*

The stones we lay on the other side will help determine whether we are worthy to reign in the kingdom. If we are faithful in "the little thing," we will be faithful over the true riches. We will join those who reign over greater treasures.

The wise take it with them.

CHAPTER 7

RUN TO WIN

There is a story about a frustrated basketball coach, Cotton Fitzsimmons, who hit on an idea to motivate his team. Before the game he gave them a speech that centered around the word *pretend*. "Gentlemen, when you go out there tonight, instead of remembering that we are in last place, pretend we are in first place; instead of being in a losing streak, pretend we are in a winning streak; instead of this being a regular game, pretend this is a playoff game!"

With that, the team went onto the basketball court and were soundly beaten by the Boston Celtics. Coach Fitzsimmons was upset about the loss. But one of the players slapped him on the back and said, "Cheer up, Coach! *Pretend* we won!"

Many of us appear to be winning in the race of life, but perhaps it is all "pretend." Standing before Christ we will soon see the difference between an actual victory and wishful thinking. We will see what it took to win and what it took to lose. We'll discover that we were playing for keeps.

Paul loved to use athletic contests as an analogy for living the Christian life. The famous Greek marathon and the Isthmian Games in Corinth were a ready illustration of how to run the race that really counts. We are running the race, Paul taught, and we are running to win.

> Do you not know that in a race all the runners run, but only one receives the prize? So run that you may obtain it. Every athlete exercises self-control in all things. They do it to receive a perishable wreath, but we an imperishable. So I do not run aimlessly; I do not box as one beating the air. But I discipline my body and keep it under control, lest after preaching to others I myself should be disqualified. (1 CORINTHIANS 9:24–27)

Let's not miss Paul's point: *Whatever makes a winning athlete will make a winning Christian.* If we were as committed in our walk with God as we are to golf or bowling, we will do well in the Christian life. We can take what we learn in our tennis lessons and apply it to Christian living. Think of the energy, time, and money spent on sports. If we would transfer such resources to the race that really counts, we would all be winners.

Society does not develop saints. There is nothing in our culture that will encourage us to have the stamina and encouragement to become winners for Christ. Indeed, we shall have to buck the world at every turn of the road; we shall have to rely on God and His people to help us develop the disciplines that lead to godliness.

Let's introduce the analogy.

In Greece you had to be a citizen in order to compete in the games. Of course, all citizens were not in the races, but if you were eligible, you had to give proof of citizenship. Just so, you have to be a citizen of heaven in order to qualify for the race that Paul speaks about.

However, there is this difference: *all* citizens of heaven are enrolled in this race. This is not optional; there are no other events offered during this time frame. You do not run this race to get to heaven; you run this race in order to receive the prize. This race began on the day you accepted Christ as your Savior.

Second, this is one race in which everyone has the potential of winning, for we are not competing with others, but with ourselves. We will be judged individually by God. To be determined is the question of what we did with what God gave us. Thus we all have our own personal finish line, our own personal coach, and our own personal final judgment.

RULES OF THE RACE

Some people don't compete in sports because they fear failure. The humiliation of coming in last is just too much for those who are sensitive to public opinion. But fearful or not, this is one race we run every day. We are best served by shirking our fears and running as best we can. Yes, this is one race you and I can win.

What are those rules that make great athletes and thus make "great" Christians? Each of us can translate them into daily living.

Discipline

When Paul speaks of those who compete in the games he uses the Greek word *agōnizomai*, from which we get our word *agonize*. "Everyone who *agonizes* in the games ..." You and I are simply unable to grasp the hours of agony that go into athletic conditioning.

In August drive past a football field and watch the young athletes sweating under the hot sun. Clad in heavy clothes, padding, and a helmet, their faces grimace with distress and even pain. If they did this because their lives were threatened we might understand. What is difficult for some of us to grasp is that they do this voluntarily. All for a trophy that will be kept in a glass case and soon be forgotten in this life, and most assuredly not remembered in the next. They voluntarily want to play, and they will torture themselves in order to win.

Athletes must give up the bad and the good and strive for only the best. They must say no to parties and late nights. They cannot have the luxury of any personal enjoyment that conflicts with their ability to concentrate and to practice. Every distraction must be eschewed. I'm told that Mike Singletary of the Chicago Bears would work out with his team, then go home and do more exercises. Then, late at night when the house was quiet, he would watch videos of opposing teams to see how he might win against them.

Translate that into the disciplines of living the Christian life. Imagine the spurt of growth we would enjoy if we were to memorize Scripture, pray, and study the opposition with the same intensity as athletes attack their game. Just think of what would happen if we were to hone our spiritual sensitivities, our spiritual appetites, and our spiritual muscles. We could take on the world.

Samson is a good example of someone who didn't discipline his body. He apparently broke his Nazirite vow when he touched the dead carcass and ate the honey that was hidden in it. He played with temptation, and eventually it ensnared him. Far from bringing his body into subjection, he followed its desires wherever they led him.

We've all met people who are gifted and even love God, but they will accomplish only a fraction of what they might do for God. The reason is that they are satisfied with too little. They are in the race, but they don't want to pay the price of winning.

There are many ways to fail in the Christian life. But all of them begin with lack of discipline, a conscious decision to take the easy route. Paul says, "I discipline my body and bring it under control." The lie is that the body cannot be disciplined, for indeed it can, especially with the help of the Holy Spirit, who gives us self-control.

I'm not asking you to add to your busy and cluttered life, but rather to substitute the spiritual disciplines in favor of the priorities you have adopted. If you had to be on dialysis every day because of kidney malfunction, you would find the time to do it. We must approach our walk with God with the same single-minded determination. Paul says, "This one thing I do!" not "These forty things I dabble in."

If you struggle with discipline, begin with this:

- Spend twenty minutes in prayer and meditation every morning before 9:00.
- Read a chapter of a good Christian book each day.
- Join a group of believers (Bible study class, prayer group, etc.) for fellowship and accountability.
- Learn to share your faith, and take the opportunities that God brings along your path.

Discipline itself does not produce godliness. We are not made spiritual by being "under the law," depending on our own strength to win God's approval. Rather, the purpose of these disciplines is *that we might learn to draw our strength from Christ.*

Direction

Two different sports help us understand what is needed to win an athletic contest: running and boxing. "So I do not run aimlessly; I do not box as one beating the air" (1 Corinthians 9:26). Imagine an official firing the gun to start the 100-meter dash and the runners all heading in different directions! A sun lover runs toward the west, another fond of mountains runs toward the east, and a third heads toward the sea. Each would be expending maximum energy, but none would win the race. Only those headed toward the finish line would qualify for the prize.

Or, says Paul, consider a boxer. If he throws punches that never hit his opponent, he is wasting his energy. If the opponent takes no hits, it matters not how fast the swing or how powerful the punch. Paul would have none of this for himself; he ran toward the goal, and he boxed so as to make every blow count.

Elsewhere, he returned to the need to keep one's eyes on the goal, to keep one's eyes fastened on Christ.

> Not that I have already obtained this or am already perfect, but I press on to make it my own, because Christ Jesus has made me his own. . . . I press on toward the goal for the prize of the upward call of God in Christ Jesus. (PHILIPPIANS 3:12–14)

Paul says he *strains* toward the goal, *grasping* for what lies ahead. No wasted energy; no tangents and detours. He will win because he keeps the finish line clearly in mind. In fact, the goal is his consuming passion.

Growing up on a farm, I knew how important it was to plow a straight furrow, especially when beginning a new field. To do so, my father would choose an object in the distance and drive the tractor toward it, keeping his eyes on the "goal." There is a story, perhaps true, of a farmer who chose his target and drove carefully toward it, but when looking back discovered that the furrow curved behind him. The story goes that he had actually fastened his eyes on a cow in the distance, and as she walked around the pasture he had followed her movements!

The goal you choose will determine how straight a line your life leaves behind. Many a man has left a crooked furrow because he chose a temporal target. "I want to be a millionaire by the time I'm thirty!" The man who chose that goal lived to see it fulfilled, but he was also divorced by the age of twenty-six!

Moses left an enduring legacy because he chose an enduring goal.

> By faith Moses, when he was grown up, refused to be called the son of Pharaoh's daughter, choosing rather to be mistreated with the people of God than to enjoy the fleeting pleasures of sin. He considered the reproach of Christ greater wealth than the treasures of Egypt, for he was looking to the reward. (HEBREWS 11:24–26)

Looking toward the reward! He had a clear view that reached well beyond Egypt and the wilderness of Sinai. He saw the eternal reward and decided to go for it. Choosing this course was more difficult than herding sheep in the desert, but it was worth it. He did not confuse the invisible with the imaginary; he knew that heaven was more real than earth could ever be. He could see more than his contemporaries.

Our best example, however, is Christ Himself. "Fixing our eyes on Jesus, the author and perfecter of faith, who for the joy set before Him endured the cross, despising the shame, and has sat down at the right hand of the throne of God" (Hebrews 12:2 NASB). He too saw beyond this life into the next. He was motivated by the prize of sitting at the right hand of God the Father. Focus is everything. Every one of us should be able to state our goals, our most fervent ambitions. We must strive toward that which will endure.

While bobbing in a boat in Lake Michigan, I became nauseated until my friend encouraged me to choose a building on the shore and keep my eyes fixed on it. I chose the Sears Tower and discovered in a few moments that I felt better. He explained that the motion of a boat confuses our balance system if we look at the very object that is causing our movement. But we can handle the ups and downs if our eyes have a fixed object that is unmoved by our own vacillations.

We all have our days when we must say, "Today I will remember the goal; I will focus on Christ no matter what storm might come my way!"

Determination

We've already referred to the passage in the book of Hebrews that tells us how to run the race. There we are given the rule book on how to run successfully. "Therefore, since we are surrounded by so great a cloud of witnesses, let us also lay aside every weight, and sin which clings so closely, and let us run with endurance the race that is set before us" (Hebrews 12:1).

You've heard Bible teachers say that this "cloud of witnesses" is a reference to those who have gone to heaven and are now watching us here on earth. But, in context, it is clear that the witnesses are the heroes of Hebrews 11, and *we are motivated, not because they see us, but because we see them!*

Specifically, we look back to men like Abraham, Joseph, and Moses and conclude that if they could run the race successfully, so can we. We learn from them that endurance is always possible if we remember where we are headed. We are to glance at these heroes and gaze on Jesus.

What are the rules of the race?

First, we must *keep our weight down.* We are to "lay aside every weight." Some people have to join a spiritual Weight Watchers group. There are some things that might not be sins, but weights, those habits and actions that take time and energy from that which is better.

Second, we are to *keep our feet free.* We must be free from the sin that does so easily "entangle" us. Sin tangles our feet, makes us stumble, and eventually will cause us to lose the race. Just think of the many people who began with a small weight or sin and ended up wounded on the sideline of the racetrack. Those of us who are still in the race have an obligation to help those who have stumbled so that they too can cross the finish line.

In the 1992 Olympics, Derek Redmond of Great Britain popped his hamstring in the 400-meter semifinal heat. He limped and hobbled around half the Olympic Stadium track. The sight of his son's distress was too much for Jim Redmond, who had been sitting near the top row of the stadium packed with 65,000 people. He rushed down flights of stairs and blew past security people, who challenged his lack of credentials to be on the track.

"I wasn't interested in what they were saying," he said of the security guards. He caught up to his son on the top of the final curve, some 120 meters from the finish. He put one arm around Derek's waist, another around his left wrist. Then they did a three-legged hobble toward the finish line.

Derek had no chance of winning a medal, but his determination earned him the respect of the crowd. His father said, "He worked eight years for this. I wasn't going to let him not finish." Whether or not his father knew it, he was acting biblically.

"Therefore, strengthen the hands that are weak and the knees that are feeble, and make straight paths for your feet, so that the limb which is lame may not be put out of joint, but rather be healed" (Hebrews 12:12–13 NASB). Some people have to be helped across the finish line. Some have stumbled over their own feet; others have been tripped by family members and so-called friends. We must help those who have fallen into the snares of the devil; we must lift up the fallen, bind up their wounds, and help them on their journey toward home.

Determination will do it.

MAKING IT TO THE FINISH LINE

Every runner knows the danger of distractions and potholes. We not only have to know how to win, but we must also know why many people have lost the race.

Please remember that chapter divisions in the Bible are not inspired! Paul does not conclude his thoughts about winning the race at the end of 1 Corinthians 9, but continues his thought into the next chapter: "For I do not want you to be unaware, brothers" (10:1). That little word *for* is a bridge that continues Paul's warning.

In chapter 9 Paul says, "But I discipline my body and keep it under control, lest after preaching to others I myself should be disqualified" (v. 27). He feared that even he might lose the race!

When he begins chapter 10 he uses the Israelites in the desert as an illustration of those who lost the race. These were people redeemed out of Egypt; they had crossed the Red Sea and had experienced the daily provision of God, and yet they fell short of the prize.

First, Paul speaks of the blessings they enjoyed. They were given all they needed to run successfully.

> For I do not want you to be unaware, brothers, that our fathers were all under the cloud, and all passed through the sea, and all were baptized into Moses in the cloud and in the sea, and all ate the same spiritual food, and all drank the same spiritual drink. For they drank from the spiritual Rock that followed them, and the Rock was Christ. (vv. 1–4)

Next, Paul describes their failure in the face of innumerable blessings. "Nevertheless, with most of them God was not pleased" (v. 5). Then follows a list of their sins: idolatry, immorality, and ingratitude. Many of these people were saved in the Old Testament sense of that word: they will be in heaven. Nevertheless, they were displeasing to God and will not win the prize.

The contrast is between their many undeserved blessings and their failures. They began the race with all the resources for the journey, yet they stumbled badly, far from the finish line. Not only did they not make it into Canaan, they never even lived successfully in the desert, where God supplied all of their needs.

The same sins beset us today. Our only hope of winning is to repent; indeed, our lives should be lived with an attitude of repentance. Ask the Holy Spirit to show you the sins that might keep you from finishing well. If Paul feared that he might be disqualified, you and I are most assuredly vulnerable.

"Say it ain't so, Ben."

That was how the venerable Canadian Broadcasting Corporation led its national radio news on Monday, September 27, 1988. Their national hero, Ben Johnson, had just tested positive for anabolic steroids and was stripped of the gold medal he had just won for breaking the record in the Olympic 100-meter race. Even as members of the Canadian Parliament were in the middle of flowery tributes to the "fastest man in the world," reports began to trickle in that Johnson had been disqualified. What made the embarrassment more acute was the fact that Johnson had just been extolled as a model "Say No to Drugs" athlete for Canadian youth.

Johnson learned that you can't win without obeying the rules. No matter how wonderfully we start, it is crossing the finish line well that counts.

We look back and say, "Abraham won; David won; Joseph won; so did a host of people who did not see deliverance but trusted God anyway." We can do the same! But let us always remember what it cost them.

Nothing fades as quickly as flowers. In the hot sunlight they last but a few hours. It was for such a wreath that the athletes competed in ancient Greece. Paul called it a "corruptible crown."

In contrast, there is an incorruptible crown given to those who serve Christ. It is guaranteed to last forever. We must covet the "prize of the high calling of God in Christ Jesus." Paul was not embarrassed to say that he desired to win the crown; he did not think it unspiritual to seek for the approval of Christ and the honor associated with it.

On a businessman's desk was this sign:

In 20 years what will you wish you had done today?
Do it now!

Do you want to win the race? Whatever it takes, just "Do it *now!*"

CHAPTER 8

STANDING IN LINE TO RECEIVE YOUR REWARD

L en was in the hospital, dying of cancer, when I had the privilege of explaining the gospel to him and he believed on Christ. During his remaining three weeks, he prayed, read his Bible, and was a blessing to those who visited him. He was not afraid to die but regretted that he had waited so long to become a born-again Christian.

What chance does he have to be rewarded by Christ since his works were so few and, for the most part, his life such a waste? Someone has said that a deathbed conversion is "burning a candle in the service of the devil and blowing the smoke in the eyes of God."

The thief on the cross had no opportunity to do good works. Perhaps he died giving praise to the One who had just promised him eternal life. That was something, but compared to a life of service, not much. Does God have a pay scale in heaven like we find in an employee handbook? Are we rewarded according to the number of days, hours, or years we serve? What happens to Christian young people killed in a car accident, or to infants who have not had the chance of doing even one good work?

Christ told a parable that has often been misinterpreted, but I believe it provides the clue to the questions we have just posed. The story comes to grips with the fairness and generosity of God and also the matter of our attitude in service. It ends with the surprise that "the last will be first, and the first last" (Matthew 20:16).

Christ had just confronted a young rich man who was not willing to admit that he had a problem with being covetous; so Christ asked him to sell everything he had and give the money to the poor so that he would have treasure in heaven. But when the young man heard this statement, he went away grieved, "for he had great possessions" (Matthew 19:22).

Christ later explained to the disciples that it was very hard for a rich man to enter the kingdom; indeed, "it is easier for a camel to go through the eye of a needle than for a rich person to enter the kingdom of God" (v. 24). Peter, bless him, thinking about what it cost the disciples to follow Christ, asked, "See, we have left everything and followed you. What then will we have?" (v. 27). Probably we would have had the same question on our minds but not the nerve to ask, "What's in it for me?"

We are the ones who are tempted to think that any consideration of rewards is self-centered. But Christ did not chide Peter for his question. After all, Christ Himself was motivated "for the joy that was set before him" (Hebrews 12:2). Just as pleasing the Father entailed a reward, even so when we in turn please Christ we are promised a reward. It is not wrong for us to strive to be thought worthy of His approval.

Christ responds to Peter's question with a lofty promise.

> Truly, I say to you, in the new world, when the Son of Man will sit on his glorious throne, you who have followed me will also sit on twelve thrones, judging the twelve tribes of Israel. And everyone who has left houses or brothers or sisters or father or mother or children or lands, for my name's sake, will receive a hundredfold and will inherit eternal life. But many who are first will be last, and the last first. (MATTHEW 19:28–30)

What a return on an investment! Mark quotes Christ as saying that such a person will receive "a hundredfold now in this time, houses and brothers and sisters and mothers and children and lands, with persecutions, and in the age to come eternal life" (10:30). Obviously, we cannot take this literally, since no one would want a hundred brothers, sisters, and mothers! Christ's point is simply that the rewards both in this life and the life to come will be out of proportion to the cost of discipleship. How would you like to put your money in a bank with a guaranteed interest of 10,000 percent!

Samuel Zwemer, famous missionary to the Muslims, lost two daughters, ages four and seven, within eight days of each other. The temperature soared regularly to 107 degrees in the coolest part of the verandah. His work was largely fruitless and fraught with great setbacks for him and his wife. Yet fifty years later, looking back on this period, he wrote, "The sheer joy of it all comes back. Gladly would I do it all over again."[1]

Many missionaries who have left houses, lands, and families bear witness to the fact that the joy of serving Christ makes up for the sacrifice. Piper writes: "If you give up a mother's nearby affection and concern, you get back one hundred times the affection and concern from the ever-present Christ. . . . If you give up the sense of at-homeness you had in your house, you get back one hundred times the comfort and security of knowing that your Lord owns every house and land and stream and tree on earth."[2]

We are asked to deny ourselves of the lesser good for the greater good. Paul was willing to say that everything was garbage in comparison to knowing Christ. And for such a commitment there is also an eternal reward. Someone has said that *the remuneration will be much greater than the renunciation.*

CHRIST'S STORY

In Israel the grape harvest ripens near the end of September, and after that the rains begin to fall. There is only a short window of time, perhaps two weeks, when the grapes can be harvested. Understandably, vineyard owners often find extra help to harvest their produce quickly. An owner can go to the marketplace and find workers willing to be paid at the end of each day. Each hopes he will be hired.

"For the kingdom of heaven is like a master of a house who went out early in the morning to hire laborers for his vineyard. After agreeing with the laborers for a denarius a day, he sent them into his vineyard" (Matthew 20:1–2).

The owner went out at 6:00 a.m. and found a group of hired hands. After some negotiations, he hired them for the standard rate: a denarius per worker per day. Off they went into the fields, doing enough work to satisfy the demands of the contract.

But there was more work to be done. So the owner went out at nine o'clock, at noon, and even at five o'clock to hire others so that the harvest would be in by sundown. He hired as many as he needed to finish the job by the end of the day, at 6:00 P.M.

When the task was finished, he asked his foreman to line up the laborers to be paid. To the astonishment of everyone, the owner requested that those who came last would be paid first. "And when those hired about the eleventh hour [five in the afternoon] came, each of them received a denarius" (v. 9).

Imagine! They worked one hour and received pay for the whole day! As they left they flashed the denarius they had been paid and word spread down the line about the generosity of the vineyard owner. The last-hired workers thrilled at the prospect of having a good supper with some money to spare. This was a man for whom they would gladly work again!

Of course, the early birds who were standing in line could hardly wait to get their wages. They did a mental calculation: If the pay is one denarius per hour, then they should receive twelve denarii. And if not twelve, they would be satisfied with ten.

They were unprepared for the disappointment that awaited them. Word spread that those who came at three o'clock in the afternoon also received a denarius; similarly, those who had arrived at noon and even at nine o'clock received but a single denarius! And now the early birds were next in line. "Now when those hired first came, they thought they would receive more, but each of them also received a denarius" (v. 10).

Unfair!

"And on receiving it they grumbled at the master of the house, saying, 'These last worked only one hour, and you have made them equal to us who have borne the burden of the day and the scorching heat'" (vv. 11–12). If they had known this was going to happen, they also would have come at 5:00 P.M. Why not do as little as you must to get what others are getting? If they were living in our day, they would have complained to the labor relations board.

But the owner had a ready reply. "'Friend, I am doing you no wrong. Did you not agree with me for a denarius? Take what belongs to you and go. I choose to give to this last worker as I give to you. Am I not allowed to do what I choose with what belongs to me? Or do you begrudge my generosity?' So the last will be first, and the first last" (vv. 13–16).

So much for that.

THE INTERPRETATION

How shall we interpret this story?

Some have thought that the denarius represents salvation. Thus, whether one is saved early in life or later, one still receives the same gift. The man who believes on Christ on his deathbed receives the same eternal life as the person who has served God for many years.

But there are serious problems with this understanding of the story. Thankfully, we do not have to work to enter the vineyard, because none of us would be qualified. This is a parable about payment for work, not about salvation by grace.

Others have suggested that this parable teaches that it is not the length of time you work, but how *hard* you work. Those who came early took long breaks, chatted while they picked the grapes, and took a three-hour lunch. So those who came at 5:00 did just as much as those who entered the vineyard at sunrise.

But we have no evidence that those who came later were better workers, while the early ones loafed. Indeed, when the early birds complained, "We have borne the burden and the scorching heat of the day," the owner did not dispute their claim.

A third interpretation says that everyone will receive the same reward. Whether you enter the vineyard as a faithful worker or a self-centered opportunist, you will in the end be rewarded the same. So the judgment seat of Christ involves nothing more than having us line up and receive our denarius.

But this cannot be Christ's meaning. Indeed, the very context of the story proves otherwise! Christ has just assured Peter and the other disciples that they would be generously rewarded because they had left all to follow Him. They would rule over the twelve tribes of Israel in the kingdom.

And, if we should envy these disciples, we are also promised that we can receive a reward if we are willing to leave father and mother and carry our cross. Whatever the reward might be, Christ said it would be much greater than whatever we give up. Clearly, everyone does not receive the same reward. Why would so many passages in the New Testament speak of rewards if we all will be equally honored when we stand before Christ?

Perhaps there is a better interpretation.

Remember that the Jews received the first invitation to the kingdom. Back in Genesis God promised Abraham that he would be great and through him all the nations of the earth would be blessed. This began a series of covenants and promises that would culminate in the coming of Christ and the eventual establishment of the kingdom. Now the Jews resented the Gentiles, who were invited by Christ into the vineyard. These newcomers were happy for the privilege and were being blessed by God.

When Jesus was criticized for befriending sinners, He told the familiar story of the prodigal son who went into the far country and squandered his living. When he returned home, the elder brother resented the generosity of the father toward his wayward sibling. After all, he was the hard worker who kept the farm going. And now the father was rewarding this scoundrel for just coming home!

The elder brother had taken his father for granted. He worked on the farm, not because he loved the father, but because of what he could get out of him. He thought that rewards should be doled out according to a payroll time chart. So much money for so many hours. And now his wayward brother comes home and the father showers him with irrational attention and joy. That was too much for the boy who had stayed home and did all the hard work on the farm.

That, I believe, is the attitude of those who came to the vineyard at 6:00 a.m. We read, "When he had *agreed* with the laborers for a denarius for the day, he sent them into his vineyard" (v. 2 NASB, italics added). They negotiated for all they could get. The others who came later served without an agreement. The vineyard owner assured them, "You go into the vineyard too, and whatever is right I will give you," and they trusted him (v. 4). It is not just a matter of how long you serve but the *attitude* with which you serve that counts. What is more, for those who serve well, the owner pays beyond their wildest dreams.

THE LESSONS TO BE LEARNED

There are several lessons that emerge from the parable, and in uncovering them we are led to the heart of what Christ attempted to communicate.

We Should Serve in Faith, Without a Contract

Haddon Robinson says that one day his son came in from the hot Texas sun and exclaimed, "Dad, I've mowed the lawn!" which, of course, is another way of saying, "Pay me!"

His father asked, "How much do you think your work is worth?" The boy refused to answer.

When pressed, he continued to evade the question, and his father insisted, "Why don't you name your price?"

To which the boy replied, "I know that if you make the decision you will give me more than I would ever ask!"

Those who came early to the vineyard named their price; the others did not. We can imagine the tone of the negotiations at sunrise. They wanted to know exactly what was in it for them. They would not set foot in the vineyard without knowing in advance what they would get in return.

The others were satisfied with the words of the vineyard owner, "Whatever is right I will give you." They felt honored to be asked to serve, and whatever the owner paid them they believed would be sufficient. They gave him the freedom to make the choice.

I've heard Christians say, "I promised God that if He gave me a better job, I would begin to tithe . . ." Or, "If God doesn't call me to Africa, I will get a good job and support ten missionaries . . ." Such bargains tie God's hands, and He cannot be generous with us. We must not try to make a deal with the Almighty; we should simply serve Him to the best of our ability and let Him worry about the results. We must seek His will and trust Him to do right by us.

We must never think we can make God obligated to us. Let us remember that God owes us nothing but eternal punishment. God has chosen to reward us, not because He owes us anything, but because He is generous. To *insist* that we receive some compensation is to miss the whole point of our Father-son relationship.

When we make a bargain with God, stipulating that He do business on our terms, we lose. He will be more gracious when we realize that He alone has the right to make the choice about our rewards. He invites us to rejoice in His promise that we will be rewarded, but He must determine what that reward will be. With His decision we shall be satisfied.

We Should Serve in Submission, Not Envy

Those early birds eyed the latecomers, envying the generous pay they had received. They resented the fact that the owner had given these loafers more money than they deserved. The vineyard owner responded, "Am I not allowed to do what I choose with what belongs to me? Or do you begrudge my generosity?" (v. 15). Unfortunately, we all too easily fall into the sin of comparison, resenting those who are above us and despising those who are beneath us. Read the pages of church history and you will soon discover that many of the conflicts were not doctrinal, but personal. Sometimes God's blessings were so unevenly distributed that one Christian envied another, scheming for his brother's demise. How much better if we could rejoice in the exaltation of others!

A friend of mine asked me if I ever had noticed how often God puts His hand on the wrong person! His point, of course, is that God often blesses some people more abundantly than we would if we were the Almighty! To be envious, or to complain that our part in the vineyard is not as great as that of someone else, is to miss the heart of service to Christ.

Charles Ryrie, author of the study notes in the *Ryrie Study Bible,* says that one day he was on a plane when the flight attendants asked some of the coach-class passengers to move into the first-class section. Unfortunately, he was not chosen to be among the fortunate. He resented having to stay put while others were asked to move toward the spacious seats.

While he sat quietly, bristling about his plight, he recalled this parable and read it. He paraphrased the words: "Friend, I am doing you no wrong. Did you not agree with American Airlines for a coach seat? Do you not have a coach seat? Is it not lawful for American Airlines to do as it wills with those who are its own? If it wishes to give first-class treatment to second-class passengers, is your eye envious because American Airlines is generous?"

We must not become envious if God is more generous to some people than we think He should be! Indeed, if He were not generous, none of us would be saved and not a one of us would be rewarded. Let us be satisfied with our place in the vineyard, no matter how obscure or unappreciated. Since whatever we receive is undeserved, we should be grateful for any pay the owner grants us.

God is sovereign in who He chooses to save; He is sovereign in the distribution of privileges and gifts. And He is also sovereign in the rewards He chooses to give us. Obviously, He does not act arbitrarily. There is a connection between our service on earth and the rewards we shall receive in heaven. But we will receive so much more than we could ever hope for.

Indeed, this leads us to the heart of the parable.

Our Reward Is Grace, Not Wages

In heaven there will be reversals: "So the last will be first, and the first last" (v. 16). With these words Christ encapsulated the central teaching of the parable. Some who have come to the kingdom late might just be ahead of those who entered early in the day.

As we have already learned, the first reason for this reversal in rank is that God takes into account the attitude with which we serve. The person who comes to faith in Christ late in life and thus enters the vineyard late in the day does not have the same opportunity to do as many good deeds as the person who grew up in the faith. But if such a latecomer serves well, he will receive much more than he could ever expect. Perhaps a lifetime of pay for a month of service. Rewards are not based on the amount of *time* in the vineyard.

If the length of time one worked in the vineyard determined our reward, none of us would want to be a martyr! We would want to go on serving Christ to accumulate more good deeds. But the fact is that God determines how long we are in the vineyard. No one is penalized because his life is cut short.

The teenager killed in an accident, the man who receives Christ as Savior while on his deathbed—these shall receive more than they could possibly hope for. Perhaps even the infant will be graciously rewarded, based on what he or she might have done if given the opportunity. These shall be rewarded above those who served God out of a sense of duty, out of a legalistic heart without a loving touch. Thus the first shall be last and the last first.

Second, it is clear that the bottom line is that the reward we receive will not be equal pay for equal service. Rather, our reward will be a hundred times greater than any work we actually have done. God will pay the legalist who has worked for a fixed price, but in the end He will compensate far beyond expectations those who have trusted Him. Our relationship with Him is not just between master and slave, but between a Father who delights in sharing His inheritance and His obedient child.

In the end we shall receive much more than we have merited; in fact, as we have already learned, we "deserve" nothing. God will give us rewards that are totally out of proportion to the work we have done. Since no one "earns" rewards anyway, we shall receive the benefits of a gracious wage. We will have hearts of gratitude for all of eternity.

Henry C. Morrison and his wife, after serving for forty years in Africa, came home by boat. Theodore Roosevelt and his entourage were also aboard; there was much pomp and revelry. The president's arrival in New York was greeted with a great delegation and fanfare. But the Morrisons felt dejected, for there was no one there to meet them. As they thought about it, they realized that those who caroused on the ship, drinking and dancing, those who were famous—they had a rousing welcome. The missionaries did not.

Understandably, the couple felt resentment. But one day the joy of the Lord returned to Mr. Morrison. He explained to his wife that he had been praying, rehearsing one more time his indignation toward God. "We are servants of the most High God and when we returned home there was no one to greet us; when those who are serving this world returned home they had a rousing welcome . . .

"Then," he said, "it was as if the Lord said to me, 'Just wait, *you aren't home yet!*'"

Whatever deprivations we have had here on earth, whatever loneliness we endure, whatever suffering comes our way for the sake of Christ—for this we shall be generously rewarded. We will stand amazed when we see that God gave us so much for so little!

We've been called to the vineyard at different times, but thanks be, we can count on being "paid" at the end of the day. And because of the generosity of the owner, some of the last shall be first and the first last. Of course, our reward will not be monetary. Rather, we shall have the joy of reigning with Christ. And it is to this ultimate reward we now turn.

CHAPTER 9

REIGNING WITH CHRIST FOREVER

A nd they shall reign forever and ever."
So says the apostle John of the Lord's bondservants who serve Him in the New Jerusalem (Revelation 22:5). Ruling with Christ is God's ultimate intention for believers; it is our highest possible privilege. "He who overcomes, I will grant to him to sit down with Me on My throne, as I also overcame and sat down with My Father on His throne" (3:21 NASB).

Those who rule with Christ are overcomers, those who have successfully conquered the challenges of this life. They have weathered the storms and have believed in God's promises against incredible odds. They have willingly suffered for His name. They have resisted the threefold seduction of pleasure, possessions, and power. These are the ones who genuinely came to believe that "the world is passing away, and also its lusts; but the one who does the will of God lives forever" (1 John 2:17 NASB).

This is the company of believers who proved that they are *worthy* of the Savior. Three times Christ used that word in Matthew 10:37–38. Although we have quoted this passage previously, we are now prepared to look at it in new light. "Whoever loves father or mother more than me is not *worthy* of me, and whoever loves son or daughter more than me is not *worthy* of me. And whoever does not take his cross and follow me is not *worthy* of me" (italics added).

Paul exhorts us to "walk in a manner *worthy* of the calling to which you have been called" (Ephesians 4:1, italics added). And again, so that you may "walk in a manner worthy of God, who calls you into his own kingdom and glory" (1 Thessalonians 2:12, italics added). We are to prove ourselves worthy of our high calling. We are, says Iosif Ton, "formed, shaped and tested for reliability, and based on our degree of trustworthiness we are given a position of responsibility in the kingdom."[1]

We cannot emphasize too often that this is not a privilege that is "earned" in the usual sense of the word. It is a gift of immeasurable grace based on our temporal efforts on earth. As we have seen, rewards are determined by our response to the opportunities (whether great or small) that are presented to us.

THE FATHER AND HIS SONS

Let us remind ourselves that God wants to produce character in us that is similar to that of Christ. The qualities seen
in Him are the ones that make for greatness in the kingdom.
As man, Christ was exalted because He had that in which
the Father found His delight. These qualities are universally
ignored by the world.

Many people in the health and wealth gospel preach that
we should live like a "king's kid." What they mean is that we
should strive for money and enjoy it; after all, the children of
a king are usually spoiled with all the amenities this world
can provide.

What they forget is that Christ was the "King's kid" who
lived a life that is directly opposite to what the health and
wealth gospel promotes. He was born into poverty and lived
without any investments in this world. And although God
might not require the same form of self-denial for us, the fact
is that Christ was as countercultural as one could possibly be.
He modeled poverty and humility; and this, He taught, was
the path to greatness.

Christ chided His disciples for confusing the blessings
of the coming kingdom with the lifestyles of earth. If they
wanted to be great tomorrow, fine; let them learn that this
could only be achieved by taking the lowest roles today. Bon-
hoeffer was right when he said, "The figure of the Crucified
invalidates all thought that takes success for its standard."

Christ had already promised the disciples that they
would rule with Him in the coming kingdom, but this was
not quite good enough for the mother of James and John.
She came to Christ with her two sons in tow, requesting that
they get to sit on Christ's left and right when the kingdom
age got under way (Matthew 20:20–28). The conversation

developed like this:

"Teacher, we want You to do for us whatever we ask of You."

"What do you want Me to do for you?"

"Grant that we may sit in Your glory, one on Your right, and one on Your left."

When the other ten disciples heard about this secret discussion they were indignant, angry that this request was made behind their backs. The other disciples wanted to compete for the two chairs next to Christ and His throne. Our Lord was not upset with their request, but He did point out that they did not understand the nature of true greatness in the kingdom.

First, He asked them whether they were willing to suffer with Him, earning their place in the kingdom. "You do not know what you are asking. Are you able to drink the cup that I am to drink?" (v. 22). They replied that they were able. This is the first test of greatness, the ability to suffer with Christ. Indeed, He was perfected through suffering, and we should be too. Greatness is not ease or luxury; it is pain and tears. As Alexander Maclaren said, every step on the pathway to spiritual progress will be marked by the bloody footprints of wounded self-love.

Christ apparently agreed that they had the determination to suffer with Him. He continues, "You will drink my cup, but to sit at my right hand and at my left is not mine to grant, but it is for those for whom it has been prepared by my Father" (v. 23). The Holy Spirit within us gives us a willingness to suffer, despite our natural hesitations and fears.

We do all we can to prevent suffering, but God nevertheless brings trials into our lives. Although He heals some from disease, many experience years of relentless pain and agony. Every affliction, it is said, comes with a message from the heart of God. Looked at from the standpoint of eternity, it is a gift to be cherished, for it enhances our eternal joy and honor.

But there is a second quality needed en route to the throne. Christ points out that greatness in the kingdom means humility and servanthood.

> You know that the rulers of the Gentiles lord it over them, and their great ones exercise authority over them. It shall not be so among you. But whoever would be great among you must be your servant, and whoever would be first among you must be your slave, even as the Son of Man came not to be served but to serve, and to give his life as a ransom for many. (vv. 25–28)

The law of the kingdom is directly opposite to that of the world. In the world, greatness is determined by the number of people whom you rule; to rule over ten thousand is better than to rule over a thousand. In the kingdom, greatness is determined by the number of people you serve. Humility is the badge of highest honor. Indeed, Christ Himself was exalted because He came not to be served, but to serve and to "give his life as a ransom for many" (v. 28).

Paul makes an explicit connection between Christ's humility and future exaltation. "And being found in human form, he humbled himself by becoming obedient to the point of death, even death on a cross. Therefore God has highly exalted him and bestowed on him the name that is above every name" (Philippians 2:8–9). His lowly submission to God is the reason why God highly exalted Him. He taught us that *the way up is down.*

Incredibly, Christ's servant role will continue in the

kingdom! Indeed, it appears as if He shall serve us when we sit down to dinner! Christ exhorts the disciples to be ready for His return, to be the first to open the door to Him when He knocks. "Blessed are those servants whom the master finds awake when he comes. Truly, I say to you, he will dress himself for service and have them recline at table, and he will come and serve them" (Luke 12:37). Serving is not just fit for earth, but also for heaven. The humility of Christ toward us should bring tears to our eyes. As Augustine said, "God humbled Himself, while man remains proud."

We serve as a stepping-stone to greatness, but serving itself is greatness; it is being like Christ. Ironically, if you want to rule with Christ, don't try to seek this reward by finding a lofty position and using it as a stepping-stone to something greater. Find a towel, a basin, and some dirty feet and take the role of a servant. Within God's good time, He may see fit to give you greater responsibility. "Humble yourselves, therefore, under the mighty hand of God so that at the proper time he may exalt you" (1 Peter 5:6). To want exaltation is fair enough, but it can only be achieved through humility. Paradoxically, *the very thing we seek, greatness, is found through its opposite, humility!*

If we wish to be great in the kingdom, we must begin by serving our spouses, our children, and any needy person we can help. We must die to our natural desire to be served and begin to serve, taking the initiative in meeting the needs of others. And if poor health or such limitations prevent us from active service, let us serve others through our prayers and encouragement.

Michelangelo, it is said, looked at a block of marble and said, "I see an angel in that block of marble." God goes into the quarry of sin, takes rough stones, and hews them into the shape of Christ. He is pleased when He looks at us and we remind Him of His only begotten Son, who was a servant.

THE NATURE OF REWARDS

When we specifically ask what rewards are, the Bible gives a variety of descriptions. The book of Revelation is filled with figures of speech that help us peer though the window to see what the inheritance of the faithful might be.

Special Privileges

Just contemplate the generosity of God:

- "To the one who conquers I will grant to eat of the tree of life, which is in the paradise of God" (Revelation 2:7).
- "The one who conquers will not be hurt by the second death" (Revelation 2:11).
- "To the one who conquers I will give some of the hidden manna, and I will give him a white stone, with a new name written on the stone that no one knows except the one who receives it" (Revelation 2:17).
- "The one who conquers and who keeps my works until the end, to him I will give authority over the nations" (Revelation 2:26).
- "The one who conquers, I will make him a pillar in the temple of my God. Never shall he go out of it, and I will write on him the name of my God, and the name of the city of my God, the new Jerusalem, which comes down from my God out of heaven, and my own new name" (Revelation 3:12).

We need not pause to interpret such passages except to say that all of them speak of special privileges or intimate fellowship with Christ. Whether it is eating, receiving a secret name, or becoming a pillar in the temple of God, all of these speak of close proximity to our Lord in heaven. John Bunyan was right when he said, "He who is most in the bosom of God, and who so acts for Him here, he is the man who will be best able to enjoy most of God in the kingdom of heaven."[2]

Some Bible scholars insist that all Christians are overcomers because these passages in Revelation do not speak of what happens to the "nonovercomers." However, the warnings to these churches make clear that some of the believers were not overcoming in their witness for Christ. Indeed, the promises are never made to the church in general, but to specific individuals within the congregation. Thus the singular pronoun: "*he* who overcomes."

We are not well served by a theology that does not recognize the possibility of serious moral and doctrinal defection on the part of believers. We've learned that Paul himself beat his body lest he be "disqualified." He lived with the healthy fear that he could end in disgrace and failure. Think about the man in the church of Corinth about whom Paul wrote, "You are to deliver this man to Satan for the destruction of the flesh, so that his spirit may be saved in the day of the Lord" (1 Corinthians 5:5). The same could be said for Paul's companions Hymenaeus and Alexander, whom he also "handed over to Satan that they may learn not to blaspheme" (1 Timothy 1:20).

Of course, these believers were legally perfect in Christ; they were overcomers, judicially speaking, for they were accepted by God on the merit of Christ. But they were not overcomers in their practical experience. God exhorts us to be overcomers of the world and its multifaceted temptations because He delights in seeing us be victorious in daily living. The fact that we are secure in Christ does not mean that we are incapable of serious failure, and with it the loss of rewards.

If you are not convinced that there will be important distinctions in the kingdom, remember that Christ spoke about those who would be "great" in the kingdom and others who would be "least" in the kingdom. Again I emphasize that there will not be two camps in heaven, the haves and the have-nots. Rather, there are probably many different levels of responsibility because there are so many different levels of obedience and disobedience.

Rewards, particularly ruling with Christ, should not be taken as a foregone conclusion for all believers. We have observed that almost every time reigning with Christ is mentioned, it is always conditional. Successful suffering, overcoming, and faithfulness are generally spoken of as the qualifications. With these come special honors.

Special Honors

Rewards are not only privileges, but also honors. Since the Scriptures speak of certain crowns being given to the faithful, some people believe that our eternal rewards are actual crowns that we will gladly lay at Christ's feet. This has given rise to the idea that our rewards or lack of them are really quite unimportant eternally. Whether we have one or many, we cast them at the feet of Christ at a great ceremony and then everyone gets on with eternity, enjoying essentially the same privileges.

> The twenty-four elders fall down before him who is
> seated on the throne and worship him who lives forever
> and ever. They cast their crowns before the throne, saying,
> "Worthy are you, our Lord and God, to receive glory and
> honor and power, for you created all things, and by your
> will they existed and were created."
> (REVELATION 4:10–11)

If we are given actual crowns in heaven, I'm sure that we shall gladly lay them at Christ's feet. But it is wrong to think that our rewards are crowns and nothing more. If we join the elders in casting our crowns before Him, I believe He shall give them back to us so we can join Him in ruling "forever and ever" (Revelation 22:5). Whatever might happen to the crowns, our rewards are eternal. Rewards are primarily not medallions, but specific honors.

Christ spoke of rewards as being "repayment," or of having "treasures," or of ruling with Him (as in the case of the disciples). Paul and John use the terminology of "crowns," but I believe that they intend this to be symbolic of our privilege of ruling with Christ. They would, I believe, be quite surprised that some interpreters think that our rewards will officially end when we throw our crowns at Christ's feet.

Although all crowns are based on faithfulness, there are different ways to be faithful. Enduring persecution might gain one person kingdom rule, whereas suffering with leukemia successfully might gain another the same privilege. Or perhaps single-minded generosity will introduce us to "the true riches."

Also, it is possible to win more than one crown. This is another indication that we should not make crowns equal to rewards. It would be odd indeed to try to fit five crowns on the same head! As you read through this list, you will see that although it might not be possible for one person to win them all, one could certainly have more than one.

What are some of the crowns? In the New Testament there are two words for "crown." *Stephanos* is a wreath crown, and *diadem* is a royal crown, the kind that Christ wears. In the passages listed below, the word *stephanos* is used, a crown given to winners.

1. *The Crown of Rejoicing*

The people we have led to Christ and nurtured in the faith are a "crown." Paul wrote, "For what is our hope or joy or crown of boasting before our Lord Jesus at his coming? Is it not you? For you are our glory and joy" (1 Thessalonians 2:19–20). This is another clue that crowns are to be understood as honors rather than a literal crown made of some cosmic metal. Meeting people we have known on earth will be a crown.

2. *The Crown of Glory*

For elders who serve well, there is special recognition. Peter wrote:

> So I exhort the elders among you, as a fellow elder and a witness of the sufferings of Christ, as well as a partaker in the glory that is going to be revealed: shepherd the flock of God that is among you, exercising oversight, not under compulsion, but willingly, as God would have you; not for shameful gain, but eagerly; not domineering over those in your charge, but being examples to the flock. And when the chief Shepherd appears, you will receive the unfading crown of glory. (1 PETER 5:1–4)

Again, this is an expression of reward for faithfulness. We should not think that elders will be identified in heaven because they are wearing a crown that is distinguishable from others. Faithfulness in being a good shepherd on earth will merit special honors from the Good Shepherd in heaven.

3. *The Crown of Righteousness*

We've already learned that this crown is given to those who eagerly await Christ's appearing.

> For I am already being poured out as a drink offering, and the time of my departure has come. I have fought the good fight, I have finished the race, I have kept the faith. Henceforth there is laid up for me the crown of righteousness, which the Lord, the righteous judge, will award to me on that Day, and not only to me but also to all who have loved his appearing. (2 TIMOTHY 4:6–8)

All Christians receive the righteousness of Christ; without it, heaven would be lost. This crown is a reference to a special enjoyment of righteousness because of a love for Christ. Paul wants us to understand that a love for Christ will attract the attention of Him whom we love.

4. *The Crown of Life*

This crown is given to those who successfully endure the sufferings associated with temptation. "Blessed is the man who remains steadfast under trial, for when he has stood the test he will receive the crown of life, which God has promised to those who love him" (James 1:12).

The same crown is given to martyrs. "Do not fear what you are about to suffer. Behold, the devil is about to throw some of you into prison, that you may be tested, and for ten days you will have tribulation. Be faithful unto death, and I will give you the crown of life" (Revelation 2:10). Blessed are those who will not give up their allegiance to Christ despite the seductions within the soul or the trials found in our path. The trials of the bride are carefully thought out by the Bridegroom! Remember, the goal is faithfulness that we might be found worthy to reign.

All Christians are given eternal life. The crown of life obviously refers to a certain enjoyment of life because of faithfulness in enduring the hardships of life. Thus we see again that the crowns are symbolic of privileges and accompanying responsibilities.

5. *Crown of Mastery*

This is a crown given to those who run the race successfully. "They do it," says Paul, "to receive a perishable wreath, but we an imperishable" (1 Corinthians 9:25b). This is given to those who have paid the price of sacrifice and discipline in running the Christian race. This is a crown fit for those who have mastered the sins of the body, having brought it into subjection.

Special Responsibilities

Now we come to the final drama, the end to which the plan of salvation was directed. As we stated in an earlier chapter, God's eternal purpose was to find a bride who would rule with Christ, joining Him on the throne of the universe.

Over what shall we rule? What will our responsibilities be? Of course we cannot answer these questions in detail, but the Scriptures give us sufficient teaching to enable us to glimpse into the future. We see through a glass darkly, but thankfully, we *do* see.

Our first opportunity for rule will be over the earth in the millennial kingdom. Christ promised twelve thrones to the twelve apostles, but there may also be other thrones that will be occupied. If not, we will be given various responsibilities, assignments commensurate with our faithfulness while living on this planet. Daniel the prophet foresaw the legacy of the saints in kingdom rule: "But the saints of the Most High shall receive the kingdom and possess the kingdom forever, forever and ever" (Daniel 7:18).

After the millennial kingdom, a new phase of eternity begins. The New Jerusalem will come down from God out of heaven. Our responsibilities of reigning with Christ will continue, but in a new sphere. "And night will be no more. They will need no light of lamp or sun, for the Lord God will be their light, and they will reign forever and ever" (Revelation 22:5).

This rule extends for all eternity. Paul argued that one of the reasons Christians should not take one another to court is because this world is practice for greater responsibility in the world to come. He writes, "Or do you not know that the saints will judge the world? And if the world is to be judged by you, are you incompetent to try trivial cases? Do you not know that we are to judge angels? How much more, then, matters pertaining to this life!" (1 Corinthians 6:2–3).

We shall judge angels, not in the sense that they need to be brought to justice, but rather in the sense that we shall rule over them. This most probably is what makes Satan so furious. The fact that sinful human beings, who sided with him in Eden, will be exalted above the angelic realm of which he was at one time a member is more than he can bear.

RULING FOREVER

When scientists began to understand the size of the universe, man's place in the cosmos seemed to diminish. After all, if the universe is 20 billion light-years in diameter, and if there are stars millions of times greater than our earth, man is but a speck of dust on the cosmic landscape. We ask with

David, "What is man that you are mindful of him, and the son of man that you care for him?" (Psalm 8:4).

The discovery of the immensity of the universe does not diminish but actually magnifies man's role in the cosmos. For if Christ is to rule over all things and we are to reign with Him, then we will be ruling over all the galaxies, affirming Christ's Lordship over the whole universe.[3]

Scientists tell us that there are as many stars in the universe as there are grains of sand on the beaches of the world. It is unthinkable that so much as one of them would wander aimlessly in space without contributing to the greater glory of God. In a way that we cannot comprehend, all things will be in subjection to Christ, and we shall be a part of His eternal rule.

Daniel predicted the final destiny of those who belong to the Almighty. "And those who are wise shall shine like the brightness of the sky above; and those who turn many to righteousness, like the stars forever and ever" (Daniel 12:3). Unworthy though we are, there we will be, reigning in accordance with Christ's instructions. Perhaps all believers will shine like stars, but some will shine more brightly than others.

We can imagine a factory worker, ignored here on earth, now exalted to the dizzy heights of rule with Christ on a celestial throne. And here is a woman, an invalid, who endured the physical pain of Parkinson's disease and the emotional pain of childhood trauma as a gift from God to refine her faith. She prayed for others, gave encouragement, and lived her life with implicit faith in her Lord. Now, in her resplendent body, she rules, not taking advantage of her new authority, but in submission to Christ. At last she understands what Paul meant when he said, "For I consider that the sufferings of this present time are not worth comparing with the glory that is to be revealed to us" (Romans 8:18). The person she was on earth determined the rewards she now enjoys.

In 1881 King Charles of Romania did not have a crown; he requested that one be made from the metal captured by the nation in battle. It was bought and paid for by Romanian lives. Just so, the crown we wear will be the result of our successful suffering with Christ on earth. He suffered immeasurably in our behalf that we might be in heaven forever. Our suffering adds nothing to the completed work He did on our behalf. But the lives we live after He has saved us prepare whatever crown(s) we will enjoy in heaven.

What if there are some Christians who do not get to rule with Christ, or are given lesser authority in the heavenly kingdom? They will not envy those above them. In fact, Jonathan Edwards says, in heaven we shall be so free of sin that we will rejoice in the exaltation of others as though it were our own! We will not regret that others are above us, but we will regret that we did not serve the Savior to the best of our ability.

Somewhere I read a story about a wealthy couple who had a son they dearly loved. Unfortunately, the mother died, leaving the care of the boy with the father. He knew that he needed help to raise the lad, so he enlisted the aid of a housekeeper, who came to take care of the boy. She came to love him as if he were her own son.

The boy was stricken with a disease and died at a young age. Soon after, perhaps because of a broken heart, the father also died. And, because no will was found, the decision was made to auction his personal effects to the highest bidder.

The housekeeper attended the auction, not because she could afford the expensive furniture or the pricey antiques. She came because she wanted a picture of the boy that hung in the living room. When the auctioneer got to it, it sold for but a few cents.

When the woman took the picture home, she noticed a piece of paper attached to the back. It was the father's last will and testament, written in his own handwriting, which read simply, "I will all of my inheritance to anyone who loved my son enough to buy this picture."

God the Father loves His Son. And if we love Him, the Father will stop at nothing to bless us, even granting us the privilege of ruling with Him. "He who did not spare his own Son but gave him up for us all, how will he not also with him graciously give us all things?" (Romans 8:32).

Yes, when we receive Christ we are graciously rewarded. And for those who are faithful there is the prospect of ruling with Him forever. That God should be so gracious to those who once were His enemies is the essence of the gospel. It is here that we encounter the mystery of God's matchless grace.

Come with me to the city of Rome with its opulent cathedrals, sculptures, and monuments. Survey the pyramids of Egypt and the splendor of the Palace of Versailles. Visit the skyscrapers of New York and the exclusive shops along Chicago's Michigan Avenue. Spend your life studying works of art and the great literature of the world.

Now compare these possessions with our eternal inheritance. The contrast is stark and gripping.

> But the day of the Lord will come like a thief, and then the heavens will pass away with a roar, and the heavenly bodies will be burned up and dissolved, and the earth and the works that are done on it will be exposed. Since all these things are thus to be dissolved, what sort of people ought you to be in lives of holiness and godliness, waiting for and hastening the coming of the day of God,

because of which the heavens will be set on fire and dissolved, and the heavenly bodies will melt as they burn! But according to his promise we are waiting for new heavens and a new earth in which righteousness dwells. Therefore, beloved, since you are waiting for these, be diligent to be found by him without spot or blemish, and at peace. (2 PETER 3:10–14)

What sort of people ought we to be in holy conduct and godliness! When Sir Walter Raleigh laid his new coat on the ground so that Queen Elizabeth might be able to walk without getting her shoes dirty, he knew that there is no price too great for royalty. Whatever he could do to honor the queen of England should be done. And whatever we can do to honor the King of kings should be done *now*. And with all that is within us.

The curtain of this earthly drama will close, but it will open in eternity. What we encounter there will have been determined, to some degree, by the life we lived on this earth. Only in this life can we impact the kind of eternity we shall enjoy. *For we are becoming today the person we will be throughout all of eternity.*

"Behold, I am coming soon, bringing my recompense with me, to repay each one for what he has done" (Revelation 22:12).

Even so come, Lord Jesus!

CHAPTER 10

THE GREAT WHITE
THRONE JUDGMENT

When I was a teenager, I developed a fervor for the game of Monopoly. I would try to buy the most expensive property and, if lucky, find my opponent paying a hefty fee for his brief sojourn on Boardwalk. But when one of us was bankrupt, we just put all the fake money and deeds back into the box. The game was over.

Is that what life is all about? Is it true that when we breathe our last everything just gets put back into the box and the game is over? Is the old bumper sticker right when it says, "He who dies with the most toys wins"?

No. Life is an *eternal* game. When it's over here, you and

I will be tenderly laid into a box, but the game we played here will continue into the life beyond. We will have to meet God. Death is not a thick wall, but a soft, yielding curtain through which we cannot see, but a curtain that beckons us nevertheless.

This book has been dedicated to a study of the judgment seat of Christ to which all Christians will be summoned. However, there is another judgment that will also be compulsory. In it the names of all those who have not received Jehovah's forgiveness will be called into account.

The Bible describes it:

> Then I saw a great white throne and him who was seated on it. From his presence earth and sky fled away, and no place was found for them. And I saw the dead, great and small, standing before the throne, and books were opened. Then another book was opened, which is the book of life. And the dead were judged by what was written in the books, according to what they had done. And the sea gave up the dead who were in it, Death and Hades gave up the dead who were in them, and they were judged, each one of them, according to what they had done. Then Death and Hades were thrown into the lake of fire. This is the second death, the lake of fire. And if anyone's name was not found written in the book of life, he was thrown into the lake of fire.
> (REVELATION 20:11–15)

We picture the scene: host beyond host, rank behind rank. The millions among the nations of the world, all crowded together in the presence of the One who sits upon the throne, the One who looks intently at each individual.

We are accustomed to human judges; we know their partial and imperfect verdicts. In the presence of the Almighty, all previous judgments are rendered useless. Many men and women acquitted on earth before a human judge will now be found guilty before God. Men who have been accustomed to perks, special privileges, and legal representation now stand as naked in the presence of God. To their horror they are judged by a standard that is light-years beyond them: the standard is God Himself. Little wonder they feel what one writer calls "unfamiliar awfulness."

A DESCRIPTION OF THE PLAINTIFFS

For the first time in their lives they stand in the presence of unclouded righteousness. They will be asked questions for which they know the answer. Their lives are present before them; unfortunately, they will be doomed to a painful, eternal existence.

What do we notice as we look at this scene?

Their Diversity

These multitudes standing before the throne are diverse in size. "I saw the dead, great and small, standing before the throne" (v. 12). Lives separate on earth come together here: the attorney and the storekeeper, the farmer and the king. Those who lived a private life on earth awake in a realm in which human differences do not matter. The dead of all the ages stand together: black, white, yellow, brown.

There is diversity in time periods and civilizations. "And the sea gave up the dead who were in it, Death and Hades gave up the dead who were in them" (v. 13). We think of those who died before Christ came to earth, those who rejected the God of Abraham, Isaac, and Jacob. Then we think of those who lived since the time of Christ, but have treated Him with benign indifference.

We think of Asia with its teeming millions. We think of the country of China, of Japan, Russia, and all of Europe. We can visualize the United States, and Central and South America. Here are people who lived during the time of the patriarchs as well as those who lived during the days of Abraham Lincoln and John Kennedy.

Not one can beg for a postponement of the court date. Every individual feels that his own soul is immortal; he knows that his existence is what is most important to him. And now it is too late to change his destiny.

This multitude is diverse in its religions. We see Buddhists, Muslims, Hindus, Protestants, Jews, and Catholics. We see those who believed in one God and those who believed in many gods. We see those who refused to believe in any God at all. We see those who believed in meditation as a means of salvation and those who believed that doing good deeds was the path to eternal life. We see the moral and the immoral, the priest as well as the minister, the nun as well as the missionary.

Their Common Experience

The books are thrown wide open and the past is recalled. Details long since forgotten are brought to light. The good, the bad, and the ugly. Many have a litany of good deeds: acts of charity, love, and sacrifice. There is the priest who conscientiously visited the people of his parish standing next to the Protestant minister who expended his life to help the poor and spread justice. There is the poor beggar and the wealthy rajah.

Their good works will be carefully recounted, but none

will have enough for admittance into heaven. But the good deeds done will make their punishment in the lake of fire more bearable. They will be judged on the basis of what they did with what they knew, or should have known; thus hell will not be the same for everyone.

How accurate will the judgment be? Jonathan Edwards says that it will be meticulous. Sinners will wish they had done just a little less evil that their punishment would be slightly more tolerable; pornographers will wish they had published fewer magazines; control freaks will wish they had been less angry and hurtful; abortionists will wish they had killed fewer pre-born infants. All of this would adjust the degree of punishment at least a bit.

> *Though the mills of God grind slowly*
> *Yet they grind exceedingly small;*
> *Though with patience He stands waiting*
> *With exactness He grinds all.*
> —*Friedrich von Logau, "Retribution"*
> *Trans. Henry Wadsworth Longfellow*

Justice is symbolized on courthouses by the figure of a blindfolded woman with scales in her hand; the point to be made is that she deals impartially, without reference to the parties involved. However, with God it is different: He judges with eyes that are wide open, eyes as of fire that can penetrate the most hardened criminal. He knows not only the individuals, but their parents, brothers, and sisters; He sees the opportunities they had and takes into account their predicament. Justice is carefully administered. Nothing will be overlooked.

Their Common Destination

Why do the good people and the bad share a common fate? Alas, the good people were not good enough! The requirement to enter heaven is that they be as good as God, and no one qualifies. Even the most devoted religious persons will discover that they fall short of the glory of God.

In addition to the book containing a list of their deeds, there is a second book called the Book of Life. Symbolically, this book is checked from top to bottom, but none of those who are here have their names written there. If their names had been in it, those fortunate souls would already be in heaven appearing at the judgment seat of Christ (discussed in the earlier chapters of this book).

We read, "And if anyone's name was not found written in the book of life, he was thrown into the lake of fire" (Revelation 20:15). They must go obediently into outer darkness. The words of Dante, long since forgotten, come to mind, "All hope abandon, ye who enter here!"

Is the lake of fire a just sentence for those who find themselves in this frightful predicament? What about those who have a raft of good deeds to show for their sojourn here on earth? Does it not appear as if the punishment is greater than the crime warrants?

We must proceed cautiously.

What if it is true, as Jonathan Edwards says, that the greatness of the sin is determined by the greatness of the being against whom it is committed? If so, then even the smallest sin is a serious affront to God. Hell exists because unbelievers are eternally guilty. No human being's suffering can ever be a payment for sin. If human suffering could erase sin, then the lake of fire would eventually end.

Also, keep in mind that the unbelievers will be judged

"according to their deeds" (vv. 12, 13 NASB). This means that they will be judged fairly; the person who never heard of Christ will be punished more leniently than the person who consciously rejected Him. The good person will be punished less severely than the criminal.

If a man grew up without an understanding of the gospel, this will be taken into account: he will be fairly judged. Blame will also be equitably distributed to his parents, who did not teach the child when he was growing up. Parents, grandparents, opportunities, and handicaps—all of this will be relevant to the final verdict.

To our way of thinking, hell might be considered unjust. But we are not asked to make up the rules by which the game of life is played. Since this is God's universe, He runs it according to His eternal purposes. We must bow to His authority, believing that He does all things well.

WHAT THE PLAINTIFFS LACKED

What binds these millions of people together is the common view that they will be accepted by God on the basis of their goodness. Virtually all the religions of the world teach that if we live moral lives, if we treat our neighbor with respect and "do the best we can," we will be able to save ourselves. The specifics may vary, but the bottom line is the same. What these people lack is the righteousness that God requires for entry into heaven.

The problem, as I have already mentioned, is that we have to be as good as God to get to enjoy eternity with Him. And since that is impossible, our only hope is to trust Christ, who died so that we might be saved by His merit. In other words, when we believe on Christ, His righteousness is credited to our account so that legally we are declared to be as perfect as God. Thus, while millions languish in the lake of fire, millions of others who have placed their trust in Christ alone will be enjoying the bliss of heaven.

It would be a mistake to think that those who appear at the Great White Throne Judgment are punished with a different standard than Christians who are enjoying heaven. God is just; He must exact the same from every sinner.

Here is the big difference: Christ bore the wrath of God on behalf of those who believe in Him. He, as the God-man, personally took the punishment of God so that those who believe in Him will be exempt from the lake of fire. Either we must personally bear infinite punishment for our sins or else our sins have to be laid upon an infinite being, namely, Christ. Either way, God is eminently just.

This explains why only those who believe in Christ will be spared the eternal wrath of God. His suffering accomplished in a few hours what purely human suffering can never do. Christ is our sin-bearer, our shelter, our Savior. He forgives us and reconciles us to God. "There is therefore now no condemnation for those who are in Christ Jesus" (Romans 8:1).

If you have never personally believed in Him, or if you are unsure whether you have, here is a prayer you can pray that will affirm your desire to believe.

Dear God,

I know that I am a sinner. I cannot save myself from my sins. I also know that I deserve Your judgment. At this moment, as best as I know how, I transfer my faith to Christ alone. I receive His death on the cross in my behalf. I am grateful that He bore my punishment, and I now accept His sacrifice for myself. I thank You that Christ died and rose again from the dead and ascended into heaven in triumph. Today I receive Him as my personal Savior. "But to all who did receive him, who believed in his name, he gave the right to become children of God" (John 1:12). Thank You for hearing me. Amen.

If you have prayed this prayer in faith, God will confirm your decision through His promises and the work of the Holy Spirit in your heart. You have now entered the family of God, with all the rights and privileges that pertain. You will appear at the *Bema,* the judgment seat of Christ, rather than the judgment at the Great White Throne.

Throughout all of eternity we will sing:

> Great and amazing are your deeds,
> O Lord God the Almighty!
> Just and true are your ways,
> O King of the nations!
> Who will not fear, O Lord, and glorify your name?
> For you alone are holy.
> All nations will come and worship you,
> for your righteous acts have been revealed.
> (REVELATION 15:3–4)

All glory to God alone, both now and forever.

NOTES

Chapter 1: Tears in Heaven

1. Quoted in Iosif Ton, "Suffering, Martyrdom and Rewards in Heaven" (Th.D. diss., Evangelische Theologische Facultiet, Haverlee/Leuven, Belgie, 1996), 477.

2. Quoted in Jim Elliff, "The Starving of the Church," *Reformation and Revival: A Quarterly Journal for Church Leadership* 1, no. 3 (1992): 116.

3. Ton, 280.

4. See also A. J. Gordon, *Ecce Venit: Behold He Cometh* (New York: Revell, 1889), 271.

Chapter 2: You'll Be There

1. Joe E. Wall, *Going for the Gold* (Chicago: Moody, 1991), 32.

2. Jim Elliff, "The Starving of the Church," *Reformation and Revival: A Quarterly Journal for Church Leadership* 1, no. 3 (1992): 115.

3. Philip Edgcombe Hughes, *Paul's Second Epistle to the Corinthians*, New International Commentary on the New Testament (Grand Rapids: Eerdmans, 1962), 180.

4. Woodrow Kroll, *Tested by Fire* (Neptune, N.J.: Loizeaux, 1977), 51.

5. Hughes, 182.

Chapter 3: What We Can Gain

1. Paul Billheimer, *Destined for the Throne* (Fort Washington, Pa.: Christian Literature Crusade, 1975), 37. The author develops the concept that the ultimate goal of our trials on earth is that we be trained to eventually reign with Christ. Some of the ideas of this chapter were generated by the reading of this challenging book.

2. Ibid., 15.

Chapter 4: What We Can Lose

1. Anthony A. Hoekema, *The Bible and the Future* (Grand Rapids: Eerdmans, 1979), 259.

2. John Murray, *Lectures in Systematic Theology*, vol. 2 of *Collected Writings of John Murray* (Carlisle, Pa.: Banner of Truth, 1977), 414–15.

3. Woodrow Kroll, *Tested by Fire* (Neptune, N.J.: Loizeaux, 1977), 108.

4. Joseph C. Dillow, *The Reign of the Servant Kings* (Miami: Schoettle, 1992), 137. This detailed volume attempts to show that while the eternal destiny of believers is secure, their rewards in heaven are conditioned on obedience. The author begins in the Old Testament and works through all relevant passages.

5. The question of whether "inheriting the kingdom" is the same as entering it necessitates a discussion well beyond the parameters of this book. R. T. Kendall, in *Once Saved Always Saved* (Chicago: Moody, 1983), gives extensive arguments to show that all Christians enter the kingdom but all do not "inherit it" (119–34). Joseph Dillow also adopts the same premise and labors to show that this interpretation is a more consistent understanding of the relevant texts.

6. Quoted in Dillow, 546.

7. Warren W. Wiersbe, *The Bible Exposition Commentary*, vol. 1 (Wheaton: Scripture Press, 1989), 92.

8. Quoted in Dillow, 532.

Chapter 6: Taking It with You

1. Willard Cantelon, *The Day the Dollar Dies: Biblical Prophecy of a New World System in the End Times* (Plainfield, N.J.: Logos International, 1973), vi–vii.

Chapter 8: Standing in Line to Receive Your Reward

1. John Piper, *Desiring God* (Portland, Ore.: Multnomah, 1986), 203.

2. Ibid., 199.

Chapter 9: Reigning with Christ Forever

1. Iosif Ton, "Suffering, Martyrdom and Rewards in Heaven" (Th.D. diss., Evangelische Theologische Faculteit, Heverlee/Leuben, Belgie, 1996).
2. Randy Alcorn, *Money, Possessions and Eternity* (Wheaton, Ill.: Tyndale, 1989), 157.
3. Joseph Dillow, *The Reign of the Servant Kings* (Miami: Schoettle, 1992), 563.

MORE BOOKS BY ERWIN W. LUTZER

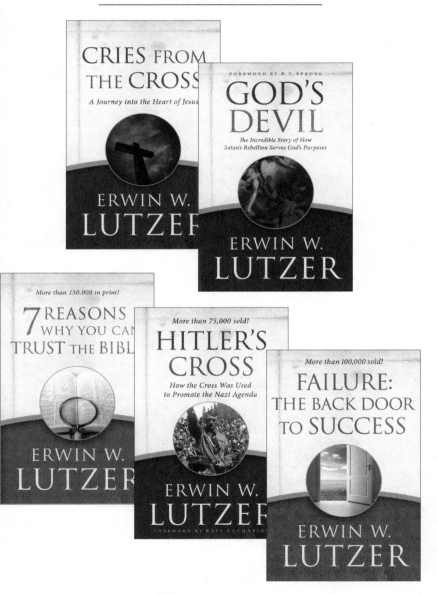

MOODY
Publishers™

From the Word to Life

MORE **ONE MINUTE AFTER YOU DIE** PRODUCTS

- Study Guide
- DVD

MOODY
Publishers™

*From the Word **to** Life*

DR. LUTZER'S AUTOBIOGRAPHY

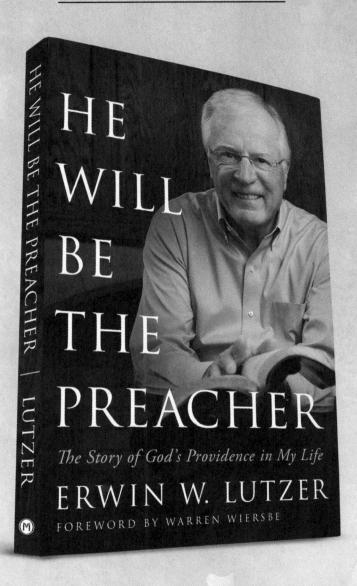

HE WILL BE THE PREACHER | LUTZER

HE
WILL
BE
THE
PREACHER

The Story of God's Providence in My Life

ERWIN W. LUTZER

FOREWORD BY WARREN WIERSBE

MOODY
Publishers™

From the Word to Life

From the Word to Life

Moody Radio produces and delivers compelling programs filled with biblical insights and creative expressions of faith that help you take the next step in your relationship with Christ.

You can hear Moody Radio on 36 stations and more than 1,500 radio outlets across the U.S. and Canada. Or listen on your smartphone with the Moody Radio app!

www.moodyradio.org